# The life of Elgar

## Musical lives

The books in this series each provide an account
of the life of a major composer, considering
both the private and the public figure. The main
thread is biographical and discussion of the
music is integral to the narrative. Each book
thus presents an organic view of the composer,
the music and the circumstances in which the
music was written.

**Published titles**

The life of Bach PETER WILLIAMS
The life of Beethoven DAVID WYN JONES
The life of Bellini JOHN ROSSELLI
The life of Berlioz PETER BLOOM
The life of Debussy ROGER NICHOLS
The life of Elgar MICHAEL KENNEDY
The life of Charles Ives STUART FEDER
The life of Mahler PETER FRANKLIN
The life of Mendelssohn PETER MERCER-TAYLOR
The life of Mozart JOHN ROSSELLI
The life of Musorgsky CARYL EMERSON
The life of Schubert CHRISTOPHER H. GIBBS
The life of Richard Strauss BRYAN GILLIAM
The life of Verdi JOHN ROSSELLI
The life of Webern KATHRYN BAILEY

# The life of Elgar

MICHAEL KENNEDY

CAMBRIDGE
UNIVERSITY PRESS

PUBLISHED BY THE PRESS SYNDICATE OF THE UNIVERSITY OF CAMBRIDGE
The Pitt Building, Trumpington Street, Cambridge, United Kingdom

CAMBRIDGE UNIVERSITY PRESS
The Edinburgh Building, Cambridge, CB2 2RU, UK
40 West 20th Street, New York, NY 10011–4211, USA
477 Williamstown Road, Port Melbourne, VIC 3207, Australia
Ruiz de Alarcón 13, 28014 Madrid, Spain
Dock House, The Waterfront, Cape Town 8001, South Africa

http://www.cambridge.org

First published 2004
Reprinted 2005

Printed in the United Kingdom at the University Press, Cambridge

Typefaces FF Quadraat 9.75/14 pt.     System LaTeX $2_\varepsilon$   [TB]

A catalogue record for this book is available from the British Library

Library of Congress Cataloguing in Publication data
Kennedy, Michael, 1926–
The life of Elgar / by Michael Kennedy.
     p.     cm. – (Musical lives)
Includes bibliographical references (p. 214) and index.
ISBN 0 521 81076 0 (HB) – ISBN 0 521 00907 3 (PB)
1. Elgar, Edward, 1857–1934.   2. Composers – England – Biography.   I. Title.
II. Series.
ML410.E41K48   2004   780'.92 – dc22   [B]   2003055733

ISBN 0 521 81076 0 hardback
ISBN 0 521 00907 3 paperback

For David Cairns

# CONTENTS

List of illustrations   page viii

Preface   x

Prologue   1

1 'Boyhood's daze'   6

2 Helen   18

3 Alice   32

4 *Caractacus*   51

5 Enigma   61

6 'The best of me'   72

7 Darkness at noon   83

8 The last oratorio   97

9 Symphony   105

10 Windflower   116

11 Second Symphony   125

12 'For the Fallen'   140

13 Brinkwells   154

14 Post mortem   163

15 Vera   179

Notes   202

Further reading   214

Index   217

# ILLUSTRATIONS

1 Elgar's birthplace at Broadheath in about 1920 (courtesy of the Elgar Birthplace Museum) 7

2 Elgar with his brother and sisters, 1878 (courtesy of the Elgar Birthplace Museum) 15

3 Elgar aged fourteen (Raymond Monk Collection) 16

4 The wind quintet, c.1878 (Raymond Monk Collection) 20

5 Elgar and Alice at Garmisch, Bavaria, 1892 (Raymond Monk Collection) 35

6 Alice Elgar and Carice, c.1902 (courtesy of the Elgar Birthplace Museum) 44

7 August Jaeger with his children, 1904 (Raymond Monk Collection) 54

8 Elgar with G. R. Sinclair and Hans Richter, c.1903 (Raymond Monk Collection) 64

9 Elgar c.1899 (Raymond Monk Collection) 65

10 Sketch for The Dream of Gerontius (Raymond Monk Collection) 76

11 Elgar with his bicycle, c.1900 (Raymond Monk Collection) 78

12 Jaeger and A. E. Rodewald at Betws-y-Coed, 1903 (Raymond Monk Collection) 90

13 Frank Schuster aboard HMS Surprise, 1905 (courtesy of the Elgar Birthplace Museum) 101

14 Elgar and his daughter Carice, c.1906 (Raymond Monk Collection) 106

15 Elgar at The Hut (Raymond Monk Collection) 110

16 Carice with her pet rabbit (Raymond Monk Collection) 113

17 'Windflower': Alice Stuart Wortley (Sir Ralph Millais) 118

18 Severn House, Hampstead (Raymond Monk Collection) 131

19  Brinkwells, Elgar's Sussex cottage (courtesy of the Elgar
    Birthplace Museum)  151
20  Elgar at Severn House, 1919 (Raymond Monk Collection)  158
21  Alice Elgar (Raymond Monk Collection)  161
22  Elgar conducting at the Wembley Empire Exhibition, 1924
    (Raymond Monk Collection)  170
23  Elgar with John Coates, 1925 (Raymond Monk Collection)  175
24  Elgar with Percy Hull at a Three Choirs Festival (Raymond Monk
    Collection)  180
25  First sketch of *Pomp and Circumstance* march no. 5 (Raymond Monk
    Collection)  182
26  Vera Hockman in 1945 (Nina Driver)  186
27  Elgar and his gramophone, 1929 (Raymond Monk Collection)  189
28  Elgar with Yehudi Menuhin and Sir Thomas Beecham, 1932
    (Raymond Monk Collection)  191
29  Elgar with Carice, Marco and Mina at Marl Bank (Raymond Monk
    Collection)  194
30  Elgar at Marl Bank, 1933 (Raymond Monk Collection)  196
31  Elgar at South Bank nursing home, Worcester, 12 December 1933
    (Raymond Monk Collection)  199

## PREFACE

My excuse for writing another biography of Elgar is that since my *Portrait of Elgar* appeared in 1968, a mass of documentation about him has been published, much of it the result of the scholarship of Jerrold Northrop Moore, whose *Edward Elgar: A Creative Life* and editions of the letters I have shamelessly plundered and to whom I offer gratitude and renewed admiration. Also, I was in my early forties when I wrote *Portrait of Elgar*. Now I am nearing eighty, so perhaps the years bring a different perspective. What they do not bring is any diminution in my love for this music or in my fascination with the character of this strange, elusive, lovable yet often dislikeable man, a flawed human being but a blazing genius as a composer.

In quoting from Elgar's letters, I have retained his idiosyncratic punctuation, with its liberal use of dashes and of ampersands, his old-fashioned spelling (e.g. 'shew' for 'show') and 'news' treated as a plural noun, as in 'these news'.

My thanks go to Catherine Sloan, Curator of the Elgar Birthplace Museum, for help with the selection of photographs, to the Elgar Will Trust and Elgar Foundation for permission to quote from Elgar's letters, to the Barber Fine Art and Music Library, University of Birmingham, for permission to quote from Lady Elgar's diaries, to Mr Raymond Monk for lending me letters in his collection written by Frank Schuster, Bruno Walter, Fritz Kreisler and Ernest Newman, to Penny Souster of Cambridge University Press for her encouragement, and most of all to my wife Joyce for her support and for her patience in word-processing my increasingly illegible handwriting.

# Prologue

Neither Edward VII nor Edward Elgar was really an Edwardian. They were Victorians. Elgar was forty-three when Queen Victoria died in January 1901, the king over sixty. The Edwardian age, we are sometimes told, was leisurely and opulent, with society at its most glittering. It was an age that seems permanently lit by golden sunshine, with glorious days at Ascot and Goodwood, with England's cricket team adorned by players such as Fry, MacLaren and Ranjitsinhji, an age of Royal Academy exhibitions and banquets, of the Entente Cordiale, of the country-house weekend. And no doubt it was for the privileged. But, like every age, it was a complex mixture. There was great wealth and dire poverty. If the king was called 'the Peacemaker', there was plenty of war being prepared. There was industrial strife on a scale that makes today's disruption seem small beer. There was intense political controversy and social change. There was unemployment and strife in Ireland. There were entrepreneurs on a major scale, such as the king's financial friends, and there were small shopkeepers and commercial quacks like H. G. Wells's characters. You will find one part of Edwardian England in Arnold Bennett's *The Old Wives' Tale* and *The Grand Babylon Hotel*, another part in Wells's *Kipps* and *Tono Bungay* and *Ann Veronica* (for the Edwardian age was also the age of the New Woman and of the suffragette), and yet another part in Bernard Shaw's *Man and Superman* and *The Doctor's Dilemma*. There was glory in the Edwardian age, in literature, painting, music and on the cricket field; there was shoddiness too, in every walk and branch of life.

Undoubtedly, though, life was more leisurely then, the countryside less spoilt, birds and butterflies more numerous, gardens more scented, most human beings less sophisticated and cynical. There was *style* in that era and most of all a degree of innocence and charm which was to be blasted away for ever by the First World War. Style and the lament for innocence are the qualities we find in Elgar. If he was in a very real sense the musical laureate of his time, it was not just in occasional works. He wrote the *Coronation Ode* for King Edward and nine years later he dedicated the Second Symphony to his memory. But the *Coronation Ode* was an occasional piece, deliberately designed as such, and a masterpiece as it happens; the symphony was a chapter of autobiography very little related to kingship or the sunset of empire.

The Elgar of the Edwardian era also wrote the *Five Part-Songs from the Greek Anthology*, a title that must have deterred many from exploring the beauties of the music it conceals. The songs epitomise the charm and lyricism of Elgar, his Tennysonian element. The frequently made and obvious comparison with Kipling is not really very apt (although Kipling is as complex as Elgar and still as misunderstood as Elgar was until a few years ago), but Tennyson is the Elgar of poetry, with the gift of imparting intense lyricism to anything he undertook. The parallels between Tennyson and Elgar are striking, both artistically and in relation to their personalities. Both were streaked by a dark strain of utter melancholy, both were supreme lyricists capable of exquisite small gems and especially of pastoral evocation. Both expressed their love of their country through love of its countryside. Few poets have written more beautifully of nature than Tennyson; no composer distils the essence of English woodland and river into music as Elgar did. Both reached a wide popular audience because they put their art at the service of popular themes and events and both suffered a critical reaction for that very reason. When I was young, Elgar and Tennyson were spoken of by intellectuals in disparaging terms. It was considered almost indecent to admire them. You would have thought that neither had written anything besides 'The Charge of the Light Brigade' and 'Land of hope and glory'.

In 1904, his personal *annus mirabilis*, Elgar might have seemed the musical representative of the age of empire and opulence. In March that year he received the almost unprecedented tribute of a three-day festival of his music at Covent Garden, with a member of the royal family present at each concert. Three months later, he was knighted at the age of forty-seven. Only seven years earlier he had been almost unknown in London, a struggling provincial musician who was still giving violin lessons to unwilling schoolgirls and serving behind the counter in his father's music shop. If this was the age of opportunity, then Elgar had made full use of it – when the opportunity arose. It was to be another twenty years before he became Master of the King's Music, but Elgar occupied that position in the public's mind from the 1904 festival, or perhaps even earlier, from the 1897 jubilee.

There remained the hurdle of a symphony. He found his way to it by a means which was certainly an Edwardian, or again more accurately a Victorian, preoccupation: the idealisation of childhood. In 1907, the year of his fiftieth birthday, he looked out some music he had written for a family play when he was twelve years old. He reorchestrated and perhaps recomposed it as *The Wand of Youth*, in two suites. If we seek a pertinent literary parallel, it is that while Elgar was working on *The Wand of Youth*, Kenneth Grahame was completing *The Wind in the Willows*. Elgar knew all about life and inspiration on the river bank and by entering that lost world of innocence and charm and sentiment, just as Grahame had, Elgar had unlocked the door that led to a symphonic masterpiece. And he did it with music that was often happy and boisterous but just as often withdrawn and lonely. Elgar himself supplied the perfect description when, by use of a pun (another Edwardian characteristic) in a letter to Arthur Troyte Griffith in 1914, he wrote of 'boyhood's *daze*'. 'Fairy Pipers' charmed to sleep the characters in the Elgar children's play, so we must accept that at the age of twelve Elgar imagined going to sleep in the exact musical terms he was later to use for Gerontius.

It was no great distance from The Wand of Youth to the second movement of the First Symphony, completed in 1908, music he asked orchestras to play 'like something we hear down by the river'.[1] Here I shall mention another Victorian-Edwardian whose most celebrated work appeared in 1904, another boy from a poor family who became one of the great literary figures of his day and, like Elgar, was always seeking the 'wand of youth', the land of lost content, 'the happy highways where I went and cannot come again'. He was James Barrie, author of Dear Brutus and, of course, of Peter Pan. If there is an Edwardian characteristic which united some of the outstanding English writers, poets and musicians of that era, it was not a dream of empire or jingoism, but this desire to escape into an idealised childhood as if the real world was too painful. I do not want to exaggerate a comparison with Barrie, but it is there and it emerged strongly in 1915 when in the midst of war Elgar poured heart and soul into music for a sub-Barrie play, The Starlight Express, adapted from a story by Algernon Blackwood. When Barrie is acted well and sincerely, his mawkishness vanishes and what may embarrass us in a lesser performance becomes magical and occasionally sinister. So it is with Elgar in his children's play and it is significant that in the score for The Starlight Express he draws heavily on The Wand of Youth.

The climax of Elgar's Edwardian period is the trilogy of works composed between 1909 and 1912 in which, to quote his own words, 'I have written out my soul . . . I have shewn myself'.[2] These are the Violin Concerto, the Second Symphony and The Music Makers. They have nothing to do with the Edwardian age in its social and historical aspects; they are the music of a private man, deeply divided against himself, his religious beliefs in tatters, his emotions torn between loyalty and devotion to his wife and another kind of love of a highly complex and noble kind for Alice Stuart Wortley; his personality at once the prey of insecurity and depression and the onrush of sudden high spirits, a man who had a deep grudge against providence for its failure to recognise him at the first glance and an equally deep scorn for the ingrained philistinism of the country which had loaded him with more honours than any other musician. Is it any wonder that the central climax of his

Second Symphony, when the violent hammering of percussion blots out the rest of the music, took its cue from Tennyson?

> And the wheels go over my head,
> And my bones are shaken with pain
>
> . . .
>
> The hoofs of the horses beat,
> Beat into my scalp and brain.

There is another celebrated passage in this symphony, the coda of the finale. Those elegiac and consolatory pages have been seen in retrospect, by those wise after the event, as an epitaph for an age that was to end on 4 August 1914. But this music enshrines more than a temporal event. Is it the benediction of the Spirit of Delight or its withdrawal? It has never been more evocatively described than by Peter J. Pirie, in an essay of 1957:

> It is a farewell to a vision that has been glimpsed but never held, to an illusion, stubbornly maintained in the face of overwhelming evidence, that the dignity of nineteenth-century society was real, its values true, its structure stable. The vision was seen by a boy in a candlelit bedroom of a country cottage . . . it was the blackcurrant tea that he mourned, and the life of a schoolboy on Malvern slopes.[3]

*The Music Makers* is a requiem for Elgar's creative psyche. It was the apotheosis of the ideals of the boy who had tried to write down what the reeds were saying and who had believed that he could thereby sway the hearts and minds of mankind. But the adult Elgar found that music did not move and shake the world. He cursed the gifts that providence had given him.

# 1 'Boyhood's daze'

In 1841 a twenty-year-old piano tuner, piano teacher and organist named William Henry Elgar moved from London to Worcester. Born in Dover, he had worked in London for the music publisher Coventry & Hollier, but it was the piano firm of Broadwood who had recommended him when a stationer called Stratfords, with a shop in The Cross, Worcester, wanted to develop its musical side and sought a tuner. He was handsome and charming. His son Edward was to say in later years: 'My father used to ride a thoroughbred mare when he went to tune a piano. He never did a stroke of work in his life.'[1] The rides took him to the country houses of Worcestershire, among them Witley Court, the seat of the Earl of Dudley and once the home for three years of William IV's widow, Queen Adelaide. Lord Dudley heard William playing the piano after tuning it and was so impressed that he offered to pay for him to have further lessons, but the offer was refused. William was, in any case, a violinist and joined various amateur ensembles in Worcester such as the Glee Club, which met weekly in the Crown Hotel. He became friends with John Leicester, a printer in the High Street, and William Allen, a solicitor. Leicester was a Roman Catholic and a member of the choir at St George's church. It was he who in 1846 put forward William Elgar's name when the organist left (even though William was Anglican). The duties, besides playing the organ, involved training the choir, choosing the music and occasionally composing. On many

1  Elgar's birthplace at Broadheath in about 1920

Sundays, instrumentalists were called in for Masses by Haydn, Mozart, Beethoven and others.

William lodged at a café in Mealecheapen Street kept by a man whose wife had been a Miss Greening. Soon he was taken into their family home in the village of Claines where he met Ann Greening, a Herefordshire farm labourer's daughter, with an avid appetite for reading, especially tales of chivalry. William and Ann were married in 1848. She accompanied her husband to church every Sunday and eventually took instruction from the priest and converted to Roman Catholicism. William would have no truck with it and wrote to his family in Dover excoriating 'the absurd superstition and playhouse mummery of the Papist; the cold and formal ceremonies of the Church of England; the bigotry and rank hypocrisy of the Wesleyan'.[2] Later he was known to have threatened 'to shoot his daughters if caught going to confession'.[3]

Children soon arrived: Henry John (Harry) on 15 October 1848, Lucy Ann on 29 May 1852 and Susannah Mary (Pollie) on 28 December 1854. They were born at 2 College Precincts, opposite the east end of the cathedral. Ann Elgar yearned for a country life and in 1856 they rented The Firs, the tiny cottage of Newbury House in the village of Broadheath, three miles north-west of Worcester. It had six rooms on two floors. There, on 2 June 1857, Edward William Elgar was born, a day, according to his sister Lucy, when 'the air was sweet with the perfume of flowers, bees were humming, and all the earth was lovely'.[4] Edward was baptised at St George's on 11 June, his sponsors being William and Charlotte Leicester.

William Elgar remained in Worcester on weekdays so the family revolved round Ann. She imbued her children with a love of nature and continually read stories and recited poetry to them. A favourite poem was 'The Better Land', by Mrs Felicia Dorothea Hermans:

> Mother! Oh, where is that radiant shore?
> Shall we not seek it and weep no more?
>
> . . .

Dreams cannot picture a world so fair –
Sorrow and death cannot enter there:
Time doth not breathe on its fadeless bloom,
For beyond the clouds, and beyond the tomb,
– It is there, it is there, my child!

Ann Elgar was not musical, but enjoyed those weekend evenings when her husband brought John Leicester and William Allen for an evening of singing round the piano. Allen always sang the baritone aria 'Di Provenza il mar' from Verdi's La traviata (which had only been premièred in 1853). But Edward was still a baby and knew nothing of this.

In the spring of 1859, with a fifth child due, the family moved back into Worcester. John Leicester had offered William a shop where people could try pianos before buying them and it was essential for William to live there. Edward was less than two years old when the family moved into 1 Edgar Street (now 1 Severn Street) where Frederick Joseph (Jo) was born on 28 August 1859. The business prospered and William sent for his much younger brother Henry to join him (in fact, rejoin, because Henry had worked as his teenage apprentice in Worcester for several years until they quarrelled). In 1860 they took over a vacant shop at 10 High Street (now demolished) as 'Elgar Bros.', though Henry was an employee rather than a partner. In the following year, the Elgars and Henry moved back into 2 College Precincts. There Edward 'played about among the tombs & in the cloisters when I cd. scarcely walk'.[5] A sixth child, Francis Thomas (Frank), was born in College Precincts on 1 October 1861. The family moved into rooms above the shop at 10 High Street in 1863, where a seventh child, Helen Agnes (Dott or Dot), was born on 1 January 1864.

Lucy and Pollie attended the dame school at 11 Britannia Square, home of a Catholic convert, Miss Caroline Walsh, and were joined there in September 1863 by Edward. Life was no longer a Broad-heath idyll. There were worries about money because William took life so easily. While Henry concentrated on the business of the shop, William always found it impossible to settle down to work on hand but could cheerfully spend hours over some perfectly unnecessary and entirely unremunerative undertaking (a trait that was very noticeable in E[dward] especially in later life) . . . But anything that promised an hour's or a day's distraction always took him away.[6]

Edward grew deeply attached to his mother, who communicated her love of literature to him, but it was his father who noticed the boy's aptitude for music when he began to extemporise on a piano in the shop, and who arranged for him to have lessons from Sarah Ricketts, a singer at St George's, and later from Pollie Tyler at Miss Walsh's school. Soon William took his son on his piano tuning rounds, in a pony and trap, and allowed him to improvise on the instrument after he had finished with it. Elgar's friend the violinist W. H. Reed wrote many years later:

> No detail or happening of those far-off times escaped him; he could tell me as we ambled about the lanes and passed these great houses, and many others too, the names of all the people who lived in them long ago, and relate to me the sayings of the members of the household, or the yarns spun for his benefit by the groom, or the old ostler who watered his father's horse.[7]

The boy achieved some local fame as an extemporiser and used to be taken to a house in College Green to play to two old ladies and their guests. Elgar recalled: 'The old people talked gravely about the music, and my favourite old gentleman (who wore many seals & such a stiff collar) said "Kozeluch was more fiery than Corelli" & that Schobert was "artificial in his Allegros". Dear Heart! how learned it seemed.'[8]

On 5 May 1864 the eldest child, Harry, aged fifteen, who 'loved botany and the study of herbs and was always making concoctions of plants',[9] died from a kidney disease after an illness lasting four weeks. Edward thus became the eldest son, especially protective of the next boy, Jo,

who was regarded as 'the "Beethoven" of the family', according to
his sister Lucy, 'having very remarkable aptitude for music in every way
from the time he could sit up in his chair'.[10] Jo, 'though very intelligent,
was curiously undeveloped in many ways and never learnt to pronounce
his words properly'.[11] His health declined throughout the summer
of 1866 and he died from tuberculosis on 7 September just after his
seventh birthday. As it happened, this was also the month of a seminal
experience for Edward. The lay clerks of the cathedral were regular
customers at Elgar Bros. and Edward, from when he was a small boy,
had gone into the cathedral to hear music rehearsed and performed
and had borrowed scores from the cathedral library. The organist was
William Done, who also conducted the Three Choirs Festival when
it was Worcester's turn. It is a little difficult to comprehend Elgar's
insistence when he was older that being a Roman Catholic had barred
doors to him. It certainly did not bar the doors of the Anglican cathedral.
The 1866 festival was Worcester's: William played in the orchestral
second violins, Henry in the violas. To distract Edward from Jo's death,
the boy was allowed to attend the rehearsal of Beethoven's Mass in C on
10 September. He was overwhelmed, not by the choral singing but by
the sound of a full orchestra. He said to his friend Hubert Leicester: 'If
I had that orchestra under my own control & given a free hand I could
make it play whatever I liked.'[12] Already he had ambitions. As he wrote
to a friend in 1921:

> I am still at heart the dreamy child who used to be found in the reeds by
> Severn side with a sheet of paper trying to fix the sounds & longing for
> something very great – source, texture & all else unknown. I am still
> looking for this – in strange company sometimes – but as a child &
> as a young man & as a mature man no single person was ever kind
> to me.[13]

No single person? His mother was constantly sympathetic but, as
Hubert Leicester recorded, 'his father and uncle were merely amused
and scoffed at these childish efforts – an attitude in which they persisted

until E. really had made his way in the world. They failed to see not only that they had an exceptionally gifted boy in the family but even that he was moderately clever at music.'[14] Meanwhile, what of general education? After Miss Walsh's dame school, Edward went to the small school at Spetchley Park built by the Catholic Berkeley family. This was two and a half miles outside Worcester on the way to Stratford-upon-Avon and the children were taught by the Sisters of St Paul. From the school windows, Edward would gaze in wonder at the tall fir trees swaying in the wind. When he revisited Spetchley Park over fifty years later, he found a score of *The Dream of Gerontius* in the library of the great house. He opened it at the page where Gerontius sings 'The sound is like the rushing of the wind – the summer wind among the lofty pines' and wrote against the music: 'In Spetchley Park 1869'. Attending this school meant long walks every day and in 1869 Edward went to Littleton House, Wick, run by a professional Catholic schoolmaster, Francis Reeve. Even this meant a two-mile journey involving daily crossing of the Severn by ferry from Cathedral Steps. Hubert Leicester, two years his senior, was already a pupil at Littleton House and the two boys' journeys cemented a friendship that was to last until Elgar's death. Leicester was impressed by his friend's maturity and later described Edward as having 'nothing of a boy about him. One great characteristic – always doing *something.* When he stopped away from school (which he did about $\frac{1}{3}$ of his time) it was not to play truant merely.'[15] The reason was his delicate health, a source of anxiety to his parents after the loss of Harry and Jo.

For Edward, memories of Broadheath were only what his siblings told him. But in 1867 they returned there in the summer holidays to stay with Mr and Mrs Doughty who owned a farm beside Broadheath Common, the back of which ran nearly down to the cottage where Elgar was born. During this visit he wrote his earliest surviving piece of music: 'Humoreske, a tune from Broadheath 1867'. He copied it into a sketchbook some years later. It opens in G major and the second of its two four-bar phrases ends in F sharp minor, a semitone down. 'Jape', Elgar wrote in his sketchbook. It is to this time that the candlelit bedroom and the blackcurrant tea belong, and the idealisation of the cottage of his birth into a symbol of that 'better land'.

Edward found the piano a limiting instrument. When he was seven or eight he accompanied his father into St George's organ loft and soon began to play, but was still frustrated by the instrument's restricted variety of colour. Dissatisfied, too, with his attempts at composition, he read books on harmony, theory and orchestration, first C. S. Catel's *Traité d'harmonie* (1802) and then Cherubini's *Counterpoint*. He found something more human in 'Mozart's Thorough-bass School' and, even more, in studying the scores of Haydn, Mozart and Beethoven in his father's shop. Beethoven's First Symphony, in particular the transition from D flat back to C in the Minuetto, 'sank into his very soul' and convinced him that 'Tallis and Byrd and Orlando Gibbons and the rest of the classic church-composers had not exhausted the possibilities . . . that Mozart and Beethoven, having attained the highest plane of emotional expressiveness, were the best models for study'.[16] He also acquired Anton Reicha's *Orchestral Primer* on 7 March 1869. Listening later that year to a Three Choirs rehearsal for Handel's *Messiah*, he was so excited by the sound of the strings in 'O thou that tellest' that he begged his father to lend him a violin from the shop. A fortnight later, by his own efforts, he could play the violin part of the Handel aria. William Elgar had helped the festival librarian to check and correct the hired orchestral parts for *Messiah* and took Edward with him. The boy added extra notes for the brass to provide added colour, but his additions were detected at rehearsal. *Elijah* and *Judas Maccabaeus* were performed in this year, and Elgar heard Sims Reeves, Charles Santley and Thérèse Tietjens for the first time. 'Now they *were* singers', he told Wulstan Atkins.[17] Edward's violin playing progressed so well that William invited him to join the Crown Hotel Glee Club, which was short of a second violinist. He and his father played the two violins and Uncle Henry the harmonium. Philip Leicester, Hubert's son, described the Dickensian scene in the long, low room of the hotel as his father recalled it:

Huge fires roar a cheery welcome. Round the walls and at numerous
small tables are seated perhaps a hundred men, of all ages and
conditions, from prosperous city fathers to young clerks. Half a dozen
buxom waitresses flit about with trays of tankards and glasses and the
air is heavy with smoke . . . At the top of the room, on a small platform,
sits the chairman, a local alderman, and at his side the stout and genial
secretary. In the corner beside them is the band – a piano, some violins,
a couple of cellos, woodwind and a solitary cornet. Near them sit two
men in evening dress, artistes from the cathedral choir.[18]

Elgar learned to smoke at these concerts and remained a smoker,
pipe, cigar and cigarette, for the rest of his life. The music, besides
glees, comprised symphonies by Haydn and instrumental works by
Corelli, Handel, Mozart, Bellini, Auber, Beethoven and Schubert. He
was especially excited by the Coronation March from Meyerbeer's Le
prophète: 'His eyes used to shine with excitement when we discussed
this', W. H. Reed wrote, 'and he hummed the strong rhythmic tune: the
strength of that triplet on the first beat of the bar gripped him.'[19]

In either 1869 or 1871 the Elgar children presented a play with music
which they performed to their parents. It was devised because of 'some
small grievances occasioned by the imaginary despotic rule of my father
and mother (The Two Old People) . . . to show that children were not
properly understood'.[20] It was set in a woodland glade, such as could be
found at Broadheath, intersected by a brook. On one side was fairyland,
on the other the 'ordinary life'. The Old People were lured over the
bridge into fairyland by moths and butterflies and little bells, but they
failed to develop 'that fairy feeling'. So fairy pipers entered in a boat
and charmed them to sleep. Elgar wrote the music for piano, two or
three strings including a home-made double bass, flute and improvised
percussion. Nearly forty years later, this music, which incorporated the
Broadheath Humoreske, became the two suites entitled The Wand of
Youth. The Humoreske 'tune from Broadheath' became 'Fairies and
Giants' and the 'Moths and Butterflies' tune was recast in A minor. Of
the latter Elgar said: 'I do not remember the time when it was not written
in some form or other.'[21] This illustrates Elgar's lifelong method of

2  Elgar (centre) aged twenty-one with his brother and sisters (l. to r.) Frank, Lucy, Dot and Pollie, 1878

composition. He always carried a sketchbook into which he jotted ideas or themes as they occurred to him. He might not use these for many years, one reason why precise dating of his compositions is difficult. It also explains why some of his word setting is awkward: the melody may have been written years earlier without any text in mind.

In 1872, before he was fifteen, Elgar composed his first song, *The Language of Flowers*, to a poem by the American James Gates Percival

3   Elgar aged fourteen

(1795–1856), and dedicated it to his sister Lucy on her twentieth birth-day. He left school this year. An ambition to go to Leipzig to study music was financially impossible, so on 26 June he started work in the office of the solicitor William Allen (the singer of 'Di Provenza il mar'). But rather than receiving instruction in the law, he found he was expected to wash the office floors. Music still occupied his free time and he was able to assist his father in his organ duties at St George's – William would leave during the sermon and go for a drink. On 14 July Edward played for the first time at Mass. Soon he was arranging music for the choir. When he attended the Three Choirs Festival in 1872 he was again impressed by the way in which Handel treated the second violins when strengthening a lead for altos, bringing that part into prominence by throwing it into the upper octave. He noticed also the 'wonderfully resonant effect' Handel obtained by the spacing of his chords in a chorus such as 'Their sound is gone out'.[22] He abandoned his job with Allen in 1873 after the upper clerk had made life unpleasant for him and became an assistant in his father's shop. This enabled him to study the scores of Beethoven symphonies. 'I remember distinctly the day I was able to buy the *Pastoral* Symphony. I stuffed my pockets with bread and cheese and went out into the fields to study it.'[23] A favourite spot for study was the churchyard at Claines, where his mother's family had lived. Here he could be undisturbed. He would also go to the point where the River Teme joins the Severn. It was there, as he told his daughter in later years, that he wished to be buried. At home he would wait until his parents were asleep, then creep downstairs to select a score to study and pore over it by candlelight with his bedclothes drawn up like a tent to prevent anyone seeing the light under the door.[24] One result of his Beethoven studies was the Credo he concocted for St George's choir in July 1873. This was composed entirely of themes from three of the symphonies. He used the opening Allegro con brio of no. 5, the Allegretto of no. 7 and the Adagio of no. 9. He ascribed it to 'Bernhard Pappenheim' (pope's home), a joke that was probably not appreciated at St George's. He also based a Gloria on Mozart's F major violin sonata (K. 547). It was around this time that he told his mother that he wouldn't be satisfied 'until I receive a letter from abroad addressed to "Edward Elgar, England" '.[25]

## 2 Helen

Elgar's musical education now began in earnest. The 1875 Three Choirs Festival in Worcester was known as the Mock Festival because the dean and chapter, egged on by the Earl of Dudley, refused to allow an orchestra into the cathedral or for charges to be made for performances there. Streets and shops were decked with black flags in protest. For Elgar the only redeeming feature was the thrilling organ playing of S. S. Wesley at the end of the evening services, particularly of J. S. Bach's 'Wedge' and 'Giant' fugues. For the rest of his life Elgar remembered the registrations Wesley had used. Wesley played on the new organ which had been installed in the cathedral in 1874.[1] On 23 November 1875 Elgar played in the second violins with his father in a Worcester Musical Society performance of Spohr's The Last Judgement. He also found a place in the orchestra (only about ten performers) which accompanied the touring opera companies that visited Worcester. Thus he came to know Bellini's Norma, Verdi's Il trovatore and La traviata and Mozart's Don Giovanni. At this time he asked the Glee Club's ensemble leader Fred Spray to give him formal violin lessons. After six months Spray told him he could not teach him anything more. When he played on 16 May 1876 in a performance of Mendelssohn's Elijah by Worcester Philharmonic Society, he was on the back desk of the first violins while his father remained in the seconds.

In September and November of 1876 he wrote his first compositions for the choir of St George's, a *Salve regina* and a *Tantum ergo*. For the Glee Club ensemble in October he arranged Wagner's overture to *The Flying Dutchman*. He replaced his father at the Glee Club both as accompanist and as arranger. Hubert Leicester remembered that this led to 'battles between father and son. Old man always great respect & fear of son's superior musical knowledge.'² Soon Edward was leading the orchestra for C. H. Ogle's concerts at Pershore and he began to give violin lessons to village children and at his old school Littleton House. In March 1877 he wrote *Reminiscences* for violin and piano, an early example of Elgar nostalgia which he dedicated to a grocer friend, Oswin Grainger. A few days after finishing the piece he attended a recital in Worcester by the German violinist August Wilhelmj, whose playing, with its big tone, inspired Elgar to save up to go to London in August for lessons with the celebrated teacher Adolphe Pollitzer. He had five lessons with Pollitzer, who urged him to stay in London and devote himself to violin playing, but as Elgar recounted later, 'I had become enamoured of a country life and would not give up the prospect of a certain living by playing and teaching in Worcester on the chance of only a possible success which I might make as a soloist in London.'³

In Worcester that same summer he was appointed 'leader and instructor' of the Amateur Instrumental Society, which had recently been formed by Oswin Grainger and others for weekly rehearsals and to accompany oratorio performances under the conductor Alfred Caldicott. Among the members were Edward's brother Frank as oboist and Hubert Leicester and his brother William as flautist and clarinettist. With another flautist, Frank Exton, and with Edward as bassoonist (he taught himself), these friends formed a wind quintet which rehearsed in a shed behind the Elgar shop. Because of the unusual composition of the quintet (no horn), Elgar wrote the music for it himself, composing it during the St George's sermon. He called these works 'Shed Music' and several followed over the next year or two. They were lost for nearly 100 years until a BBC broadcast in 1976. Although not mature Elgar, they are delightful pieces and show remarkable

4   The wind quintet, c.1878: back row, William Leicester (clarinet), Elgar (bassoon),
Hubert Leicester (flute); front row, Frank Exton (flute), Frank Elgar (oboe)

craftsmanship and a sense of instrumental colour that never deserted him. They are the forerunners of the vignettes of the Enigma Variations. Elgar dedicated them to members of the quintet and under the generic titles of *Harmony Music*, *Promenades* and *Intermezzi* gave them fanciful individual titles such as 'Mme Toussaud's' (*sic*), 'Evesham Andante', 'Mrs Winslow's Soothing Syrup' (a remedy advertised on the back of sheet music), 'Hell and Tommy', 'Somniferous', 'The Alphonsa' (Hubert Leicester's sister), 'Noah's Ark' and 'The Farmyard'. Some years later Elgar wrote on the bassoon part of one of these works: 'I like the Shed on the whole, but the *Intermezzi* are "mine own children".' On the bassoon part of *Harmony Music* no. 2, completed in April 1878, he wrote 'Nelly Shed'. This is taken to be a reference to Helen Jessie Weaver, the seventeen-year-old daughter of William Weaver, who had a thriving boot and shoe business at 84 High Street, although the family home was in Mayfield Road. The family comprised five children from Weaver's first marriage, Helen being the youngest (she was thirteen when her mother died), and the son born in 1877 to his second wife, who was twenty-eight years his junior. Elgar was friendly with Frank Weaver, the fourth child and second son, born in 1855, who played the violin in some of the same ensembles. When William Weaver died in 1880, Frank took over the business.

In 1878 Elgar had more lessons from Pollitzer. This time he showed the violinist some of his compositions. Pollitzer gave him an introduction to August Manns, conductor of the Crystal Palace concerts ('no single person was ever kind to me'!). Manns gave him a pass to attend rehearsals and Elgar was thus enabled to hear some of the important new works which Manns introduced. But it involved a logistical exercise from Worcester:

> I rose at six – walked a mile to the railway station, – the train left at
> seven; – arrived at Paddington about eleven; – underground to
> Victoria; – on to the Palace, arriving in time for the last three-quarters
> of an hour of the rehearsal; if fortune smiled, this piece of the rehearsal
> included the work desired to be heard; but fortune rarely smiled and
> more often than not the principal item was over. Lunch, – Concert at

three; – at five a rush for the train to Victoria; – then to Paddington; – on to Worcester arriving at ten-thirty. A strenuous day indeed; but the new work had been heard and another treasure added to a life's experience.[4]

He was twenty-one in June 1878. The Three Choirs Festival was again in Worcester and this time the orchestra was allowed into the cathedral. Elgar played in the second violins. One of the works rehearsed was Mozart's G minor symphony (K. 550) and this stimulated Elgar to rule a score for the same instruments and with the same number of bars. Within that framework he wrote music which followed the same outline in the themes and the same modulations. Although he completed only the minuet, it was a discipline from which he learned much.

For some years Elgar and his father had played in occasional concerts given for the inmates of the County Lunatic Asylum at Powick. The asylum doctors believed in the therapeutic effects of music, formed an ensemble of players from their staff and hired a conductor to instruct the players and to compose items for Friday evening dances. The post became vacant in 1878 and Elgar submitted a minuet scored for Powick's instrumentation: flute, clarinet, two cornets, euphonium, bombardon, two violins, double bass and piano. He was appointed music director from 1 January 1879 at £30 a year, with five shillings (25p in today's currency) for each quadrille or polka he might compose. He was now working at Powick one day a week, playing in ensembles far and near, teaching his violin pupils, leading the Amateur Instrumental Society, playing at Glee Club meetings, playing at St George's, serving in the shop occasionally, slipping up to London for concerts – and composing. His visits to London had fired his enthusiasm for the music of Schumann after he heard Hans von Bülow play the Fantasy and the Joachim Quartet play the A minor string quartet.

For one of the asylum dances in 1879 he wrote a set of quadrilles which he called *Die junge Kokotte* and dedicated to Miss J. Holloway, the band's pianist. Another of his titles, for a set of five quadrilles, was *L'assomoir* (sic), an allusion to Emile Zola's novel *L'assommoir* published in 1876–7. The last of the five was incorporated in 1908 into the second *Wand of Youth* suite as 'Wild Bears'. Elgar's sketchbooks at this time contain many themes which went into later works: the Minuet, 'Moths and Butterflies', the March and 'Wild Bears' from *The Wand of Youth*; a sarabande for wind quintet which he planned to use in the opera *The Spanish Lady* in the 1930s; a piano piece *Douce pensée* which became *Rosemary* in 1915; an Andante in Shed no. 6 which became *Cantique* in 1912; ideas which went into *The Black Knight* and *King Olaf*; a phrase that was to become the orchestral opening of 'Sabbath Morning at Sea' in *Sea Pictures*; and a quadrille that became 'When corals lie' in the same work. Elgar continued his work at Powick until 1884. It left its mark. In a letter to Ernest Newman in June 1917, he wrote: 'A lunatic asylum is, after the first shock, not entirely sad; so few of the patients are aware of the strangeness of their situation; most of them are placid & foolishly calm; but the horror of the fallen intellect – *knowing* what it once was & *knowing* what it has become – is beyond words frightful.'

During 1879 Elgar left his parents' home at 10 High Street to live at 35 (now 12) Chestnut Walk with his sister Pollie and her husband William Grafton, who had been married in April. The eldest Elgar daughter, Lucy, was engaged to Charles Pipe, but since he was not a Catholic there was opposition to the marriage, probably from Ann Elgar. At any rate, in August 1880 all was resolved when Pipe was received into the Catholic Church. The following month he and Elgar went to Paris for a brief holiday (Pipe had been there three times before). Elgar went to the Madeleine to hear Saint-Saëns play the organ. He also found time for a brief dalliance. Writing in 1933, he mentioned that 'in passing through the pine-scented forest of Fontainebleau I had come to a turn of the road leading to Barbizon. The scent recalled a romance of 1880, and I nearly – very nearly – turned to Barbizon.'5 Back home the next set of Powick quadrilles was called *Paris*, with titles such as 'Châtelet', 'Café des ambassadeurs' and 'Là, Suzanne!'. Miss Holloway was again the dedicatee.

Meanwhile Elgar's knowledge of music was broadening. On visits to London he heard works by Berlioz – the *Francs-juges* overture, *Lélio* and *Nuits d'été*. The last-named was preceded by Wagner's overture to

Die Meistersinger. The conductor was Hans Richter. That was in October 1881. Before then, in the spring, Elgar wrote a march, Pas redoublé, and an Air de ballet which Caldicott conducted at a concert of the Amateur Instrumental Society, with Elgar leading the orchestra. In September he was at the last desk of the first violins in the Three Choirs Festival orchestra in Worcester. Among the new works was a cantata, The Bride, by Alexander Mackenzie, performed in the College Hall. The impact it made was recalled fifty years later: 'Here was a man fully equipped in every department of musical knowledge, who had been a violinist in orchestras in Germany. It gave orchestral players a real lift . . . Then I had the honour to meet the composer the following morning and actually shook hands with him.'[6] He always retained an affection for Mackenzie, whom he did not regard as a pillar of the academic establishment. In 1933 he persuaded Adrian Boult to revive Mackenzie's Violin Concerto in a BBC concert. Of the two real pillars, Parry and Stanford, he had admiration and respect for Parry as man and musician but not for Stanford, even though Stanford did much to promote his music at the turn of the century. Elgar felt he was shunned by academics and never got over it.

Elgar's Air de ballet was repeated by the Amateur Instrumental Society on 20 February 1882 and a new Pas redoublé march was played. The Air de ballet was played again on 11 August at a concert for delegates to a meeting in Worcester of the British Medical Association. Among the members was Dr Charles Buck, an amateur cellist. He and Elgar struck up a friendship and Buck, who was thirty, invited Elgar to spend a holiday at his house, Cravendale, in Giggleswick, near Settle, Yorkshire. Elgar took up the offer at the end of the month, on the 28th. While there he played in a piano trio in which Buck's mother was the pianist. For them he wrote the piece he called Douce pensée. Perhaps this was a 'sweet thought' about Barbizon. When in 1915 he arranged it for piano and for small orchestra he called it Rosemary ('That's for remembrance'). The holiday was a success. The two bachelors played tennis and golf, walked, stalked cats and smoked (Buck had fifty pipes).[7]

On return to Worcester, Elgar succeeded Caldicott as conductor of the Amateur Instrumental Society and was engaged as a violinist in

William C. Stockley's Birmingham concert orchestra which gave an annual series of winter concerts. Stockley was also conductor of the Birmingham Festival Choral Society and the festival's chorusmaster. Elgar saved enough money for a fortnight's visit to Leipzig over the Christmas holidays, a venture which precipitated one of the most mysterious episodes of his life. In October 1882 he had written a polka called *La blonde* which he inscribed 'H. J. W. vom Leipzig gewidmet' ('Dedicated to H. J. W. of Leipzig'). This was Helen Weaver, who had gone to Leipzig Conservatory to study the violin. It is not known exactly when she went there, but it seems likely that the polka was a present for her to wish her well. Elgar arrived in Leipzig on 31 December 1882 to stay in the *pension* where Helen and her younger friend Edith Groveham were also staying. This was arranged with the approval of Helen's brother Frank. Elgar packed a lot into two weeks, seeing Anton Rubinstein's opera *Die Makkabäer* and Wagner's *Tannhäuser* and *Lohengrin*, and attending rehearsals of the Gewandhaus Orchestra in the old Cloth Hall. He 'got pretty well dosed'[8] with Schumann ('my ideal!'), hearing the Overture, Scherzo and Finale, Symphony no. 1 and Piano Concerto, Brahms, Rubinstein (Ocean Symphony), and Wagner's Prelude to Act 1 of *Parsifal* (the opera had first been performed less than six months earlier). There were also musical evenings at the *pension*. He gave Helen a copy of Longfellow's *Hyperion*, about student life in Heidelberg, a book he and his mother enjoyed.

   Whether Edward proposed to Helen during that visit is yet another unknown fact in their relationship. No letters survive. In March 1883 he attended the Wagner memorial concert at the Crystal Palace, noting in his copy of the programme that Isolde's *Liebestod* 'is the finest thing of Wagner's that I have heard up to the present'. Around this time his sister Pollie moved to a house called The Elms at Stoke Prior near Bromsgrove, so he left Chestnut Walk to live with Charles and Lucy Pipe at 4 Field Terrace. He completed an orchestral work, *Intermezzo: Sérénade mauresque*, which was performed on 4 April at a Worcestershire Musical Union concert conducted by the Reverend Edward Vine Hall and on 13 December at a Stockley concert in Birmingham. At the end of May he heard Berlioz's Requiem at the Crystal Palace.

Charles Buck invited Elgar to Settle again in the summer but Elgar replied on 1 July that 'the vacation at Leipzig begins shortly; my "Braut" arrives here on Thursday next; remaining 'till the first week in Septr; of course I shall remain in Worcester 'till her departure'. Presumably the engagement became 'official' during the summer, although it is curious that Elgar said nothing about it in any letter to Buck, to whom he usually wrote lengthily and effusively. When Helen returned to Leipzig, he went to stay with Buck and on return wrote another polka which he called *Helcia*. In November Helen cut short her Leipzig studies to return to Worcester. Her stepmother had been ailing since 1880 and had moved to a smaller house at 3 (now 6) Arboretum Road. 'Well, Helen has come back!!', Elgar wrote to Buck. 'Mrs Weaver is so ill, dying in fact, so the child thought it best to return & nurse her; so we are together a little now & then & consequently happy.'

Mrs Weaver died from pulmonary tuberculosis on 13 November. Helen did not return to Leipzig. She went with Elgar's mother to Birmingham on 13 December to hear the *Sérénade mauresque*. Elgar wrote to Buck on 14 January 1884:

> I had a good success at Birm. despite what the papers say . . . I have *no money* – not a cent. And I am sorry to say have no prospects of getting any . . . My father was ill just before Xmas which made it dismal; the younger generation at the Catholic Ch. have taken an objection to him & have got him turned out of the Organist's place; this he has held for 37 years!! . . . Frank gets on . . . it seems to me that the only person who is an utter failure in this miserable world is myself . . . Miss Weaver is remaining in Worcester & the little Music &c that we get together is the only enjoyment I get & more than I deserve no doubt.

'Miss Weaver' seems oddly formal. This letter is an example of Elgar's typical self-pity. But composition usually pulled him out of his Slough of Despond and he wrote *Sevillana* which was played at a Worcester Philharmonic Society concert on 1 May 1884 and at a Crystal Palace concert conducted by August Manns on 12 May, the first music by Elgar to be heard in London. (Manns later repeated it.) By then Helen had broken off the engagement after nine months. Why? Again, no one knows. It has been suggested that there were objections because of their different religions – Anglican and Catholic. This is extremely unlikely since no one had objected to the engagement. Ann Elgar was happy to go to a concert with Helen, and the wife and children of Helen's brother Frank became Catholics and Frank himself later became a convert. It is more likely that Helen saw that Elgar had no money and no prospects. Elgar did not at once tell the news to Buck (who had just announced his own engagement), writing on 21 April: 'My prospects are about as hopeless as ever.' Buck inquired about Helen and was told: 'Miss Weaver is very well. I do not think she will remain in Worcester much longer now.' It was not until 20 July that he wrote: 'Things have not prospered with me this year at all, my prospects are worse than ever & to crown my miseries my engagement is broken off & I am lonely. Perhaps at some future time I may come out of my shell again but at present I remain here; I have not the heart to speak to anyone.' If Helen did leave Worcester, no one knows where she went, although it has been suggested by Wulstan Atkins that she took a teaching post in Yorkshire, staying in Bradford with Edith Groveham.[9]

Sevillana had been played at the Crystal Palace at an afternoon concert. In the evening there was a Richter concert at which Elgar heard the first British performance of Brahms's Third Symphony and was profoundly impressed. On another visit to London, he heard Wilhelmj play Beethoven's Violin Concerto. Afterwards he asked Pollitzer if he himself could ever be 'first-class'. Pollitzer answered: 'No'. Being in a 'very desponding state', as he told Buck, he went to Scotland on 11 August and visited Mull, Iona, Ballachulish and Inverness. On Loch Etive on the 15th he met a girl with his own initials – E. E. – from whom he parted on the 22nd. While with her he wrote Une idylle for violin and piano, dedicated to 'E. E., Inverness'. To Buck's inquiry when the work was published he replied: 'Miss E. E. at Inverness is nobody – that is to say that I shall ever see again.' He returned to Worcester to play at the third desk of the first violins at the Three Choirs Festival in September when Dvořák conducted his Stabat mater and Symphony in D (now known as no. 6). Dvořák's music, he told Buck, 'is simply ravishing, so tuneful & clever & the orchestration is wonderful; no matter how few instruments he uses it never sounds thin'.

A month later, for no known reason, Elgar resigned from his band-master's post at Powick. He negotiated with Schott in Regent Street, London, to publish his Romance in E minor for violin and piano, which thus became his op. 1. He signed away his copyright for a shilling (5p today) and twenty free copies. He also sent some of his works to the directors of the Covent Garden Promenade Concerts. They agreed to devote a morning to rehearsing them. He went to conduct them, but Sir Arthur Sullivan arrived unexpectedly to run through a selection from one of his operas. He took up all Elgar's rehearsal time and that was that. In February 1885 he was working on a 'Scottish' overture, which he later abandoned, and had 'a big work in tow' (unidentified), projects which, as he again told Buck, 'serve to divert me somewhat & hide a broken heart'.

Was the 'broken heart' due to Helen? Six months later he wrote a song beginning:

> Through the long days and year
> What will my lov'd one be,
> Parted from me?

And ending:

> But, while my darling lives,
> Peaceful I journey on,
> Not quite alone.

A few days later he journeyed on to stay in Settle with Buck and his wife. During the holiday he began a courtship of Sarah Anne ('Annie') Wilkinson-Newsholme of Hellifield Green, six years his senior. If mar-riage was ever contemplated, the idea was scotched by her wealthy father, who saw Elgar as merely a penniless musician. After the Settle holiday, Elgar wrote to Buck: 'Miss W. is going to New Zealand this month – her lungs are affected, I hear, & there has been a miserable time for me since I came home.' The 'I hear' implies that there was no personal contact with Helen.

New Zealand, a thirteen-week voyage away in 1885, had no reputation for tuberculosis sanatoria, although its milder climate was an attraction. Why Helen decided to go there has never been explained. In August 1890 she married John Munro, a bank manager, in Auckland. A son, Kenneth, was born in July 1891. He was killed in action in France four days before his twenty-fifth birthday in 1916. His sister, Joyce, was born in 1893 and died of tuberculosis in 1921. Helen died of cancer on 23 December 1927.

Although Jerrold Northrop Moore's comprehensive biography *Edward Elgar: A Creative Life* gave the facts of the Elgar–Weaver relationship, it was the book by Elgar's godson Wulstan Atkins that propounded the theory that 'this experience had profoundly affected much of Elgar's music',[10] a big claim. Apparently in about 1932 Elgar had told Wulstan Atkins's father, Sir Ivor Atkins, organist of Worcester cathedral 1897–1950 and a close friend of Elgar, about the engagement and how it had been broken off 'by mutual consent'. Elgar did not say that the revelation was confidential – why should it have been? – but Sir Ivor kept it to himself and asked his son not to reveal it until 1984, fifty years after Elgar's death, 'to avoid any possible distress' (to whom?).

Ivor Atkins believed that the three asterisks in the 'Romanza', the thirteenth of the Enigma Variations, are a disguise for Helen as the real 'friend pictured within' and that the clarinet's quotation from Mendelssohn's *Calm Sea and Prosperous Voyage*, with its Leipzig association, is a reference to her departure for New Zealand. This was no doubt why, when he chose the music for Elgar's memorial service in Worcester cathedral on 2 March 1934, one of the four extracts he selected from the Variations was '(* * *)', together with the theme, 'C. A. E.' (Lady Elgar) and 'Nimrod'. Atkins could not believe that Lady Mary Lygon of Madresfield Court, whom Elgar said was the inspiration for the 'Romanza', could have given rise to this variation 'with all its depth and tenderness'. Another Elgar confidant, the critic Ernest Newman, wrote in 1956 that

> it is time we heard the last of the old legend that the subject of this variation was Lady Mary Lygon . . . A present-day listener to the *Enigma* must surely be devoid of all sensibility if he does not see that, whoever the human subject of the no. 13 variation may have been, it is a poignant brooding upon some personal experience or other that had made a profound and enduring mark on him . . . A study merely of Elgar's scoring of the variation should make it clear to any person of more than average sensitivity that he was here dwelling in imagination on somebody or something the parting from whom or which had at some time or other torn the very heart out of him.[11]

Newman, of course, also wrote that Elgar on his deathbed had spoken five tragic words to him that had 'a particular bearing . . . on that passion of his for public mystification of which the most remarkable outward expressions were the two "enigmas" – that of the Variations and that of the "Soul" enshrined in the violin concerto'.[12] Newman claimed that he had been told by a friend of Elgar that the real subject of the 'Romanza' was the same as the 'Soul' whose identity is concealed by the use of five dots in the quotation on the concerto's score: 'Aquí está encerrada el alma de . . . . .' ('Here is enshrined the soul of . . . . .'). Wulstan Atkins followed suit and put forward Helen Weaver as the answer to both enigmas.

Elgar knew Lady Mary Lygon through the Madresfield music festivals and she became friends with him and his wife. Writing notes about the Variations in 1927, nearly thirty years after they were composed, he said that the asterisks in '(* * *)' 'take the place of the name of a lady who was, at the time of composition, on a sea voyage'.[13] His memory let him down, for Lady Mary Lygon did not accompany her brother Earl Beauchamp to Australia on his appointment as governor of New South Wales until 11 April 1899, two months after the Variations had been fully scored. But sketches for the variation refer to it as 'L' and at one point he contemplated reintroducing 'L. M. L.' in the finale. He wrote to her in Sydney on 25 July 1899: 'The *Variations* (especially no. 13) have been a great success for me under Richter.' Why the asterisks? Almost certainly, out of superstition, to avoid attaching someone's initials to no. 13.

Helen Weaver was definitely not on a sea voyage 'at the time of composition', but that does not mean Elgar could not have been thinking of her at the time of composition. Did his 'heartbreak' last all that time? Perhaps it did if he was still talking about it to Newman's informant all those years later. But does the music of the 'Romanza' variation really suggest that the 'very heart' had been 'torn out of him'? One's response can only be subjective, but to my ears 'Nimrod' and 'B. G. N.' are more expressive. We must remember that Elgar liked cryptic puzzles, secret codes, anagrams and crosswords. He liked them in his emotional life, too.

# 3 Alice

In October 1885 Elgar took over the duties of organist at St George's from his father's successor. 'I hate it', he told Buck, 'the choir is awful & no good to be done with them.' He wrote and arranged short Litanies for them. In April 1886 he went to a Liszt concert at the Crystal Palace at which the composer was present. And he continued to teach, although he had fewer pupils because of competition from a German violinist in Malvern. There was, however, one new pupil for piano accompaniment: 'Miss Roberts. 1st lesson. Oct. 6th'.

Caroline Alice Roberts was thirty-eight in 1886. She was the daughter of Major General Sir Henry Roberts, of the Indian army, who died in 1860, and she lived with her mother at Hazeldine House, Redmarley. She had studied the piano in Brussels and harmony with C. H. Lloyd, organist of Gloucester cathedral. She had also written poetry and two novels, the first published in 1879, the second in 1882. How soon she and Elgar discovered a mutual attraction is not known, but a few weeks after meeting her he began to set a translation of a poem by Charles, Duc d'Orléans:

> Is she not passing fair,
> She whom I love so well?[1]

In fact Alice Roberts was not particularly 'passing fair'. She was very short, dumpy and pleasant-looking rather than attractive.

On 24 February Elgar played in the Birmingham première of Verdi's Requiem and on 25 May he went to a Richter concert in London to hear the British première of Bruckner's Seventh Symphony – 'Fine intro.', he wrote in his programme, as well he might. He was more taken with the extracts from *Die Walküre*: 'Brass telling through all the strings – most weird & witchlike hurry-scurrying through the air' – that was the Ride of the Valkyries. When his song *Through the long days* was published by Stanley Lucas in 1887, he inscribed a copy 'to Miss Roberts' on 21 March. He was invited to tea at Redmarley to meet Lady Roberts. A few days later Lady Roberts died suddenly and he lent Alice, who was Anglican, his copy of Newman's poem *The Dream of Gerontius* into which he had copied the markings made by General Gordon in the copy he had been given before leaving for Egypt in 1884. These markings were widely circulated after Gordon's murder at Khartoum. Alice obtained a copy of the poem for herself and recopied the Gordon markings.

At the 1887 Three Choirs Festival in Worcester, Elgar played in the first violins in works by Cowen, Sullivan and Stanford. Later in the year he started a Ladies' Orchestral Class with sixteen violinists. He began and abandoned a violin sonata, wrote a four-movement orchestral suite (which he conducted at a Stockley concert on 23 February 1888) and also completed a suite of *Three Pieces* for strings ('Spring Song', 'Elegy' and 'Finale'), which were played in Worcester conducted by Rev. Edward Vine Hall on 7 May 1888. 'I like 'em (the first thing I ever did)', he wrote to Buck. They inspired Alice to poetry ('mystically the music swells, / Floats on and on and ever tells / Of joy and love and yearnings past'). She had moved to live in Malvern at a house named Saetermo, nearer to her piano lessons. Elgar set a poem Alice had written in 1880, and the song, *The Wind at Dawn*, was published in May in the *Magazine of Music*. Then, while on holiday with Charles Buck in Settle in August, he wrote a piano piece, *Liebesgrüss* (*Love's Greeting*). He dedicated it 'à Carice' (Caroline Alice) and on 22 September he became engaged to 'dearest A.' and gave her a pearl ring. Dearest A.'s relatives were horrified. She was marrying a penniless musician – no doubt after her money – who was also Roman Catholic and the son of a tradesman. One of her aunts cut her out of her will. For Elgar the most wounding aspect was the label of tradesman. He wrote some years later:

> Now – as to the whole 'shop' episode – I don't give a d – n! I know it has ruined me & made life impossible until I what you call made a name – I only know I was kept out of everything decent, 'cos 'his father keeps a shop' – I believe I'm always introduced so now, that is to say – the remark is invariably made in an undertone.[2]

It is impossible to know what truth there was in this, but he believed it all his life; and, of course, it is true that not only tradesmen and shop-keepers but musicians were regarded as social inferiors in Victorian England and for many years afterwards.

After a courtship of two and a half years, the marriage was fixed for 8 May 1889, Alice agreeing to a Catholic ceremony at Brompton Oratory, London. They had decided to live in the capital and rented a house – 3 Marloes Road, Kensington. Meanwhile, Elgar sold Liebesgrüss, under the French title Salut d'amour, to Schott for two guineas (£2.10) and later arranged it for violin and piano, for cello and piano and for small orchestra. It became almost his best-known piece of music, a favourite in restaurants everywhere, but its intrinsic melodic charm has defied all over-familiarity.

Elgar left for London on 4 May, his father seeing him off at the station. On the night before the wedding he went to The Yeomen of the Guard with his Uncle Henry. His only other relations present in the side chapel next morning were his sister Pollie and her husband Will Grafton. His sister Lucy Pipe and her husband Charles, with whom Elgar had lodged for several years, were not there because 'no invitations were issued'. The honeymoon was spent on the Isle of Wight. 'This is a time of deep peace & happiness to me after the vain imaginings of so many years & the pessimistic views so often unfolded to you on the Settle highways have vanished!', he wrote to Buck. They returned to London on 28 May. They had little money, but Alice's small income was enough to enable her still to employ the maid she had had at Redmarley.

5   Elgar and Alice at Garmisch, Bavaria, 1892

It was also enough to enable them to attend concerts and operas. Although the move to London was a failure as far as promoting Elgar's career was concerned, it was important for his musical education. The Richter concerts they heard in June 1889 contained Brahms's Third Symphony, Dvořák's Symphonic Variations, Parry's Fourth Symphony and the closing scene of *Götterdämmerung*. At Covent Garden they heard *Die Meistersinger* three times, *Don Giovanni*, *Carmen*,

Verdi's *Otello*, Gounod's *Roméo et Juliette* and Rossini's *William Tell*. The lease on their Kensington house expired at the end of July and Alice's cousin William Raikes and his wife offered them the use of their house Oaklands in Upper Norwood from October. So they returned to Saetermo in Malvern for the rest of the summer, during which they had chamber music sessions with some of Elgar's old pupils and with their pianist friend Hew Steuart-Powell and his friend the cellist Basil Nevinson. Other musical evenings involved Mrs Harriet Fitton and her daughters Hilda and Isabel. Elgar began to make sketches for a choral work to be called *The Black Knight*, with words by Longfellow from *Hyperion*.

Their home in Upper Norwood gave the Elgars easy access to the Crystal Palace concerts where they heard Manns conduct Brahms's Second Symphony and Mendelssohn's overture *Calm Sea and Prosperous Voyage* – and Elgar's *Salut d'amour*. Later Manns conducted the Suite in D twice and rehearsed the *Three Pieces* for strings. At Oaklands Elgar installed a grand piano and a small organ (his father came to tune them both) and composed *Eleven Vesper Voluntaries*, which were published by Orsborn & Tuckwood. He also wrote two part-songs, *O happy eyes*, to words by Alice, and *My love dwelt in a northern land*, to a poem by Andrew Lang. Lang at first refused permission for its use, so Alice wrote alternative words to fit the music. The poet later relented and the part-song became the first of many Elgar works to be published by Novello's. In November Elgar was invited to compose an orchestral work for the Three Choirs Festival in Worcester. In March 1890 they moved into 51 Avonmore Road, West Kensington. To secure the tenancy Alice sold her pearls to Spink & Co. On 6 April Elgar began to compose the 'work for Worcester', although this may have been a false start, since on 25 May the diary entry reads: 'Commenced *Froissart*.'[3] He had discovered the reference to Jean Froissart, the fourteenth-century author of the *Chronicles of Chivalry*, in Walter Scott's *Old Mortality* and he headed his score with a Keats quotation: 'When chivalry lifted up her lance on high'. Sketches for the overture show Elgar's characteristic method of composition: a mélange of interrelated themes which he brought together as the vision of his work matured in his mind. He would sometimes begin in the middle or switch from one movement or section to another. The moment always came when he knew exactly how it should all work out. *Froissart* was completed in July 1890. 'I do not think it will be liked', he wrote to Frank Webb in Worcester. 'I find in my limited experience that one's own friends are the people to be most in dread of.' He sent the full score to Novello's, who agreed to publish it on condition that he assigned them the copyright without payment.

On 14 August, Alice, then in her forty-second year, gave birth to a daughter, Carice Irene. Elgar's parents went to London to see their granddaughter a few weeks later and Ann Elgar accompanied her son when he took Carice for her Catholic baptism at Brook Green. The next day William Elgar went with Edward to the first London rehearsals for the Worcester Festival where *Froissart* had a run-through. Edward played in the first violins for the rest of the rehearsal. He conducted the first performance in the Public Hall, Worcester, on 10 September. In the audience was Ivor Atkins, the twenty-one-year-old assistant organist to G. R. Sinclair at Hereford cathedral. The music thrilled him and he wrote: 'I knew that Elgar was the man for me, I knew that I completely understood his music, and that my heart and soul went with it.'[4] This is the first recorded example of the extraordinary immediate personal rapport that thousands of people have experienced when listening to Elgar's music, or perhaps Alice's reaction to the *Three Pieces* for strings was the first. Many years later, Elgar told Ivor Atkins's son Wulstan about this meeting:

After conducting it [the overture] I retired to the artists' room below the platform, and I was alone there when suddenly the door opened and a tall young man with red hair came in and shook my hand. He was too nervous to speak and so was I. But the eager excited look in his eyes told me that at least one musician had fully understood my music and had made it his own. No word passed between us, but we both knew that a real friendship had begun.[5]

Alice did not go to Worcester for *Froissart* because she was recovering from childbirth, but she joined Elgar afterwards in Herefordshire where they stayed with R. B. Townshend and his wife, who was the sister of Mary Frances (Minnie) Baker, an old friend of Alice. Elgar liked Townshend, who had 'a trick of finishing up a rather tall-sounding story with an impressive "I'm telling *you*" to convince you of the truth of it'.[6] Townshend's brother-in-law was William Meath Baker of Hasfield Court. Minnie Baker was eventually to become the second wife of the Reverend Alfred Penny and thus the stepmother of Dora Penny, known to Elgar as 'Dorabella'. The 'friends pictured within' of the Enigma Variations were beginning to assemble. Most of them Elgar knew through Alice and he was already becoming conscious of the consequences of marrying into a class one or two rungs higher up the social ladder than his own – and of marrying an upper-class woman with only a small income. He still had to travel to the Midlands from London to play in orchestras such as Stockley's (which performed *Froissart* on 5 February 1891) and to give violin lessons. He and Alice saw quite a lot of his parents, but – for reasons unknown – she never went to Stoke Prior to visit his sister Pollie. He dressed like a country gentleman and tried to avoid carrying a violin case so as not to show that he was a professional musician. In the 1920s he told the violinist Jelly d'Arányi that when he was younger he disliked being described as 'Mr Elgar the composer'. 'Mr Elgar, gentleman' would have been enough.[7]

The Elgars returned to London for the winter of 1890–1, a winter described by Elgar in a letter to Frank Webb as 'truly awful: the fogs here are terrifying & make me very ill'. He began to write a violin concerto but soon abandoned it. He made no progress and was despondent at having to resume his old life as a peripatetic violin teacher, involving weekly journeys to Worcester. They decided to quit London and found a semi-detached house in Malvern Link called Forli, the birthplace of the Italian painter of angel-musicians Melozzo da Forli, which they took on a year's lease and moved into in June 1891. In spite of their lack of money, Alice persuaded Elgar to buy a Gagliano violin from Hill's in Bond Street and this led to a virtuoso violin piece, *La capricieuse*, dedicated to one of his pupils.

They spent New Year of 1892 at Hasfield Court, where Elgar became inseparable from the Wagner-loving W. Meath Baker. In spite of writing to Charles Buck that he was not composing much but 'hoped to sometime', Elgar was finding encouragement from the friendship of twenty-seven-year-old Hugh Blair, assistant organist at Worcester cathedral and conductor of the Worcester Festival Choral Society (Elgar led its orchestra). One evening at Forli, Elgar played him the abandoned sketches of *The Black Knight* and Blair promised that he would produce it at Worcester if Elgar would complete it. As a kind of 'dummy-run', he first set Longfellow's 'Spanish Serenade' for mixed chorus, two violins and piano, adding an orchestral accompaniment later. Novello's accepted it for publication, on condition that the piano part was simplified. Before resuming work (in April) on *The Black Knight* – writing on the title page 'Words by Longfellow, music by Edward Elgar (if he can)' – Elgar converted his 1888 pieces for strings into the Serenade in E minor. Like *Froissart*, this is one of the first of his works to be recognisably 'Elgarian'. In *Froissart*, Atkins had responded strongly to the exuberant colours of the orchestration and the spiritually romantic cast of the melody, epitomised in later works by the direction 'nobilmente'. In the Larghetto of the Serenade we hear the Elgar of the slow movements of the symphonies, in which he combined yearning for the unattainable with a blissful sense of meditative resignation, while the outer movements have that open-air lightness of touch, plus a vein of fantasy, which is to be heard in parts of the Variations, in *The Wand of Youth* and in many of the short pieces. He sent the Serenade to Novello's, who thought it 'very good' but rejected it on the grounds that 'this class of music is practically unsaleable'. Elgar rehearsed it with the Ladies' Orchestral Class he conducted in Worcester.

Meanwhile there was great excitement because Minnie Baker had invited the Elgars to accompany her to the Bayreuth Festival. Enough of the vocal score of *The Black Knight* was completed by 23 July for him to leave it in London for Novello's to look at. They crossed to Ostend on 25 July and travelled to Cologne, Bonn (visiting Beethoven's birthplace) and Mainz. In Bayreuth they stayed for five days at 7 Ludwigstrasse. They heard *Parsifal* twice, *Tristan und Isolde* and

*Die Meistersinger.* From Bayreuth they went to Nuremberg, Munich (where they stayed in the Hotel Vierjahreszeiten), Lindau and Heidelberg. From Heidelberg Elgar wrote to his mother that a torchlight procession of students 'did remind me of Hyperion & the beer scandal etc. etc.' They were back in London on 15 August, the day after Carice's second birthday. Elgar went to the offices of the German publisher Breitkopf & Härtel who accepted the Serenade. Back in Malvern, he finished *The Black Knight* by the end of September. Novello's accepted it in November and the orchestral full score was delivered to them on 26 January 1895.

Over Christmas at Hasfield, Townshend taught Elgar to play golf, a further stage in his conversion to a 'gentlemanly' lifestyle. But even this was to cause social embarrassment. Fixing rounds with Townshend, Hugh Blair, R. P. Arnold and Basil Nevinson had to be accommodated to Elgar's teaching schedule.

1892 had been a good year. 'Thank God for one beautiful year', Alice wrote in her diary. 'It has been more beautiful than ever with my beloved.'[8] He had added Worcester Girls' High School to his teaching commitments and also gave the pupils a series of lecture-recitals on Beethoven's violin sonatas. Since 1891 he had also been teaching at another girls' school, The Mount in Malvern, where the new headmistress was twenty-five-year-old Rosa Burley, who has left us one of the most penetrating and insightful portraits of Elgar at this time in his career (although the impression that she was in love with Elgar and jealous of others cannot be entirely discounted).[9] She soon discovered that he was a bad-tempered teacher and that the girls were afraid of him:

> I have never known anyone who changed so abruptly and completely . . . He had a habit of speaking of Malvern in the condescending manner of a country gentleman condemned to live in a suburb . . . He told me of post after post which would have been open to him but for the prejudice against his religion, of golden opportunities snatched from his grasp by inferior men of more acceptable views. It was a subject on which he evidently felt very bitter for he embroidered it at great length.[10]

One of his violin pupils at The Mount, Mary Beatrice Alder, recalled in a BBC interview in 1973 that Elgar once said to her: 'Great musicians are things to be ashamed of.'

On 7 April 1893 the Reverend J. Hampton conducted Herefordshire Philharmonic in the first performance of the *Spanish Serenade*. Alice's diary entry is in the intimate baby-talk which they used together: 'My darling Star's *Spanish Serenade* given – most lovely – A. vesy proud & everyone admiring.' Eleven days later, Elgar conducted *The Black Knight* at a Worcester Festival Choral Society concert, as Blair (the work's dedicatee) had promised. The local press – the only reviewers present – were complimentary. Elgar had boldly and perhaps rather over-ambitiously described it as a 'symphony for chorus and orchestra' rather than as a cantata. Other Midlands choral societies took it up but some found it too difficult. The music is a big advance on *Froissart*, the first of the four movements, or scenes, an example of the ceremonial style that he was to make his own, vigorous, colourful and confident, aptly descriptive of the mediaeval castle where the King sees his son defeat all comers in the tournament. In the second scene the unknown Black Knight, 'a Prince of mighty sway', rides in to a sinister motif on lower strings and brass. The third scene is the first ripe example of the pastoral Elgar of the Woodland Interlude in *Caractacus*, tinged with an exotic Spanish element such as one hears in *Sevillana* and the *Spanish Serenade*. It is arguably too agreeable as illustration for the 'measure weird and dark' which the Black Knight dances with the King's daughter, causing her to swoon. In the finale, the weakest movement, it is again the orchestration which takes centre stage at the banquet when the Black Knight offers golden wine to make the King's son and daughter whole again but from which they die. 'Take me too', the King implores, but the Black Knight replies, 'Roses in the spring I gather', giving Elgar the excuse for a quiet ending. It is possible that Elgar was here thinking of his two dead brothers, a link with Mahler whose early cantata *Das klagende Lied*, on a similar subject, may also have been inspired by the death of his siblings.

Throughout the 1890s Wagner was the most potent influence on Elgar. When he acquired a vocal score of *Tristan* on his thirty-sixth birthday, he wrote in it: 'This Book contains the Height, – the Depth, – the Breadth, – the Sweetness, – the Sorrow, – the Best and the whole of the Best of This world and the Next.' He and Alice went to a Covent Garden performance in June. They planned another German holiday. Rosa Burley was also going there and suggested rooms in Munich. They booked at 13 Gluckstrasse. But they spent the first fortnight, from 5 August, in Garmisch at the guest-house of an English family, the Slingsby-Bethells. They loved the Alpine area, its walks and flowers. They walked to the villages of Hammersbach and St Martins. In St Martins, at an inn called Die drei Möhren, they watched the Bavarian Schuhplättler dancers. To the accompaniment of a zither, the dancing involved vigorous hand-clapping over and under the legs.

The holiday had been timed to coincide with the Wagner festival in Munich in mid-August and during the fortnight in the city from 17 August they heard Die Meistersinger, the complete Ring, Die Feen, Tristan and Tannhäuser. Most were conducted by Hermann Levi. After each performance they adjourned to the Hofbrauhaus to discuss its merits. Rosa Burley records that Elgar thought the brass playing was coarse and 'was immensely tickled by the all-too-generous proportions of the Rhinemaidens and . . . always hoped that the ropes which supported them would give way'.[11]

This holiday was the first occasion on which Rosa could observe the Elgars closely. Her pupil, Alice Davey, who accompanied them, noticed that Elgar spent hours writing notes about what he had heard, and remarked of Alice, 'My word, doesn't she keep him at it?' Rosa thought Alice's attitude to Edward was 'that of the doting mother of a gifted son rather than a wife'. Edward she found unrecognisable because he relaxed, laughed and enjoyed himself, and would sometimes say with a groan, 'Oh think of Malvern'. He felt at ease in Bavaria, where the principal religion was Roman Catholicism. They visited art galleries, museums and the Nymphenburg Palace, rode on horse trams, ate in beer gardens and went to Starnberger See and saw King Ludwig's lakeside villa.

When they were in Partenkirchen during the Garmisch part of the holiday, Elgar sent a postcard to Carice for her third birthday: 'Best birthday wishes from Father and Mother. Here is a nice little chamois and a Bavarian man. Love E. E.' Carice had been sent with her nurse to Minnie Baker's house. She came low on her parents' list of priorities. Rosa Burley described her as

> a very beautiful little girl with flaxen hair and a roseleaf complexion. But the expression on her face troubled me, for it was one of profound sadness. She never smiled or laughed; and when I learned that from the first she had been taught never to make the least noise for fear of disturbing her father, I understood her unnatural look of resignation.[12]

Elgar spoke freely towards the end of his life to Vera Hockman about his wife's attitude to their daughter. As soon as possible she was sent to a boarding-school, but was allowed home on Sundays after Mass:

> She was subject even then to further instruction and correction from her mother, a major general's daughter who expected high standards of self-discipline. Holidays were not infrequently spent with various friends and relations while her parents were absent on musical jaunts abroad. Carice grew up a repressed, shy and dutifully obedient child, who rarely smiled or laughed. She was often unkindly teased at school over her unusual name and the dowdy clothes her mother insisted she wore. The usual childhood illnesses meant not only prolonged confinement in bed, but not even being allowed to look out of the window; and the summer months at Birchwood were, on Alice Elgar's insistence, the time for cold baths in water taken straight from the water-butt with all its creepy-crawlies.[13]

Elgar himself was less of a martinet. A series of the postcards, usually signed 'Faser', that he sent her as a child has been published.[14] There is the occasional one from 'C. A. E.', who also sometimes added a postscript to Elgar's, such as 'Lovely day, much love'. Elgar

6   Alice Elgar and Carice, c.1902

shared Carice's love of her pets, and when she was older, in 1908, she accompanied her parents on their long stay in Italy. When I knew Carice in the 1960s she never criticised her mother except to say that she thought Alice stupidly kept certain friends, such as Ernest Newman, away from Elgar; and she once remarked that she thought she was perhaps the only woman of whom her mother might have been jealous.

Rosa Burley noted with surprise in Munich that Elgar never spoke 'of the teaching and playing by which he really earned his living'. He never mentioned during the holiday that on return he would play in the festival orchestra in Worcester. On his copy of the programme of the Three Choirs Festival he wrote: 'I played 1st Violin for the sake of the fee as I cd. obtain no recognition as a composer.' He was thirty-six. At that date Mahler, born 1860, was at work on his Second Symphony, the First having had two performances. Richard Strauss, born 1864, had completed his first opera, *Guntram*, and was about to compose *Till Eulenspiegel*.

At the end of 1893 Elgar tried to recast a theme from a violin sonata (abandoned in 1887) as an Andante religioso, but again abandoned it until Hugh Blair requested it for a special service to celebrate a visit to

Worcester by the Duke of York (later King George V). Elgar completed it for the service on 9 April, calling it *Sursum corda*. Scored for organ, strings, brass and timpani, it is another early example of Elgar's special gift for noble ceremonial music. The writing for brass in *Sursum corda* was the result of hearing so much Wagner, but Elgar had the genius to absorb influences without allowing them to obliterate his own musical personality. When we hear *Sursum corda*, we exclaim 'Elgar!' Because of recurring throat trouble, he did not conduct the first performance. Throat and eye ailments constantly afflicted him, often when he was under pressure to start a new work. This suggests a psychosomatic cause.

On 11 April he composed five bars and an introduction for what became *Scenes from the Saga of King Olaf*. In June he made an arrangement of the Good Friday Music from *Parsifal* for Worcester Girls' High School and on 21 July Alice was received into the Roman Catholic Church at St George's. Six days earlier she wrote in her diary: 'E. with Sagas all day – booful.' But progress was slow and was interrupted by the seven-week summer holiday. Carice stayed with Rosa Burley and the Elgars made for Garmisch, meeting Mrs Fitton and her daughter for a few days before exploring new waters. Elgar played golf, played football with the Slingsby-Bethell boys and, when it rained, organised charades and musical chairs. He also tried to photograph Alpine thunderstorms. On a postcard to his mother, Alice added a postscript: 'E. looks so well, a straw hat & he bought a delightful cloak in Munich in which he looks like a magician!' They returned via Munich, hearing *Götterdämmerung* and *Die Meistersinger*, and Frankfurt, where they visited Goethe's house. Back in Malvern he composed two part-songs, *The Snow* and *Fly, Singing Bird*, to Alice's words, and sold them to Novello's for twelve guineas, his biggest fee so far. A request from the Midlands choirmaster Charles Swinnerton Heap for a big choral work sent him back to Longfellow's 'Saga of King Olaf', but Alice, spurred by the sale of the part-songs, urged that he should write more of them and suggested that their Bavarian holidays could provide a subject. Together they wrote six poems capturing the spirit of the Schuhplättler dances, giving each a subtitle relating to one of their favourite haunts, thus: 1. 'The Dance (Sonnenbichl)', 2. 'False Love (Warnberg)', 3. 'Lullaby (In Hammersbach)', 4. 'Aspiration (Bei St Anton)', 5. 'On the Alm (True Love, Hoch Alp)', 6. 'The Marksmen (Bei Murnau)'.

In From the Bavarian Highlands, Elgar composed a touching tribute to the Victorian domesticity he enjoyed with Alice at that time. Four years later, in the Enigma Variations, he immortalised their Malvern circle in much the same way. After 1900 some of the innocence went out of his musical autobiography: as the world outside claimed more of him, pain and tensions entered the music which are wholly absent here. The songs were completed in April 1895 in the original version for four-part chorus and piano accompaniment. In this form the companionable, intimate atmosphere of the music – 'so pert and spirited and tuneful', as Sir George Grove described it – is most fully realised, but no one would wish to forgo the apt and colourful alternative orchestral accompaniment which Elgar provided in 1896 or the version for orchestra only of nos. 1, 3 and 6, published in 1897 as Three Bavarian Dances.

Alice's help was practical. She often wrote in the words for him, at the same time putting in the bar-lines and writing the names of the instruments at the beginning of each page. What she did not do is what she is shown doing in Ken Russell's television film – ruling the stave lines. Elgar could always afford printed manuscript paper, to which he had ready access at the shop.

On 10 April Elgar began to compose his organ sonata for Hugh Blair, beginning with what became the Allegretto (second) movement. Blair wanted the work for a service on 8 July to be attended by a convention of American organists. They had come to Worcester to hear the result of joining together, by means of an experimental 'electric' action, the nave organ of four manuals and fifty-one stops with the quire organ of three manuals and forty-three stops. Most of the sonata was written during June. Rosa Burley described the 'sequence of moods' which afflicted Elgar when he was composing: first a period of great exaltation over the conception of the work and the commission . . . This was always followed by a period of black despair over the intractability of the material and the utter impossibility of ever getting it into a satisfactory shape. An immense amount of encouragement, accompanied by assurance that he was the only person able to do it, and reminders that it at all costs must be done, had now to be expended in order to shift him into the next phase – which was one of increasing hope and enthusiasm.[15]

The sonata was completed on 3 July, which left Blair five days to learn it and master its difficulties. Not surprisingly, the first performance was a mess. As will be seen, Elgar was to make a habit of delivering his final thoughts too late for adequate rehearsal. The sonata was the most ambitious work he had attempted, grandiose, poetic and imaginative. The very characteristic theme of the slow movement dates from 1887 when it belonged to a proposed orchestral suite.

Also in the spring of 1895 Elgar was commissioned to compose a choral work for the 1896 Worcester Festival. He chose the subject of the blind man whose sight was restored by Christ. The libretto was to be written by the Reverend Edward Capel-Cure, who chose the title *Lux Christi*. It reached Elgar in Garmisch in August, during a fortnight spent at the Slingsby-Bethells' Villa Bader. This year an Elgar 'benefit' cricket match was organised before they went on to Munich, where Elgar developed throat trouble and they went to only one opera, *Der fliegende Holländer*. Awaiting his return was a request from Swinnerton Heap for a big choral work for the North Staffordshire Festival (which could not afford a composer's fee) in October 1896. Elgar decided this should be the *Saga of King Olaf* and returned to his sketches, completing the vocal score on 21 February 1896. After a week correcting organ sonata proofs for Breitkopf & Härtel and orchestrating the *Bavarian Highlands* for Joseph Williams (Novello's having rejected it) he started in earnest on *Lux Christi*, completing the vocal score on 6 April. He took both scores, even though *Lux Christi* was unfinished, to Berthold Tours, music editor of Novello's, on 31 March. Tours demanded cuts in *King Olaf*, particularly the passages linking the episodes so that individual numbers might later be issued separately. Elgar agreed, but was annoyed, and removed thirty pages. Novello's agreed to publish both works but only if a subvention of £60 was paid out of King Olaf royalties and £40 out of Lux Christi. Alice guaranteed the money.

Elgar orchestrated Lux Christi between 5 May and 20 June. Novello's had jibbed at the title's flavour of Roman Catholicism and Elgar agreed to The Light of Life. Tours again demanded cuts. On 22 June Elgar began the orchestration of King Olaf. It was a hot summer and he worked in the garden in a tent, finishing the task on 23 August. The oratorio's first performance was on 8 September, after Elgar had spent a few days in Settle with Charles Buck. It was well received, the tenor solos being sung by Edward Lloyd, but Capel-Cure's libretto came in for criticism. The words 'Hadst Thou a Son, O Lord', in the Blind Man's Mother's solo, were deemed 'somewhat deficient in reverence' by Edward Vine Hall, precentor of the cathedral, writing in the Worcestershire Echo. The words and some of the solo parts were revised for a Worcester Festival performance in 1899. Once one has heard The Light of Life one should no longer be surprised by the Italianate fluency of the writing for solo tenor in The Dream of Gerontius (1900) – the tenor part in The Light of Life was, after all, revised only a few months before Elgar began Gerontius – nor by the assurance with which the orchestra is handled in the later work, nor by the imaginative use of the choir. There are many passages prophetic of Gerontius and The Apostles and of the choral writing in The Spirit of England of twenty years later. There are other passages, notably the tenor's 'As a spirit didst Thou pass before my eyes', where the music seems to belong to a Massenet opera. There is a fugue – 'the British public would hardly tolerate oratorios without a fugue', Elgar told a journalist in 1896[16] – and the Blind Man's worship of Christ in the closing section is expressed in an orchestral passage which is the most exquisite piece of mature Elgar in the work. The luminous and striking orchestral writing preceding Christ's 'Father, I will that they be with Me' is the sign of the hand of genius on the score. In other passages there are signs that Elgar was under pressure while composing. Part of the opening Meditation was taken from the introduction to an abandoned setting of part of Psalm 91, another solo for Christ was commandeered from *King Olaf*, and a draft opening of the tenor solo 'O Thou, in heaven's home' began as *Ophelia's song*, a setting of words from *Hamlet*, Act 4, Scene 5 ('And will he not come again?').

*King Olaf*, although it has its passionate adherents, is to my mind a much less satisfactory work. Elgar asked a Malvern friend, H. A. Acworth, to help with adapting Longfellow's poem. One can sympathise with Rosa Burley when she wrote that her 'heart sank when I realised that Longfellow was once more to serve as librettist and my hopes were not encouraged by a study of the poem. *Olaf* is a wretchedly muddled story, in which there is neither consistency of character nor unity of plot.'[17] Only too true, and although there are some vivid orchestral passages and stirring choral episodes, the libretto is so risible that Elgar's melodic inspiration seems to have deserted him, especially in the feeble music for the women in Olaf's life. As in *Froissart* and *The Black Knight*, the idea of chivalry seems to have been in the forefront of Elgar's mind while he composed the work. The first performance was at Hanley on the morning of 30 October 1896 conducted by Elgar. Edward Lloyd missed all the rehearsals and at the performance something went wrong when he sang 'And King Olaf heard the cry'. An already nervous Elgar lost his grip and the performance was saved by the leader of the orchestra, Willy Hess, who leapt to his feet and conducted with his bow.[18] But Alice noted in her diary, 'Glorious King Olaf is a magnificent triumph', and the critics were full of praise, one (unidentified) describing Elgar as 'the greatest English genius since Purcell'. The wisest was Arthur Johnstone of the *Manchester Guardian*, who, after a Hallé performance in 1898, found the work 'fragmentary and incoherent', mainly because the text was in places 'unfit for any kind of musical treatment', but forecast that 'something of lasting value' would follow when Elgar found the right subject. August Manns conducted the first London performance at the Crystal Palace on 3 April 1897. Whatever its shortcomings, *King Olaf* did more than any previous work to bring Elgar's name to the forefront of English musical life. There was also a valuable by-product for Elgar. As a result

of the bad feeling between him and Berthold Tours, Novello's trans-
ferred his affairs to a younger editor, August Johannes Jaeger, a German
emigré who had lived in England since December 1878, when he was
eighteen.

That was a welcome change. But another, bigger change was less
welcome. Acworth wrote to him afterwards: 'In one respect I am sorry
for you. You have now the obligation of living up to a great reputation,
a reputation which if I read the critics aright places you at the head of
living composers, & high wrought expectations are difficult to satisfy –
and such all your work will henceforth evoke.'[19] From 10 High Street
came a poem from his mother: 'The Genius has won its much [sic], /
And Fame is crowning thee.' Edward went to see her and, as she told her
friend Winifred Whitwell, put his head in her lap and said he could not
cope with it.[20] To Swinnerton Heap he wrote one of his self-dramatising
letters – 'I cannot afford to write any more . . . the rest of my life will
only be "it might have been".'

# 4  Caractacus

After the success of the *King Olaf* première, Elgar spent a week in London and went through the score of the cantata with August Manns, who offered a Crystal Palace performance if there were financial guarantees. Novello's offered some and Elgar said he would provide the rest as long as Alice did not know. (It cost him £38, as the audience was not large.) But at least Novello's regarded him as a good prospect and suggested to him that, in view of Queen Victoria's forthcoming diamond jubilee, he should write an *Imperial March* and a short cantata about St George, the text of which they had commissioned from a Bristol writer, Shapcott Wensley. Elgar accepted both commissions, which again appealed to his chivalric vein. He sent Novello's a sketch of the march on 7 December 1896. One of the publishing staff, Henry Clayton, objected that it 'contains so many short phrases of two bars & even one bar; & we are of opinion that it would be enormously improved if you could re-model the march with a view to including in it phrases say sometimes of eight bars'. Elgar acquiesced, sent a revision on 9 January 1897 and accepted twenty guineas. The march is not a jingoistic piece. Although its opening is marked 'pomposo', the theme is almost reticent and the second subject has the dancing lightness we first encounter in *Sevillana*.

The Banner of St George is 'a ballad' for chorus and orchestra. A maiden is daily fed to the dragon. Eventually it is the turn of the King's daughter, who is willing to meet her fate but is saved by St George. He slays the dragon but then rides off to do good deeds elsewhere. As Jerrold Northrop Moore has pointed out: 'In none of Elgar's choral works with subjects of his own choosing does the hero live happily ever after with the heroine. Always there is renunciation, and often death, after whatever victory has been achieved.'[1] It is a better work than might be imagined. The expansive opening section, mainly quiet and lyrical music, describes the unhappy Land of Sylenë. For the fight with the dragon, the orchestration takes on a Wagnerian (*Meistersinger*) tinge; there is a luscious melody for St George's renunciation and a patriotic epilogue, 'It comes from the misty ages', for which Elgar cannot quite summon the grandiloquence the text invites.

Sending the piano solo version of the music to Novello's on 9 January, Elgar mentioned 'terms', adding: 'I should not have mentioned the last item but that the Term will shortly re-commence & it will depend entirely on this matter whether I return to teaching or continue to compose – or try to.' Novello's were to become used to this kind of threat over the years. The fully orchestrated score of the march was sent off on 6 February. The vocal score of the *Banner* was completed on 14 February, the full score on 15 March. The march's first performance was conducted by Manns at the Crystal Palace on 19 April. It was played in the Queen's Hall on 25 April and at a royal garden party during the June week of jubilee celebrations. *The Banner of St George* was first performed on 18 May in London by the St Cuthbert's Choral Society conducted by Cyril Miller.

Elgar performances began to multiply, not only of the jubilee works but of *The Light of Life*, *King Olaf* (at Bishop Auckland conducted by Nicholas Kilburn, in Worcester conducted by Elgar, in Hanley conducted by Heap and in Manchester, Liverpool and Bradford conducted by Frederic Cowen) and his part-songs. On 30 May, three days before his fortieth birthday, he set a three-verse poem by Alice each verse of which ended with the refrain 'Love alone will stay'. Shortly before this he had been asked by the Hereford cathedral organist, George Sinclair, to compose a Te Deum and Benedictus for the opening service of the

Three Choirs Festival in September. He took a sketch on 5 June to play to Sinclair (who found it 'very, very modern', but liked it). The full score was completed on 31 July and sent to Novello's. Four days later he received an enthusiastic letter signed by A. J. Jaeger whose function was publishing manager but who acted as artistic adviser to the directors of Novello's, few of whom were musicians. 'You praise my new work too much', Elgar wrote to him, 'but you understand it.' Jaeger apologised for Novello's 'wretched' payment for the work (fifteen guineas) to which Elgar responded: 'What I feel is the utter want of *sympathy* . . . Now my music, such as it is, is alive, you say it has heart – I always say to my wife (over any piece or passage of my work that pleases me): "if you cut that it would *bleed!*" You seem to see that, but who else does?'

Elgar had now found a ready ear into which to pour his self-pity, his spleen and also his enthusiasms and high spirits. He was uplifted when Jaeger wrote: 'I claim qualities for you which I fail to see in *all* other British composers. *Heart* above all things! The other "coming man" is Coleridge-Taylor.'

The Elgars had not had a Bavarian holiday in 1896 but hurriedly decided to revisit the Slingsby-Bethells in Garmisch in August 1897, travelling via Cologne and Munich. Elgar arrived in Munich with a 'badsley headache', as Alice described it, but attended a performance of *Tristan* conducted by Richard Strauss, whom they met afterwards. Next day they went to Garmisch. To a 'fancy ball' on 18 August Elgar went in Japanese costume. They returned to Munich on 1 September and heard *Don Giovanni* conducted by Strauss in the Cuvilliéstheater. Next evening they heard *Der fliegende Holländer* and returned home by way of Cologne.[2] Just before leaving for this holiday, Edward and Alice visited his mother on 4 August while she was staying at Colwall. Looking at the Herefordshire Beacon, Ann Elgar exclaimed: 'Oh! Ed. Look at the lovely old Hill. Can't we write some *tale* about it?' This implanted the idea for a new cantata, perhaps about the British chieftain Caractacus who, it was said, made his last stand against the Romans at the top of the Beacon. But first there was the Hereford first performance of the Te Deum and Benedictus on 12 September (preceded by the

7 August Jaeger (right) with his children Edward and Maimie and Professor S. S. Sanford outside Jaeger's home, 37 Curzon Road, Muswell Hill, 1904

*Imperial March* as an organ voluntary). Jaeger was there and, although critical of the performance, found it 'your finest, most spontaneous & most deeply felt & most effective work'. Sinclair may have found it 'modern', but today it sounds more secular than sacred, a continuation of *The Banner of St George* but more inspired, perhaps because the text is so much better. This was Sinclair's third festival; but it was the first for Herbert Brewer of Gloucester and Ivor Atkins of Worcester (successor to Hugh Blair, a victim of alcoholism). Thus the celebrated triumvirate of Elgarian Three Choirs organists came together for the first time. But although Elgar was long associated with the festivals and became their focal figure, he wrote few works for them, and none of these was major.

In late October 1897 Elgar twice conducted his orchestration of three of the *Bavarian Highlands* songs at the Crystal Palace, first as *Characteristic Dances*, then as *Three Bavarian Dances*.[3] While in London he sold to Novello's for ten guineas a piece for violin and piano called *Evensong*, which they published as *Chanson de nuit*. Then he returned to teaching and to the discovery that his friends had formed a new choral and orchestral society, the Worcestershire Philharmonic, for him to conduct. Martina Hyde and Winifred Norbury were the secretaries, the committee included Earl Beauchamp's sister Lady Mary Lygon, and the Three Choirs organists were honorary members. Their motto was 'Wach' auf!', and each concert began with this Wagner chorus from *Die Meistersinger*. For the first concert (7 May 1898) Elgar chose Humperdinck's *Die Wallfahrt nach Kevlaar*, in German. One of the orchestra described Elgar as 'a fine conductor . . . but he is at the mercy of his moods . . . He can bear much provocation with patience and little provocation with no patience at all. If a violin player drops her mute there is a "rumpus"; on the other hand, he is unsparing in his care for detail.'[4]

Towards the end of 1897 Elgar learned that Leeds was likely to ask him for a work for its 1898 festival in early October. He considered but rejected St Augustine as a subject and then favoured an orchestral work with the stories of Augustine, King Canute and Caractacus forming a suite of *Mottoes* from English history. But Leeds wanted a cantata for its chorus, so he decided on Caractacus as the (again chivalrous) subject and in January 1898 signed away his copyright for £100. He had left himself barely eight months until performance before he composed a note. Meanwhile, Jaeger, after attending a performance of *King Olaf*, had sent him good advice:

> I think the work has one great fault which the audience notice muchly: the absence of a developed broadly melodious lyrical movement with the 'fat' given to the *chorus* where the ear can *rest* & just drink in *quietly* moving strains of a broadly melodious type . . . There is *too much* 'going on' in *Olaf* . . . the ear is allowed *no rest*. You are always 'at it' in splendidly dramatic style . . . I do feel this want of *repose*.

For the *Caractacus* libretto he again enlisted H. A. Acworth, who provided love interest by supplying Caractacus with a daughter, Eigen, whose lover Orbin was a member of a 'half-priestly order of minstrels'. Orbin is expelled after protesting against the Arch-Druid's deliberate deception of Caractacus by ignoring the gods' warnings of disaster. He joins Caractacus's army, which is routed by the Romans. Caractacus and his soldiers are taken to Rome where Emperor Claudius is so impressed by Caractacus's eloquence that he pardons them. The final chorus – 'The clang of arms is over' – has been a stumbling-block for the squeamish. Somewhat incongruously, since the cantata is about a British defeat, the end of the Roman Empire is foreseen, to be supplanted by the evangelistic paternalism of the British Empire. Yet Elgar (perhaps ironically) based the music of this chorus on the thematic material of the Arch-Druid's deliberately false prophecy of Caractacus's victory.

He began to compose *Caractacus* early in 1898. He tramped over the Malvern Hills and followed the Druid path along the top from end to end. On one of these walks, near Storridge, he came across a small unoccupied cottage, Birchwood Lodge, which reminded him of his birthplace. It was in the midst of woodland and had wonderful views of the Severn Valley. A short lease was negotiated and Elgar and his wife moved in for the summer. It provided the solitude and quiet he needed in order to work and he loved the birds and animals in the woods. He was never happier than at Birchwood, and its atmosphere is reflected in Caractacus, which is predominantly pastoral. Other composers – Cowen, Stanford, Mackenzie and Sullivan – were writing similar works. Some may contain better individual items than Caractacus, but Caractacus is by far the best work of any size that Elgar had so far composed. There is, for instance, the introduction to Scene 3, the Woodland Interlude, one of those uniquely Elgarian fresh-as-dew, bruised-innocence pieces, like Chanson de matin, which defy analysis of their power to move and delight the sympathetic listener. (The music for it existed in a sketchbook of 1887 where it was part of an intended suite – it might have been written even earlier.) He quoted a few bars from it in a letter from Birchwood, adding: 'This is what I hear all day – the trees are singing my music – or have I sung theirs? I suppose I have.'[5] When in 1934 he supervised from his deathbed a recording of extracts from Caractacus, he asked for the Woodland Interlude to be repeated twice. It was almost the last music he heard.

Manipulation of leitmotif is perhaps more flexible in King Olaf, but Caractacus, while designedly much simpler and more straightforward, is more mature as an expression of Elgar's personality. It is also Elgar in his happiest orchestral vein, with iridescent splashes of colour, endearing fragments of detail and a continuous pulse of broad lyrical string tone. He had wanted, as sketches reveal, to use four saxophones ('beautiful and expressive') in Scenes 1, 2 and 6 but 'difficulty in getting players, rehearsing and extra expense prevented my experiment coming to a hearing'.[6] As Simon Mundy has pointed out, there is in Caractacus an echo of the seventeenth- and eighteenth-century masques and semi-operas, linking it with the King Arthur of Purcell and Dryden.[7]

He had his customary throat trouble and depression while compos-ing, telling Nicholas Kilburn on 29 March that 'I have just arrived at hating what I have done & feeling a fool for having done it', and writing to Joseph Bennett, the Daily Telegraph's critic and a librettist: 'I hope some day to do a great work – a sort of national thing that my fellow

Englishmen might take to themselves and love.' Evidently he did not feel that *Caractacus* filled the bill – he still hankered after St Augustine and hoped Bennett would provide a libretto. He let Novello's have the vocal score scene by scene so that the Leeds chorus could learn it (he told Jaeger that it was 'the first time I have had "scenes" ordered like barrels of beer'). The vocal score was finished on 12 June, the orchestration on 21 August. He was cutting it fine. Asked by Brewer for a short work for the Gloucester Festival in September, he recommended Coleridge-Taylor instead. The result was the Ballade in A minor. There was a slight *contretemps* in June when the German-born Jaeger objected to the truculent reference in the final chorus of *Caractacus* to 'menial tyrants'. Elgar replied: 'Any nation but ours is allowed to war whoop as much as they like but I feel we are too strong to need it – I did suggest that we should dabble in patriotism in the Finale, when lo! the *worder* (that's good!) instead of merely paddling his feet goes & gets naked & wallows in it.' He followed this up in July with: 'I knew you would laugh at my librettist's patriotism (& mine). Never mind. England for the English is all I say – hands off! There's nothing apologetic about me.' Nothing tactful, either, but there it is. Efforts to claim Elgar for liberalism are in this instance doomed to failure. He went fox-hunting, too. But he changed 'menial' to 'jealous'.

Permission was given for Elgar to dedicate *Caractacus* to Queen Victoria. Help in correcting vocal score proofs came from Isabel Fitton and Winifred and Florence Norbury from Sherridge. A niece of the Norburys later gave a vivid picture of the scene:

> W. N. and Lady Mary Lygon (who was a lively intelligent creature) could keep him in order and *make* him work as well as amuse him. My little aunt [Florence Norbury] and Dora [Penny] could run with him, bicycle, climb hills, fly kites . . . His work and well-being was everything to [Mrs Elgar], and I believe she *made* these friendships with other women – all young and attractive – who could do the parts she couldn't always manage. She was almost *too* sweet with him . . . My aunts always said he was lazy and would never have done anything with his music but for his wife.[8]

Elgar took chorus rehearsals in Leeds in August and went to London in September to rehearse soloists and to attend Three Choirs rehearsals ('Queen's Hall seemed to be reeking with humbug & sham', he told Jaeger, and complained also of 'the twaddle & mutual admiration' of a Three Choirs Festival). In London Jaeger tried to cheer him up by comparing Elgar's uncertainties with Beethoven's and followed this up with a long letter (lost) rebuking Elgar for his ingratitude for his great gifts. The talk and the letter were soon to be commemorated in 'Nimrod'.

The final Leeds rehearsal was on 1 October. Parry and Sullivan (the festival conductors) and Gabriel Fauré were present, as were Basil Nevinson, Hew Steuart-Powell, Nicholas Kilburn, George Sinclair, Lady Mary Lygon and Rosa Burley. The first performance was on the 5th with Medora Henson, Edward Lloyd, Andrew Black and John Browning as soloists and Elgar conducting. The audience was enthusiastic, the critics less so. Rosa Burley thought Elgar left Leeds 'with the air of one who has fought – and is inclined to think he has lost – a heavy engagement'.[9] She was right. He had told Novello's he had been approached for the 1900 Birmingham Festival, another prestigious triennial event, and they had suggested he should write something easy like *The Banner of St George*. This, combined with the chore of returning to teaching, was too much. He let off steam to Jaeger on 20 October:

> No – I'm not happy at all: in fact never was more miserable in my life – I don't see that I've done any good at all: if I write a tune you all say it's commonplace – if I don't you all say it's rot. Well, I've written *Caractacus*, earning thro' it 15 *shillings a week* while doing it & that's all – now if I will write any *easy*, small choral-society work for Birmingham . . . your firm will be 'disposed to consider it' . . . No thank you – no more music for me – at present.

Later in this letter he mentioned a proposal that he should write an orchestral work about General Gordon, whose murder at Khartoum in 1885 had shocked the nation:

'Gordon Sym.' I like this idee [sic] but my dear man why should I
try? . . . I have to earn money somehow & it's no good trying this sort of
thing even for a 'living wage' & your firm wouldn't give £5 for it – I tell
you I am sick of it all: why can't I be encouraged to do decent stuff & not
hounded into triviality.

But three weeks later he wrote: 'Now as to Gordon: the thing possesses
me, but I can't write it down yet.'

Caractacus was the summit of Elgar's diamond jubilee music. Its
Triumphal March led a separate life in concert programmes and helped
to establish Elgar as a kind of unofficial national musical laureate,
an impression that remains to this day. Yet curiously none of Elgar's
ceremonial music has become part of the national heritage except for
two adaptations – 'Nimrod' from the Enigma Variations and 'Land of
hope and glory', originally a tune composed as the trio of an orchestral
march which had words fitted to it only later. The Coronation March he
wrote for King George V in 1911 is a rarity, fine as it is, and has never
equalled the success and popularity of Walton's Crown Imperial. He wrote
nothing that has rivalled Handel's Zadok the priest nor Parry's I was glad
(in every coronation since Edward VII's in 1902). The Coronation Ode
(1902) is a rarity, too, even the setting of 'Land of hope and glory' as it is
found in this score. There is the additional irony that Parry's Jerusalem
is sung usually with the orchestration supplied by Elgar.

# 5 Enigma

Having renounced music forever (again), Elgar wrote to Jaeger on 24 October 1898:

> Since I've been back I have sketched a set of Variations (orkestry) on an original theme: the Variations have amused me because I've labelled 'em with the nicknames of my particular friends – *you* are Nimrod. That is to say I've written the variations each one to represent the mood of the 'party' – I've liked to imagine the 'party' writing the var: him (or her) self & have written what I think they would have written – if they were asses enough to compose – it's a quaint idea & the result is amusing to those behind the scenes & won't affect the hearer who 'nose nuffin''. What think you?

Elgar was clearly in high spirits, as his jocular spelling indicates. The story goes – according to J. A. Forsyth and Basil Maine[1] – that he returned from teaching at Rosa Burley's school, The Mount, on Friday 21 October 1898, had dinner, lit a cigar and improvised at the piano. Alice remarked, according to what Elgar is said to have told Maine, 'That's a good tune.' Elgar 'awoke from the dream: "Eh! tune, what tune?" And she said, "Play it again, I like that tune". I played and strummed, and played, and then she exclaimed: "That's the tune".' According to Forsyth, Alice asked, 'What is that?' and was told: 'Nothing – but something might be made of it.' Elgar then told her:

'Powell would have done this, or Nevinson would have looked at it like this.' Then, 'Who is that like?' Alice's answer: 'I cannot quite say, but it is exactly the way Billie Baker goes out of the room.' Oddly, there is no mention of this in Alice's diary – she does not mention the Variations until 11 January 1899.

The tune, we may assume, was the 'original theme', whether invented on the spot or something that he had been toying with in his mind no one can say. But he had already thought of how it would be varied to depict H. D. Steuart-Powell, Basil Nevinson and W. M. Baker. By 24 October, as his letter shows, he had thought of 'Nimrod' ('Jäger' is German for 'hunter' and the biblical Nimrod was 'a mighty hunter': Genesis 10.9) and Dora Penny claims that when she visited Forli on 1 November she saw the sketches of 'C. A. E.' (Alice Elgar), 'R. B. T.' (Townshend), 'Troyte' (the Malvern architect A. Troyte Griffith), 'Nimrod' and herself as 'Dorabella' (Elgar's nickname for her, after the character in Mozart's *Così fan tutte*).[2] But the recollections of Dora Powell (as she became) are unreliable in matters of strict chronology. The autograph sketch for 'R. B. T.' – which Elgar called a scherzo – was originally headed 'I. A.' (Ivor Atkins) and when the substitution was made, the music was not altered. 'Dorabella', an intermezzo, is derived from a theme composed in the 1880s for a projected orchestral suite. Elgar himself pointed out that it had 'only the slightest connection' with the original theme.[3]

This idea of a portrait gallery of his friends obviously fired Elgar's imagination from the start. There are twelve friends, because 'C. A. E.' is his wife and the finale 'E. D. U.' is himself ('Edoo' was Alice's pet name for him), and perhaps there are only ten since one variation is about a dog and another about a house. Some whom one might have thought would be included are not there – his boyhood friend Hubert Leicester, for example, Charles Buck, even Rosa Burley (who remarked 'I am the theme', whatever she meant by that). He planned but did not write a variation on Nicholas Kilburn, and it is said, on scanty evidence, that he contemplated variations on Sullivan and Parry, but they would have led him into parody. We may assume he chose those whose idiosyncrasies suggested music to him, whether it was a stammer ('Dorabella'), a certain way of playing the piano ('H. D. S.-P.' and 'Troyte'), slamming a door ('W. M. B.'), cello playing ('B. G. N.'), viola playing ('Ysobel'), or 'gracious personalities' in an eighteenth-century house (Sherridge, where 'W. N.' – Winifred Norbury – and her sister Florence lived). 'Nimrod' has a further musical association. It commemorates Jaeger's pep talk about Beethoven and some have discovered an allusion in the opening bars to the slow movement of the Pathétique piano sonata. However, the descending sevenths in the fifth and sixth bars of Schumann's Second Symphony are echoed in bars 13 and 14 of 'Nimrod' and it has been suggested that this may be an allusion to Düsseldorf, Jaeger's home town with which Schumann was closely associated.[4] When Frederick Ashton made the Variations into a ballet in 1968, Elgar's daughter Carice went to a performance and told Ashton: 'I knew them all and I disliked them all except Troyte.' Presumably she did not include her parents in this sweeping condemnation!

Research by Julian Rushton indicates that 'W. N.' and 'G. R. S.' were the last to be sketched.[5] This supports the belief that the incident when Sinclair's bulldog Dan fell into the Wye occurred during the weekend of 29 October–1 November 1898, when Elgar was in Hereford for Sinclair's thirty-fifth birthday and his fiftieth organ recital in the cathedral. Rushton also suggests that 'G. R. S.' was for a time fifth in the running order, with 'Nimrod' and 'Dorabella' eleventh and twelfth and 'B. G. N.' thirteenth.[6] The 'Romanza' variation '(* * *)' was sixth until it moved to thirteenth.

The initial impetus seems to have slackened. On 11 November Elgar wrote to Jaeger: 'The Variations go on slowly but I shall finish 'em some day.' It was in this letter that he mentioned being possessed by the Gordon Symphony. But four days earlier he had been assured of 'the principal place' in the 1900 Birmingham Festival. Writing to Jaeger on 17 December, he was 'very sick at heart over music'. But what he meant was that he was sick of Novello's, who seemed uninterested in his 'big works' but wanted pieces like Edward German's Henry VIII dances and

8  Elgar with G. R. Sinclair (left) and Hans Richter (seated), c.1903

'I can't write that sort of thing.' Yet, besides Birmingham, Worcester asked for the *Gordon Symphony* for September 1899 and the Norwich Festival asked for a *scena* for the young contralto Clara Butt. Neither offered a commission fee. Elgar called on Clara Butt in her London flat on 9 January 1899, but she was having a bath and refused to see

9 Elgar c.1899

him. He complained to her manager and five days later he showed her the sketches of what became *Sea Pictures* and included the setting of Alice's 'Love alone will stay'. Butt's manager was Narciso Vertigliano, anglicised to Nathaniel Vert, who was also Hans Richter's agent. He agreed to approach Richter with the idea of his giving the first performance of the Variations in London. While in London, Elgar called on Jaeger and his bride, showed him the Variations sketches and told him about Richter. Jaeger then told Parry, who knew Richter well, and Parry lent his support. Thus encouraged, Elgar returned to Malvern on 17 January and completed the sketches. He began the full score on 5 February and finished it on 19 February, fast work for him. So fast that he wrote the wrong date ('Feb. 18, 1898') on the autograph score. (Alice ruled the bar-lines, paginated the score sheets and wrote in most of the instruments' names.) Two days later he sent the score to Vert to pass on to Richter. Elgar then made a piano transcription which he sent to Novello's in mid-March. This contains, in 'Nimrod', Elgar's first use of the direction 'nobilmente', although he does not use it in the orchestral version, where this variation is marked 'moderato', changed by Elgar to 'adagio' after the first performance. ('Nobilmente' first occurs in an orchestral score in *Cockaigne*.)

On 9 March Elgar heard from Vert that Richter had received the score. He was in St Petersburg but on return would 'look through the work and he says "that he shall be only too pleased to promote the work of an English artist"'.[7] By 24 March Elgar was able to write to Ivor Atkins that Richter would definitely conduct the first performance on 19 June. This letter was from the new house, Craeg Lea (an anagram of E., A. and C. Elgar) on the Wells Road south of Great Malvern into which they had moved on 21 March.

So far, it will have been noticed, the word 'Enigma' has not been mentioned. Although the work is not called Enigma Variations on the score, this is how it is now universally known. How and why? The manuscript score arrived back from Richter towards the end of March and was delivered to Novello's on 8 April. Around this time, perhaps while Elgar was in London between 17 and 22 March and saw Jaeger, he apparently asked that the word 'Enigma' should be written above the original theme. This was done in pencil, probably by Jaeger (the writing is certainly not Elgar's). The 'Enigma' is the seventeen bars of the theme. This must have been talked about, because on 10 April C. A. Barry, who provided the programme notes for Richter's concerts, wrote to ask Elgar for information about the variations. He was himself a composer and told Elgar that many years earlier he had written variations which contained some kind of 'trick'. 'You won't guess it', he added, 'so I am glad to think that there is something enigmatical about my variations as well as yours.' In another letter on 30 April he told Elgar: 'Novello's have sent me proof sheets . . . of your Enigma (which I cannot guess) and Variations.'[8] Elgar provided Barry with some information, which Barry quoted more or less verbatim in his programme note:

> 'The Enigma I will not explain – its "dark saying" must be left unguessed, and I warn you that the apparent connection between the Variations and the Theme is often of the slightest texture.' Then the trouble starts: 'Further, through and over the whole set another and larger theme "goes" but is not played . . . So the principal Theme never appears, even as in some late dramas – e.g. Maeterlinck's L'intruse and Les septs princesses – the chief character is never on the stage.'[9]

What did he mean? The 'principal Theme' does appear. It is beyond doubt that it – the Enigma – is Elgar himself. He used it in place of a signature in letters to 'Dorabella', and when he quoted it in 1912 in The Music Makers he explained that 'it expressed when written (in 1898) my sense of the loneliness of the artist'. As for 'dark saying', that is a reference to the Webster's Dictionary definition of 'enigma'. The chief character, in the person of Elgar, is on the stage throughout the work. 'Another and larger theme "goes".' He hinted this was a well-known tune rather than an abstract idea. People have ingeniously been trying to guess the tune ever since, a harmless but pointless recreation since the secret, if there was one, died with him. Elgar added further mystification when he told F. G. Edwards, editor of the Musical Times, who wrote an article about him in the October 1900 issue, that 'it is possible to add another phrase, which is quite familiar, above the original theme'. Phrase is an ambiguous word. The odds are on there being a mystery tune, since several times during the rest of his life Elgar encouraged that belief. But he loved puns, acrostics, secret codes and crossword puzzles. He also loved pulling people's legs. And he was an early practitioner of the art of publicity.

The theme itself, with its alternating phrases of G minor and G major, is a breathtakingly haunting invention. Loneliness, wistfulness, halting uncertainty are all there. In its pristine simplicity – the first six bars are scored for strings only and in the next thirteen only woodwind and horns are added – it offers perhaps the most profound musical example of self-analysis. Elgar wrote of it in 1929:

> The alternation of the two quavers and two crotchets in the first bar and
> their reversal in the second bar will be noticed; references to this
> grouping are almost continuous . . . The drop of the seventh in the
> Theme (bars 3 and 4) should be observed. At bar 7 (G major) appears the
> rising and falling passage in thirds which is much used later.[10]

For a concert he was to conduct in Turin in October 1911, Elgar wrote a note (preserved at the Elgar Birthplace Museum) in which he said:

> This work, commenced in a spirit of humour & continued in deep
> seriousness, contains sketches of its composer's friends. It may be
> understood that these personages comment or reflect on the original
> theme & each one attempts a solution of the Enigma, for so the theme is
> called.

Elgar interrupted composition of the Variations on 23 and 24 January 1899, when he took his orchestral suite of 1888, revised three of its four movements and sent it to Novello's as *Three Characteristic Pieces*, op. 10, asking them to print it before April so that he could give a copy to the dedicatee, Lady Mary Lygon, who was due to sail to Australia then, accompanying her brother Earl Beauchamp, who had been appointed governor of New South Wales. On 7 February he composed a madrigal, *To her beneath whose steadfast star*, as one of a group by various composers dedicated to Queen Victoria on her eightieth birthday. (It was sung at Windsor Castle on 24 May. Elgar was present.) On 6 March he completed an earlier violin and piano piece as a companion to *Chanson de nuit*, calling it *Chanson de matin*. On 20 April he conducted the first London performance of *Caractacus*. In the same month he told Worcester Festival Committee not to expect the *Gordon Symphony*. 'Just let it drop', he told Ivor Atkins. 'The reason is merely the pecuniary one & this is insurmountable.'

Richter's first rehearsal of the Variations was on 3 June in St James's Hall, and while in London Elgar gave Edward Lloyd the sketches of a new song, *The Pipes of Pan*. A second rehearsal of the Variations took place on 17 June, with a third on the morning of the day of the first performance, the 19th. So Richter had prepared it thoroughly. The première was a triumph.[11] Richter took Elgar to dinner afterwards with Ivor Atkins and Sir Alexander Mackenzie. Alice received a letter a few days later from Elgar's mother: 'What can I say to him, the dear one – I feel that he is some great historic person – I cannot claim a little bit of him now he belongs to the big world.'[12]

In the conductor's room after the first performance, Elgar, Atkins and Jaeger discussed the work. According to Atkins, Jaeger said the finale was too short and Richter agreed that it could be further developed.[13] Elgar appeared to be hurt. However that may be, Jaeger – who in the *Musical Times* of 1 July 1899 wrote of the work's 'effortless originality . . . and, most important of all, beauty of theme, warmth and feeling' – wrote to Elgar a few days later suggesting changes in the finale and adding that Richter had criticised it. Elgar tetchily rejected Jaeger's suggestion and 'should really like to know *how* you heard Richter was disappointed', but by 7 July he was sketching an extension and five days later it was done. He added ninety-six bars and an optional part for organ. It was first played at the work's third performance, given at the Three Choirs Festival in Worcester on 13 September. Richter first conducted the new ending in London on 23 October. The original ending was not played again until Sir Frederick Ashton used it for his ballet in 1968. As first composed, the finale, 'E. D. U.', recalled both 'C. A. E.' and 'Nimrod'. It ended at cue 76. Elgar's extension brought back the Enigma theme in the rhythmic pattern in which it had appeared in 'G. R. S.' He further elaborated the Enigma theme, wrote a grandiose statement of the 'E. D. U.' theme and ended with a peroration on the Enigma theme, all lasting barely ninety seconds.

Interestingly, Elgar had at one time contemplated recalling the 'Romanza' variation ('Introduce LML' he wrote in his sketches) with also a return in E flat of the Mendelssohn quotation. The further enigma surrounding the 'Romanza' has been discussed in chapter 2. It remains to reiterate here that, whoever else might have been in Elgar's mind, all the documentary evidence shows that Lady Mary Lygon was the subject of the thirteenth variation. Why, then, not put '(L. M. L.)' instead of '(\* \* \*)'? Because he knew that some people might be superstitious about being no. 13. A little mystery also surrounds no. 11, 'G. R. S.' Some believe that the variation, particularly in the double basses and bassoons in bars 2 and 3, represents G. R. Sinclair's skill on the Hereford organ pedalboard. Elgar, however, unequivocally stated in his pianola notes that it has

> nothing to do with organs or cathedrals or, except remotely, with G. R. S. The first few bars were suggested by his great bulldog Dan (a well-known character) falling down the steep bank into the River Wye (bar 1); his paddling upstream to find a landing-place (bars 2 & 3) and his rejoicing bark on landing (second half of bar 5).

Why should this not be true? The word 'Dan' is written over bar 5 in the sketches. Elgar loved dogs. Buck had given him a collie, Scap, in 1885 and Elgar's letters are full of Scap's adventures. But Alice did not like dogs and when they were married in 1889 Elgar had to leave Scap with his sister Lucy until the dog's death in 1892. Dan seems to have been born in 1895 or 1896. The date of birth – 6 July 1898 – on his gravestone in Sinclair's garden is obviously wrong because there is a photograph of him with Sinclair, Elgar and others dated 1896. (He is an unusual looking bulldog, more like a bull terrier. Bulldogs are said not to be able to swim, but a bull terrier could cope with the Wye.) Whenever Elgar called on Sinclair, he wrote a musical fragment in the visitors' book. These he called 'The Moods of Dan', the first being inscribed on 5 June 1897, the last in 1903 (Dan died on 1 July that year). Themes which found their way into *The Dream of Gerontius* (the 'prayer' motif), *In the South*, *Crown of India* and *The Spirit of England* began as 'Moods of Dan'. Sir Percy Hull, Sinclair's assistant and eventual successor, wrote to Dora Powell in 1944: 'This double third passage (bar 5 of G. R. S.) was quoted in "Moods of Dan" long before the Variations were written and it was also used in *King Olaf* between the letters O and P in the accompaniment to the words "they found the watchdog in the yard".'[14] But I suppose, as W. H. Reed wrote, 'it is quite possible that the composer saw also something in common in these two boon companions, the master and his dog, the one paddling away in the river and the other pedalling away on his organ in the cathedral'.[15]

All this is part of the folklore of the Variations. It is not only the music we love but the puzzles and controversies inseparable from it. But what music! It is a work that stays perennially fresh. Its scoring is miraculous, pellucid, witty, delicate, colourful, touching. It incorporates the private whistle with which Elgar announced to Alice that he had come home, the difficulties an amateur violist had with crossing the strings, a dog's bark, a friend's laugh, the throb of a liner's engines, and it contains in 'Nimrod' the most eloquent commemoration of friendship ever written, which can speak to us nationally or personally. I see no reason to modify the opinion I expressed in *Portrait of Elgar*: 'the greatest orchestral work yet written by an Englishman'.

# 6 'The best of me'

The Variations put Elgar on the European musical map. Richter's championship led other conductors – Fritz Steinbach, Felix Weingartner, Alexander Siloti, Richard Strauss and Gustav Mahler – to take them up over the next decade. But the work did not make him rich. For the first time, Novello's offered him a royalties agreement – nothing on orchestral performances, fourpence a copy on sales of the complete piano arrangement, smaller royalties for the sale of separate movements. Elgar was 'greatly disappointed' and asked for at least sixpence a copy ($2\frac{1}{2}$p today). Novello's refused but suggested he should retain the copyright. Elgar eventually accepted the original offer. Hitherto he had accepted the system by which publishers bought a work outright for all its editions rather than offering a royalty based on sales and performances. Composers in the 1890s subsisted on publishers' purchases or commission fees. Today they have royalties and performing rights from performances, sales, broadcasting and recordings, in addition to commissions.

In July 1899 the Elgars went to New Brighton where Granville Bantock had amazingly established a series of concerts of modern English composers. Elgar had agreed to conduct the Variations (with original ending) and others of his works on the 16th. In New Brighton he met Bantock's friend Alfred Rodewald, a wealthy Liverpool merchant and patron of music. Rodewald was a friend of Richter and founder and conductor of the Liverpool Orchestral Society. On this occasion, the Elgars stayed with the Bantocks, whose daughter Myrrha later recalled:

> Many arrangements were necessary for [Elgar's] comfort, including an apparatus for his nightly tea-making. Elgar's wife was absolutely devoted to him and surrounded her husband with a ring-fence of attention and care that was almost pathetic . . . My newly-married mother was, I am sure, awed by Mrs Elgar, with her array of rugs, shawls and cushions, extra body-belts and knitted bedsocks for Edward's comfort. One evening Helena [Mrs Bantock] noted with astonishment no fewer than seven hot water bottles being filled for his bed on the occasion of Elgar complaining of a slight chill.[1]

During the rest of the summer – a famously hot one – he orchestrated *Sea Pictures* for Norwich. 'Dorabella' bicycled forty miles to Worcester to see him. On 11 August he went to London to go through the songs with Clara Butt and the following day had a flaming row with Novello's. This was not over his royalties agreement but because he had discovered to his fury that Novello's had sent Richter's manager Vert a bill for thirty shillings (£1.50) for hire of parts for the extra rehearsal of the Variations. The extra rehearsal, he pointed out to Jaeger, had cost Vert £40. Alfred Littleton, Novello's chairman, told Elgar that Vert ought to have 'got the extra rehearsal out of his men for *nothing!!*' Elgar was deeply shocked 'at the sheer brutality of the idea'. He took *Sea Pictures* to Boosey & Co., who bought the copyright for £50 with a royalty of three-pence a copy on sales of published separate songs. Littleton made some amends by agreeing to print the full score of the Variations and all the orchestral parts instead of expecting orchestras to rely on manuscript copies.

At the Worcester Festival in September, Elgar conducted *The Light of Life* and the Variations, both in revised form. Suffering from a heavy cold, he conducted the first performance of *Sea Pictures* at Norwich on 5 October. For years English critics discussed these five songs only in terms of the poems. True, they are not great poems but what matters is how Elgar treated them. No one seemed to notice that the orchestration showed the same advance as that of the  Variations and that Elgar had broken new ground in writing an orchestral song cycle. Only Berlioz's *Les nuits d'été* and Wagner's *Wesendonck-Lieder* were well-known examples of the genre – certainly not Mahler's at that time. Each of the songs has something distinctively Elgarian to offer, from the impressionism of 'Sea Slumber Song' to the religious ecstasy of 'Sabbath Morning' and the flamboyance of 'The Swimmer', while it is doubtful if he ever set words and music more felicitously than in 'Where corals lie'

'Clara Butt sang *Sea Pictures* well', Elgar told Jaeger, and was 'dressed like a mermaid'. Two days later she sang four of the songs, with Elgar at the piano, in London in St James's Hall. After this he went to the Sheffield Festival to conduct *King Olaf*, there was Richter's second performance of the Variations, and he sat to the sculptor Percival Hedley for a bronze bust commissioned for the music room at 22 Old Queen Street, Westminster, by Leo Francis (Frank) Schuster, a wealthy patron and admirer of his music, whom he had met the previous May. But when he returned to Malvern from these occasions, it was still to teaching schoolgirls the violin at The Mount.

His main concern was what to write for the Birmingham Festival. For several years he had been contemplating a setting of Cardinal Newman's poem *The Dream of Gerontius*. He again thought of it for Birmingham but decided it was too Roman Catholic. He also again rejected St Augustine as a subject. But what about the Apostles? There was the possibility of a trilogy but there was not enough time. Even so, he wrote a theme for Judas and sent it to Jaeger in November. But depression took over and he wrote to the chairman of the festival orchestral subcommittee, G. H. Johnstone, giving up the commission. Johnstone turned up at Craeg Lea on New Year's Day 1900 to say he would be responsible for publishing negotiations for a new work and there would be no objection to *The Dream of Gerontius*. On 12 January Elgar went to Birmingham Oratory to ask permission from Newman's executors to abridge the poem which is in a prologue and six sections. Elgar barely shortened the prologue – Part 1 of his work – but cut the remaining 730 lines to 300 for his Part 2. Johnstone called on Littleton at Novello's and on 23 January Littleton agreed to publish *Gerontius* and to pay £200 for all rights and a 'fair proportion' on sales 'after the £200 has been cleared'. The breach was healed. On 5 February Elgar wrote to Jaeger: 'I am setting Newman's "Dream of Gerontius" – awfully solemn & mystic . . . That Judas theme will have to be used up for death & despair in this work.' It became the Angel of the Agony's solo.

It is tempting to believe that *Gerontius* subsumed Elgar's idea for a *Gordon Symphony*. By coincidence Newman wrote the poem in 1865 in memory of a friend called John Joseph Gordon, who had died aged forty-one in 1853. General Charles Gordon admired the poem and had a copy with him when he was killed at Khartoum in 1885. His annotations were copied into books owned by others and, as already related, Elgar lent Alice his annotated copy in 1887 and also received another copy on his wedding day in 1889. Although Elgar told Worcester he could not write the *Gordon Symphony* for the 1899 festival because he could not afford to, the real reason was that he did not feel ready to compose an orchestral work on that scale. *Gerontius*, with its Gordon associations, solved the problem for him.

Elgar completed the composition sketch of *Gerontius* on 6 June 1900. He had sent the score in batches to Jaeger so that the choral parts could be prepared (they had to be sent to Germany for engraving). He interrupted work only to fulfil some conducting engagements such as *Sea Pictures* at the Crystal Palace and again at a Philharmonic Society concert (the first time he conducted for the society – 10 May 1900). While composing he was in a kind of trance. This was his religion and he felt it deeply. He wrote to Nicholas Kilburn:

> I think you will find Gerontius far beyond anything I've yet done – I like it – I am not suggesting that I have risen to the heights of the poem for one moment – but on our hillside night after night looking across our 'illimitable' horizon (pleonasm!) I've seen in thought the Soul go up & have written my own heart's blood into the score.

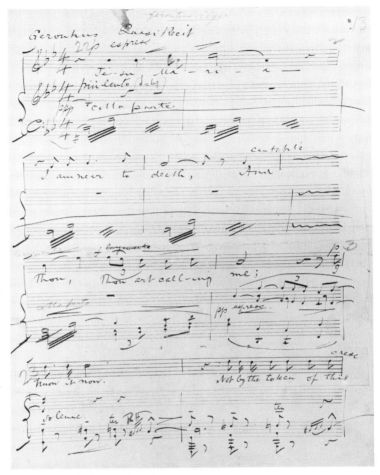

10  Sketch for *The Dream of Gerontius*

After reading part of the score, Jaeger wrote to Elgar: 'I have not seen or heard *anything* since *Parsifal* that has stirred me & spoken to me with the trumpet tongue of genius as has this part of your latest & *by far* greatest work.' Later Jaeger was to accuse him of evading the moment when Gerontius sees God. As with the finale of the Variations, Elgar at first fought a rearguard action, but he then wrote the series of devastating orchestral chords which precede Gerontius's 'Take me away', exactly what Jaeger had suggested: 'a few gloriously effulgent chords given out by the whole force of the Orchestra in its most glorious key'. Knowing just how to provoke Elgar into action, he had added: 'To suggest the glory of the momentary vision need not have been blasphemous either. But I grant you, it needed a Wagner or R. Strauss to do that, nobody else could dare attempt it. No! as I know now, not even E. E.'

Orchestration took until 3 August. He wrote a Ruskin quotation at the end of the manuscript beginning: 'This is the best of me.' Even more significant was another phrase: 'This I saw and knew.' With the subject of Gerontius Elgar had found something that stirred his creativity far more than chivalry lifting up its lance for King Olaf, Caractacus's warriors and St George. Here, with 'a man like us . . . no end of a worldly man in his life, & now brought to book', as he described Gerontius in a letter to Jaeger, Elgar had seen a reflection of his inner self, not only his religious beliefs (as far as we know them) but the thoughts of death (suicide) and what might lie beyond.

On the score he also wrote: 'Birchwood. In summer.' For relaxation while working, he and Alice had been learning to ride bicycles. He went for rides in company with Rosa Burley who remembered that 'he was very difficult and one never knew quite what would be the mood of the afternoon . . . I found that he was particularly touched by birdsong and that he loved and knew all the little creatures that darted in and out of the hedges.'[2] Dora Penny saw another side of him that summer:

When E. E. was at the top of his form, meals used to be exciting. He kept up a running fire of absurd remarks, comments, chaff and repartee. I often laughed so much that I could hardly eat and was positively afraid to drink. Also it did not help matters to have the Lady [Alice] at the bottom of the table – not always completely approving, particularly if Carice was present – putting in remarks to try to check the flow: 'Oh, Edward dear, how can you?' or 'Oh, Edward, really!' 'Cheer up, Chicky!' was all she got for her pains.[3]

11  Elgar with his bicycle 'Mr Phoebus', c.1900

This was the Elgar who enjoyed practical jokes and illustrated his letters and the sketches for his music with drawings of cats and mice and other creatures.

The first performance of *Gerontius* was on Wednesday morning, 3 October 1900. It was a near-disaster, as has often been recounted. But it was not surprising. The chorus had had too little time to learn their far from easy parts because Novello's had been behindhand in engraving them, and this was because Elgar had been so late correcting them. Jaeger kept warning him of disaster ahead. Novello's also had to prepare the scores and parts for Parry's *De profundis* and Coleridge-Taylor's *Hiawatha* trilogy at Birmingham and the new works for the Hereford Festival in September. The orchestral rehearsal in London on 23 September was the first time Richter, who was to conduct 'at the composer's request', had seen the complete work and he, the orchestra and soloists – Edward Lloyd, Marie Brema and Harry Plunket Greene – were not much more than sight-reading. At the combined rehearsal in Birmingham six days later, the Demons' Chorus came to grief. The chorus did not take it seriously and Elgar insulted them. Richter studied the score all weekend but it was too late in spite of an extra choral rehearsal on 1 October. Almost certainly he had not expected a score of such innovation and difficulty. In any case, according to what one reads in letters by Wagner and Strauss, he was inclined to be lazy. To be fair to him, as conductor of the festival he also had to prepare and conduct over the four days *Elijah*, Parry's *De profundis*, the *Hiawatha* trilogy (which he called rubbish), *Israel in Egypt*, *Messiah*, Bach's *St Matthew Passion*, Dvořák's *The Spectre's Bride* and miscellaneous orchestral works. To be fair to the chorus, too, which apparently sang badly throughout the festival, its chorusmaster Swinnerton Heap had died suddenly aged fifty-three in June and Stockley, aged seventy, had been called from retirement to take his place. The complexities of *Gerontius* were far beyond him.

The majority of the critics, while realising that the performance was totally inadequate, recognised that *Gerontius* was a work of genius, as did several visitors from Germany. But Elgar was in despair. He wrote to Jaeger on 9 October: 'Providence denies me a decent hearing of my work: so I submit – I always said God was against art & I still believe it: anything obscure or trivial is blessed in this world . . . I have allowed my heart to open once – it is now shut against every religious feeling & every soft, gentle impulse *for ever*.' Less than three weeks later: 'I really wish I were dead over & over again but I dare not, for the sake of my relations, do the job myself.' It was characteristic Elgar self-dramatisation, self-pity and depression. But he knew he had composed a masterpiece. In no previous English choral work had the orchestra had such a prominent part, being used as in a Wagner opera almost as the leading character. In no previous English work – and surely in no work of oratorio character – had soloists, chorus and orchestra been blended into such an organic whole. The tenor part of Gerontius has in places an Italianate lyricism. Yet there was also a Handelian splendour in the great choral set piece 'Praise to the holiest in the height'. Elgar was right to tell Jaeger that Gerontius was unclassifiable as oratorio or cantata – 'there's no word invented yet to describe it'.

On return to Malvern, where he had by now given up nearly all the hated teaching, he found an offer of an honorary doctorate of music from Cambridge University. This had been engineered by Charles Villiers Stanford, whose music Elgar scorned and whom he had mocked in the Demons' Chorus, evolving a cipher on the name 'Satanford'. His first inclination was to refuse because he could not afford to buy the robes, but he accepted and the degree, together with one for Frederic Cowen, was conferred on 22 November. Alice wrote next day to Elgar's mother: 'I wish you could have seen E. he looked so perfectly beautiful, really it is the only word, in his robes with a strong light on his face.'⁴ The robes had been hired, but Rodewald of Liverpool raised the money among Elgar's friends to buy him his own, made to measure. Rodewald also offered to support Elgar financially while he composed a symphony, but it was still too early for that.

Notwithstanding post-Gerontius depression, Elgar had begun a new work almost immediately. The Philharmonic Society had asked him for an orchestral work and he planned a concert overture (in effect a tone poem). He told Jaeger on 4 November: 'I call it "Cockayne" & it's cheerful and Londony – "stout and steaky".' The title was actually Cockaigne, an old name for London, and the idea had come to him 'one dark day in the Guildhall . . . I seemed to hear far away in the dim roof a theme, an echo of some noble melody.' He completed the score on 24 March 1901. It was another advance in his orchestral writing, an English equivalent of the Meistersinger overture in encapsulating the soul of a city: the dignity of Guildhall aldermen, the cheekiness of Cockney urchins, military bands marching down the Mall, lovers in the park, the work's most eloquent theme marked 'nobilmente'. He dedicated it 'to my many friends, the members of British orchestras'. There had been a further squabble with Novello's over *Gerontius* royalties, so he offered it to Boosey. He conducted the first performance on 20 June 1901 and sent the score to Richter, telling him: 'Here is nothing deep or melancholy – it is intended to be honest, healthy, humorous and strong but not vulgar.' Richter, who had become conductor of the Hallé Orchestra in October 1899, conducted *Cockaigne* in Manchester in October 1901 to Elgar's intense admiration. Abroad, Weingartner took it up, as did Strauss to whom Elgar sent some tempo directions.

But *Cockaigne* was not the only music he was writing at New Year 1901. Three days after the *Gerontius* fiasco, on 6 October 1900, Alice wrote in her diary: 'E. working at Pomp & Circ. Marches – not vesy well and raser depressed.' The Boer War was still raging and was not going well for Britain. Elgar had 'some of the soldier instinct' in him and perhaps felt that this was the time to lift morale with military marches. He began to compose the A minor march (now known as no. 2) and then to write another in D major. On 12 January 1901, ten days before the death of Queen Victoria, he wrote to Jaeger: 'In haste & joyful (Gosh! man I've got a tune in my head).' The tune was the trio section of the D major march (*Pomp and Circumstance* no. 1) which is also the tune of 'Land of hope and glory'. Elgar contemplated using it for a larger work. Alice wrote to Jaeger on 20 January: 'I think there cd. be no nobler music than the Symphony. I long for it to be finished & have to exist on scraps.'[5] Clearly Elgar was working on sketches for a symphony in this year: he told Richter in August that he was 'trying to write' a symphony and that it would be dedicated to Richter, 'but I have much to do to it yet'. He decided the great tune would not fit into a symphony, but when in 1907–8 he at last started to write his First Symphony he began it with a solemn march tune.

He did not hurry with the two marches, completing them in April 1901. He played the D major march to 'Dorabella' in May, telling her, 'I've got a tune that will knock 'em – knock 'em flat', and on another occasion he called it 'a tune that comes once in a lifetime'.[6] He did not realise it then, but he had composed Britain's second national anthem. At this stage, though, it was still the trio section of a march. The two marches were first played in Liverpool by Rodewald and his orchestra (to whom no. 1 was dedicated) on 19 October. Three days later, with Elgar absent through a misunderstanding, Henry Wood conducted them at a Queen's Hall Promenade Concert. After no. 1 'the people simply rose and yelled', Wood wrote.[7] He had to play it twice more.

Another Elgar march had its first performance on 21 October, but in Dublin. This was part of the incidental music he had written for George Moore and W. B. Yeats's play *Diarmuid and Grania* (which he called *Grania and Diarmid*). Moore had asked Elgar for a funeral march for the death of Diarmuid and he received a noble seven-minute piece memorably described by Yeats as possessing 'heroic melancholy'. Elgar also provided some atmospheric horn calls and a song, *There are seven that pull the thread*. Encouraged by Moore, he contemplated an opera, but the idea went no further than had his idea earlier in the year for an opera based on Maurice Hewlett's novel *The Forest Lovers*. His other work in 1901 was a *Concert Allegro* for piano, written for Fanny Davies to play at a recital on 2 December, and the orchestration of Herbert Brewer's cantata *Emmaus*, as an act of friendship, in time for the Gloucester Festival. The dean had forbidden performance of *Gerontius* because of its Roman Catholicism, allowing only the Prelude and Angel's Farewell which Elgar had arranged without the choral part. Elgar had conducted an abbreviated version with the Worcestershire Philharmonic on 9 May.[8]

The year ended in happiness for him when on 19 December Julius Buths, who had attended the Birmingham performance, conducted *Gerontius* (in a German translation) in Düsseldorf. Buths was the city's music director and since 1893 had conducted the Lower Rhine Festival. He was an enthusiast of Delius's music. In spite of an inadequate Angel, the performance was a triumph and proved that the Demons' Chorus was singable. Elgar rubbed it in to Novello's: 'This disproves the idea fostered in Birmingham that my work is *too difficult*.'

# 7 Darkness at noon

A picture of Elgar at Birchwood in 1901 comes from the composer Arnold Bax, who was seventeen when he was taken to meet him:

> Hatless, dressed in rough tweeds and riding boots, his appearance was rather that of a retired army officer turned gentleman farmer than an eminent and almost morbidly highly strung artist. One almost expected him to sling a gun from his shoulder and drop a brace of pheasants to the ground . . . He was not a big man but such was the dominance of his personality that I always had the impression that he was twice as large as life.[1]

Another young man, William Roberts, met Elgar when he was a dinner guest of Rodewald in Liverpool while the Elgars were staying. Roberts was beginning to write music criticism under the pseudonym Ernest Newman, which he then adopted (though not legally) as his name. Newman wrote fifty-four years later:

> He gave me even then the impression of an exceptionally nervous, self-divided and secretly unhappy man; in the light of all we came to know of him in later years I can see now that he was at that time rather bewildered and nervous at the half-realisation that his days of spiritual privacy – always so dear to him – were probably coming to an end; while no doubt gratified by his rapidly growing fame, he was in his heart of hearts afraid of the future. I remember distinctly a dinner at Rodewald's

at which Mrs Elgar tactfully steered the conversation away from the topic of suicide . . . she whispered to me that Edward was always talking of making an end of himself.[2]

Before he went to Düsseldorf, Elgar wrote to Jaeger: 'I want a sketch book bound in Human skin to write some of the things I am doing now.' Among his sketches were ideas for 'a brilliant piece for string orchestra' which had come to him in the summer when he spent five days in Cardiganshire and heard distant singing on the island of Ynys Lochtyn. As the year 1902 began he reworked some old pieces as the two Dream Children, music which holds the essence of the solitary Elgar: 'we are only what might have been'. But his larger concern was to write something to mark the coronation of Edward VII in June. A plan to convert Caractacus into an opera was rejected by Covent Garden and discouraged by Jaeger. Sir Walter Parratt, Master of the King's Music, sent him verses by A. C. Benson, a master at Eton, urging him to set them. Elgar agreed and he and Benson devised the Coronation Ode. Prompted by Clara Butt, Elgar planned a final movement for soloist, chorus and orchestra using the tune of the trio of the D major march. Within a week Benson had written a finale beginning 'Land of hope and glory'. Elgar finished the work in April and at once began to orchestrate it, at the same time making his arrangement of God Save the King. Benson suddenly remembered that he had omitted any reference to Queen Alexandra and added a new movement, 'Daughter of Ancient Kings'. The Coronation Ode is a superb example of occasional music. The opening 'Crown the King' is Elgar at his most grandiloquent, but with prayers for peace interspersed among the majesty and with a poetic coda based on 'Land of hope and glory'. A martial bass solo, 'Britain, ask of thyself', is followed by the exquisite 'Hark upon the hallowed air', for soprano and tenor with a lightly scored accompaniment. Its tragic mood carries over into a devotional quartet, 'Only let the heart be pure'. A third movement in this meditative style – 'Peace, gentle peace', for the four soloists, small orchestra and unaccompanied chorus – gives way to the finale. The text of 'Land of hope and glory' differs in the *Ode* from that of the song (there is no 'wider still and wider' and no 'God who made thee mighty'), and the setting is a reminder that the wonderful tune has a strong vein of melancholy and that Elgar once considered setting Kipling's 'Recessional' ('Lo, all our pomp of yesterday / Is one with Nineveh and Tyre').

With the *Ode* delivered to Boosey, Elgar crossed the Channel to attend the second German performance of *Gerontius* which Buths was to conduct on 20 May at the Lower Rhine Festival in Düsseldorf. With him, besides Alice, were Henry Wood and Arthur Johnstone, critic of the *Manchester Guardian*, who had been the first to appreciate Elgar at his true worth. The performance was an even greater success than the previous one. Ludwig Wüllner again sang Gerontius, Johannes Messchaert sang the bass roles and the Angel was the young English mezzo-soprano Muriel Foster, who was to make the role her own. After Part 1, Elgar was recalled twenty times. At a dinner next day,[3] Richard Strauss (who had conducted Liszt's Faust Symphony in the same programme as *Gerontius*) made a speech in which he was less than complimentary about English composers in general but ended by raising his glass 'to the welfare and success of the first English progressivist, Meister Edward Elgar, and of the young progressivist school of English composers'.[4] Elgar was overjoyed. He and Alice left Düsseldorf for a fortnight's holiday in Eisenach with Rodewald. Returning to London they found Strauss there for a concert of his works and they had dinner together. A few days later the coronation was postponed because of the king's appendix operation. But the Honours List still appeared: a baronetcy for Parry and a knighthood for Stanford. The *Pall Mall Gazette* deplored the omission of Elgar.

There was still no move to perform *Gerontius* in London, Manns having decided that it was too difficult for the Crystal Palace. But Atkins had put it into the Worcester Festival programme for September 1902 with Elgar conducting. 'You must come to Worcester to hear what *Gerontius* might be – the building will do it', Elgar wrote to Jaeger. In

April, however, the clergy (headed by Bishop Gore) made it a condition that references to the Virgin Mary, souls in purgatory, Masses on earth and other Roman Catholic doctrine should be removed.[5] Elgar contacted Father Neville, Newman's executor, who gave his permission for the changes. Elgar did not object to them; his attitude was the same as Jaeger's:

> Novello's don't mind what small alterations or omissions are made if only the performance takes place. The book of words will be printed at Worcester and the festival people therefore are responsible for whatever violence is done to the work (text or music). We shall advise the alterations being quietly made & nothing said about it.

The soloists were left to overcome the lacunae in the text as best they could. The performance was on 11 September and Elgar conducted in mourning black with tears running down his cheeks, his mother having died on 1 September at the age of eighty. Muriel Foster, John Coates and Plunket Greene were the soloists. This was Coates's first Gerontius (he came in as a last-minute substitute for William Green) and he remained Elgar's favourite interpreter of the role. It had poured with rain all morning but the cathedral was packed by 3,100 people, many of them standing. Afterward Alice gave a lunch at the house they had rented for the week in College Green, a house where Elgar had improvised for its owners forty years earlier. Worcester continued to perform Gerontius in this mutilated form until the Second World War. At Gloucester it was not performed in full until 1910, after the retirement of a dean who had totally forbidden the work in 1901, 1904 and 1907. In Hereford the text has always been sung complete (from 1903), although there was initial clerical opposition.

The song 'Land of hope and glory' was first performed at a coronation concert in the Royal Albert Hall in June of 1902, with Clara Butt as the soloist. It swept the nation. In August, Elgar, Alice and Carice spent a fortnight's holiday at Rodewald's holiday 'cottage' at Saughall near Chester, together with the Bantocks and Newmans. The Coronation

*Ode* had its postponed première at the Sheffield Festival on 2 October. *Gerontius* was performed at the same festival. Elgar performances were now becoming social events. Elgar's wealthy admirer Frank Schuster was in Sheffield and introduced him to one of the local MPs, Charles Stuart Wortley, and his wife Alice, a daughter of the painter Sir John Millais. Performances of the *Ode* followed in Bristol, London (three times) and Leeds. The Elgars stayed with Schuster in London when the Meiningen Orchestra came to London and Fritz Steinbach conducted the Variations. The Stuart Wortleys were again there, with their friends Admiral Lord Charles Beresford and the art critic Claude Phillips. Schuster has been vividly described by Siegfried Sassoon:

> Unable to create anything himself, he loved and longed to assist in the creation of music. He wanted to create artistic history; but could only do so by entertaining gifted people . . . He was something more than a *patron* of music, because he loved music as much as it is humanly possible to do. In the presence of great musicians he was humble, bowing before them in his Semitic way, and flattering them over-effusively because he knew no other way of expressing his admiration . . . He lacked essential good-breeding and was always the Frankfurt Jew among aristocrats. But when it came to the performance of first-rate music he became first-rate – as an amateur.[6]

In the autumn of 1902, Elgar was busy sketching music and fashioning a libretto for the 1903 Birmingham Festival commission he had accepted. He was to write an oratorio on the subject of the Apostles and he consulted ecclesiastical friends such as Canon Charles Gorton, rector of Morecambe, about the text as well as resorting once again to Longfellow (his *The Divine Tragedy*). Gorton ran the Morecambe competitive festival and had paid Elgar £100 for a new choral work. In November Elgar wrote for him the part-song *Weary wind of the west* and immediately followed it with the clumsily named but extremely fine *Five Part-Songs from the Greek Anthology* for male chorus. These he dedicated to Sir Walter Parratt in gratitude for the idea of the *Coronation Ode*. He also made sketches for *Cockaigne* no. 2, which he called *City of Dreadful Night*.

He planned *The Apostles* as a trilogy: 'the schooling of the Apostles, the earthly result and the result of it all in the next world – Last Judgement'. This time, he was sure, there could be no accusations of too much Catholicism, in spite of his use of Gregorian chant. Negotiations with Novello's over publication and royalties were being handled by G. H. Johnstone who, at the end of October 1902, was beginning to be worried that no music had yet been composed and the première was less than a year away. Johnstone eventually obtained handsome terms: £500 on delivery of the full score, £500 after the sale of 10,000 copies and then a royalty.

Elgar was in London in early December for the première of Strauss's *Ein Heldenleben*, conducted by the composer, and attended a dinner party for Strauss. At Christmas came a gift of the complete *Encyclopaedia Britannica* (thirty-five volumes) in a revolving bookcase. He was delighted but the gift soon vanished. Carice told 'Dorabella' that 'Mother had to send it away quite soon. Father would turn it round so!'[7] Alice no doubt saw it as a time-wasting threat to the more important activity of composing. By 23 March 1903 Elgar was only halfway through Part 1 of *The Apostles*, over an hour's music. He had to break off time and again to rehearse and conduct the Worcestershire Philharmonic in the *Bavarian Highlands* and Worcester Festival Choral Society in the *Coronation Ode*. He rehearsed *Gerontius* in Hanley on the same night as Richter conducted it with the Hallé in Manchester. These were only two of several *Gerontius* performances that spring which proved that it had survived the unhappy first performance – in Liverpool, Birmingham, Bristol, Middlesbrough, Chicago, New York and Danzig. The first London performance was in the new Westminster Cathedral on 6 June. It was a success but it was also another interruption and five days later Alice wrote in her diary: 'E. very badsley & dreadfully worried &c.' It was the day of Carice's confirmation, but neither parent attended, leaving it all to Rosa Burley.

Elgar had reason to be worried. He kept asking Jaeger for parts of the score to be returned so that he could revise them and he involved himself in negotiations with Birmingham because he had hoped for foreign male soloists such as Wüllner, Van Rooy and Messchaert. On 24 June he went to London for a performance of the *Coronation Ode* attended by the king and queen. This was the first time Edward VII had heard it. Alice recorded that he spoke to Elgar in the interval for 'quite a long time' and told him 'how he liked his music & and in his illness used to have some of his favourite pieces played to him once & sometimes more than once a day', but Lady Maud Warrender recalled that the king slept during the *Ode* but woke up for 'Land of hope and glory'.[8] On that same day Jaeger wrote to point out that 'we should have got Part 1 to Birmingham long ago, but the corrections are so *fearful* and so *upsetting*'. Elgar's response was to tell Novello's and Birmingham – in both cases using Alice as intermediary – that he would produce only Parts 1 and 2 of *The Apostles*. Part 3 'much of which was written first, you can have any time later'. Because of recurrent eye trouble, his doctor forbade him to work. That, he told Littleton of Novello's, was the sole reason for his decision. But his eyes were well enough for him to begin the task of orchestration and he took the full score with him in July to Rodewald's holiday cottage Minafon near Betws-y-Coed in North Wales. While the others drove round in Rodewald's new car, Elgar scored *The Apostles*, showing each sheet to Rodewald as he finished it and altering passages to please his host.

The first performance in Birmingham Town Hall on 14 October, conducted by Elgar, was a social as well as a musical event. Elgar's friends were there – the Stuart Wortleys, the Speyers, Frank Schuster, Lord Northampton, Rodewald – as well as the Birmingham Chamberlain clan. The hall was full. The work was received by the critics with respect rather than enthusiasm, although Johnstone of the *Manchester Guardian* noted that 'vague hostility . . . has given way almost universally to the recognition that he [Elgar] is one of the great originals in the musical world of today'. Elgar is one of a handful of composers whose

12  Jaeger and A. E. Rodewald at Betws-y-Coed, 1903

music can be likened to a crystal on which the sunlight plays so that its shape, colours and intensity seem constantly to vary. The music is so alive that it demands that the response should never be stereotyped and fixed but should be as fluid and flexible as the music. It is particularly hazardous to take up prepared positions on *The Apostles* and its successor *The Kingdom*. Familiarity with them leads to deeper understanding and intensified admiration. Several critics after the first performance of *The Apostles* described it as an 'advance' from *Gerontius* and from the standpoint of harmonic language and of architectural grandeur they were right.

A significant feature is Elgar's sympathetic treatment of the two 'flawed' characters, Judas and Mary Magdalene. Elgar followed the view of Judas as a zealot who overreached himself in the certainty that Jesus would save himself by a miracle – he betrayed him to force him into a display of supernatural power. To the most moving music in the work, Judas sings: 'We shall be hereafter as though we had never been . . . our name shall be forgotten in time and no man have our work in remembrance.' Whatever the theological aspect, this was the right musical interpretation of Judas for the kind of composer Elgar was. Elgar told Canon Gorton: 'To my mind, Judas's crime and sin was despair.'[9] Despair was something Elgar knew well. How much more successful he was with Judas's anguish than with Mary Magdalene's repentance. Elgar succeeds in his avowed aim of making the Apostles the dominant theme of the work. Christ is given some beautiful music, but he and what he does remain secondary to the way in which the Apostles are affected. In Gethsemane, Judas's actions hold the stage. Similarly the crucifixion is dwelt upon only as it affected Mary and John. In many of the multitude of themes, there is that sense of painful suffering so characteristic of Elgar's music.

The solemn opening phrases foretell at once the size and grandeur of his ambitious design: they launch us on a long and eventful journey which is enhanced by the vivid musical depiction of the landscapes we pass: night and dawn in Jerusalem, the stormy sea of Galilee, darkness at noon. But this is incidental to the spiritual and emotional power of Elgar's inventive genius as he challenges comparison with the subject matter of Bach's Passions in music which time and again overwhelms the listener with its transcendental qualities of compassion, insight and radiance. For these purposes he used a Strauss-size orchestra. In addition to a full complement of the 'normal' orchestra he included bass clarinet, double bassoon, organ, shofar and, among the percussion, small and large gongs, antique cymbals, glockenspiel, tambourine and triangle. These forces ensure the magnificence of the ending when the music broadens to a great *nobilmente* climax at the words 'the power of God', with the orchestra thundering out the 'Spirit of the Lord' theme from the Prelude decorated by a rejoicing brass counterpoint of quaver triplets. Thenceforward there is a gradual and radiant diminuendo, the air is filled with Alleluias from earth and heaven and a halo of string sound surrounds the last stately and profound Alleluias, which end with a swelling chord of E flat major.

When Elgar returned to Malvern, Littleton wrote to say that as only two of the three parts had been delivered, Novello's would pay two-thirds of the sum agreed. G. H. Johnstone of the Birmingham committee wrote to Elgar: 'Please remember that I am responsible to you for the amount & will find you the balance until they *have* paid it.'[10] Shortly afterwards, Novello's paid up the full £500. At the same time Alice told Frank Schuster that there ought to be an Elgar festival. He saw Higgins of Covent Garden who proposed a three-day festival in March 1904, with Richter – who had declared *The Apostles* to be 'the greatest work since Beethoven's Mass in D' – as its director and the Hallé as the orchestra. Elgar had renewed his promise of a 'Symphony in E flat dedicated to Hans Richter'. More sketches were made and put into the green linen-bound book marked 'Symphony'. But they went no further at present.

In November 1903 Elgar was due to go to Liverpool for one of Rodewald's concerts. But his friend developed influenza with complications and became paralysed and unconscious. On the 9th Elgar went by train to Liverpool to find that Rodewald had died just before midday. He was devastated and on return home wrote to Jaeger one of his most self-dramatising letters:

> I broke down & went out – & it was night [a deliberate reference to Judas] to me. What I did, God knows – I know I walked for miles in strange ways . . . I know I went and looked at the Exchange where he had taken me – but it was all dark, dark to me although light enough to the busy folk around . . . I went to my room & wept for hours – yesterday I came home without seeing anyone & am now a wreck & broken-hearted man.

Diana McVeagh, in a perceptive essay, has drawn a parallel between this letter and verses from Tennyson's In Memoriam (e.g. 'Dark house, by which once more I stand / Here in the long unlovely street'), written as an elegy for the poet's friend Arthur H. Hallam.[11] This has been further explored by the American writer Byron Adams in a provocative but reasoned article in which he writes of 'the erotic centrality of Hallam in Tennyson's poem' and argues that 'Elgar's chief emotional outlet – one tolerated, if barely, by English society – was his intimate and passionate friendship with such men as August Jaeger, Frank Schuster, Ivor Atkins and W. H. Reed. To these men he poured out his heart in letters filled with an almost "amatory tenderness" and to them he dedicated much of his music' (an exaggeration).[12] Elgar's trip to Liverpool, Adams believes, 'can be seen as a moving, instinctual protest against the conventional strictures that bound him, played out in the terms of one of the few homoerotic narratives available to him, Tennyson's In Memoriam'. If, that is, Elgar recognised it as a homoerotic narrative. Friendships between men in Victorian times were often expressed in more emotional terms than are customary today. In some cases, no doubt, these represented suppressed homoerotic tendencies. We can have no idea if this applied to Elgar. We know nothing of his views on homosexuality. His friend Schuster was homosexual and Elgar later befriended Oscar Wilde's son Vyvyan Holland, who was not homosexual, and Siegfried Sassoon, who was. But 'befriended' is the only word. Elgar was liberal in his attitudes to mankind's frailties, but any attempt to claim him as a thwarted homosexual is doomed to failure, not least because of his known susceptibility to women. As Adams concedes: 'It is highly unlikely that Elgar ever considered consummating his intense feelings for his male friends, if he indeed ever acknowledged to himself the merest possibility of such "abnormal" and, by the standard of the times, self-destructive behaviour.' Far from 'amatory tenderness', Elgar's letters to Jaeger and Atkins are mostly in terms of almost schoolboyish playfulness and teasing, when they are not strictly practical. (Atkins and Elgar often wrote to each other as 'Firapeel' and 'Reynart' and adopted the style of Caxton's 1481 version of *Reynard the Fox*, a rather tiresome but certainly not homoerotic literary conceit.) Adams courts risibility when he cites *Falstaff* to suggest that 'Elgar may have conceived of himself as Shakespeare's eponymous character [so far so good], a device that would have enabled him to displace his own homoerotic yearning onto the ageing knight who loves Prince Hal and is sternly rejected.' It is safer to regard Elgar's reaction to Rodewald's death as severe emotional shock at the sudden and totally unexpected loss – Rodewald was forty-three – of a friend whose musical skills and advice he admired and valued. That dark day in Liverpool is commemorated in sketches made at this time for a symphony in E flat that were eventually to become the Larghetto of the Second Symphony. Just before leaving for a holiday in Italy, Elgar wrote to Ivor Atkins: 'I've been into the Cathedral, which I have known since I was four & said "farewell" – I wanted to see you. I am sad at heart & feel I shall never return!' He was, as his music tells us, a very emotional man.

In Italy they rented a house in Alassio. It was wet and windy. Rosa Burley brought Carice to join them for Christmas. Efforts to write the symphony failed and instead he began a concert overture for the Covent Garden Festival, calling it a 'Fantasia Overture', then 'From the South' and finally *In the South (Alassio)*. He began it with a theme that he had inscribed in Sinclair's visitors' book in 1899 as 'Dan triumphant (after a fight)'. The place name Moglio provided another theme, shepherd's piping another and, one particular afternoon, 'in a flash it all came to me – the conflict of the armies on that very spot long ago, where now I stood – the contrast of the ruin and the shepherd – and then, all of a sudden, I came back to reality. In that time I had composed the overture – the rest was merely writing it down.'[13] The opening key was E flat, the key of Strauss's *Ein Heldenleben* and never had Elgar's music sounded more Straussian than in this invigorating first section. The sound picture of the 'strife and wars' of ancient times is among Elgar's strongest passages and nothing is more Elgarian than the 'canto popolare', with its entrancing viola solo. The complete work, in effect a tone poem, is one of Elgar's most brilliant, colourful, accomplished and least neurotic works.

They left Alassio on 30 January, a few days early because Elgar had been invited to dine with the king at Marlborough House. He completed orchestration of *In the South* on 21 February and dedicated it to Schuster, in gratitude for his part in bringing the Covent Garden Festival to fruition. As usual, he had worked on a ridiculously tight schedule and poor Jaeger said he could not possibly have the parts printed and corrected (in Leipzig) in time for the Hallé to rehearse them on 9 March in Manchester. Elgar, helped by Alice and Carice, corrected all the parts himself in Malvern on 5, 6, 7 and 8 March, then went to Manchester. This meant that Richter had no time to study the score and could not conduct the first performance.

For the duration of the festival, an event almost unprecedented for an English composer, the Elgars stayed with Schuster. At a dinner party given by their host on the previous evening Elgar sat between Lady Maud Warrender and the Countess of Radnor. Elgar, according to a fellow guest, Henry Wood, was 'in one of his very silent and standoffish moods'.[14] Schuster proposed his health – 'with his heart in his voice', Alice wrote – but Elgar, instead of replying, continued talking to Lady Radnor 'and probably had no idea his health had been drunk', as Wood noted. Next day, 14 March, he attended the king's levée and in the evening the festival opened with *Gerontius*. The king and queen attended. There was a blue canopy over the stage and the back of the stage was arranged to represent a baronial hall. The following evening, with the king and queen again present, Richter conducted The Apostles. On the third evening, the queen attended. Richter conducted Froissart, the Variations and extracts from Caractacus and Elgar conducted In the South after the interval.

This was high summer for the tradesman's son from 10 High Street, Worcester. He was elected to the Athenaeum under Rule 11 (special invitation to those of 'distinguished eminence' in science, literature or the arts). His proposer and seconder were Stanford and Parry. Durham and Leeds offered him an honorary doctorate of music and on 24 June (three weeks after his forty-seventh birthday) came the announcement of a knighthood, conferred on the recommendation of the music-loving prime minister, Arthur Balfour. In addition, he and Alice were to move from Craeg Lea to Plas Gwyn, a larger house a mile outside Hereford. Felix Weingartner conducted Gerontius in London (with Gervase Elwes singing Gerontius for the first time) and Alice and Elgar went to Cologne to hear Fritz Steinbach conduct The Apostles. In Hereford there were new bicycle rides to enjoy and an Aeolian harp was fixed on his study window. Yet he wrote to Richter, 'I sometimes wonder if I shall invent any more music', and to Schuster, 'I see nothing in the future but a black stone wall against which I am longing to dash my head.'

# 8 The last oratorio

Plas Gwyn (Welsh for White House) was, as Alice appreciated, a house suitable for a knight of the realm, but it was expensive. May Grafton, eldest (twenty-four) daughter of Elgar's sister Pollie, went to live with them as his secretary and to look after Carice, who was in her last term at The Mount. Elgar was busy conducting and the only music he wrote was the *Pomp and Circumstance* march no. 3, dedicated to Atkins, to whom he had given a sketch of the trio section in 1902. He went to Cologne to hear Steinbach conduct *In the South* and to Mainz and Rotterdam where Fritz Volbach conducted *The Apostles*. Weingartner conducted *In the South* in Berlin. One of the musicians who had done as much as anyone to further Elgar's reputation on the Continent, Richard Strauss, conducted a concert of his own works in Birmingham on 20 December 1904 and Elgar delivered a eulogy of him at a dinner afterwards, thereby returning the compliment from Düsseldorf in 1902. There is an interesting comparison between Elgar and Strauss in a letter of 2 July 1903 from Jaeger to Emily Harding, a friend of Muriel Foster:

> I swear by Elgar though he *can't* write love music. All *his* love scenes are 'bread and butter miss' cum 'college Boy' calf-love scenes, though nice enough music. But E's oratorios are great and *elevating*, pure and ennobling, and that's what we want, or what I want from Art (with a capital A). R. S.'s technique is a marvel and he carries everything before

him with that alone. Elgar could never give us the rush of unbridled
passion which we find in Strauss, hence his music will never appeal to
the amateur and uncultured as his German colleague does. And therein
lies Strauss's danger, I fear.[1]

At the time of Strauss's visit it had just been announced that
Elgar would be the first occupant of the newly endowed chair of music
at Birmingham University at an annual salary of £400. The donor,
Richard Peyton, had stipulated – not without misgiving – that the chair
should first be offered to and accepted by Elgar. For his part, Elgar
stipulated that he should not be expected to live in Birmingham and
that he should not give more than six lectures in the first year. He had
refused the offers of professorships at the Royal Manchester College of
Music and Leeds University and was wary of academic life. News of the
Birmingham appointment provoked an 'odious' letter from Stanford,
leading to a long period of hostility between them.

Elgar let it be known that he was at work on a pantomime-ballet
based on Rabelais's *Gargantua* and *Pantagruel*. But 1904 had seen the
formation of the London Symphony Orchestra, self-governing but
with Richter as conductor. The orchestra asked Elgar for a new work
to be played at an all-Elgar concert planned for March 1905. Jaeger
wrote to him in October: 'Why not a *brilliant* quick String Scherzo . . .
a real bring-down-the-house torrent of a thing such as Bach could
write . . . It wouldn't take you away from your *big* work for long.' For
some years Jaeger had suffered from tuberculosis and was to leave for
Davos in Switzerland to spend the winter there. He wrote to Elgar on
8 January:

shall be away for *months* . . . I am relieved to say that the firm are
behaving liberally to me . . . I worry also over your *music*, for I fear greatly
that we shall get less & less out of you. This is the danger of success
artistic & social! (especially social, of course). I grieve over it & so do all
those who most sincerely love & admire you. We know you *must live*, but
England *Ruins* all *artists*.

Whether this barb spurred Elgar we cannot know, but on 26 January he wrote to Jaeger at Davos: 'I'm doing that string thing . . . Intro. & Allegro – no *working-out* part but a devil of a fugue instead. G major & the sd. divvel in G minor . . . with all sorts of japes & counterpoint.' He returned to the sketches he had made at Ynys Lochtyn in 1901, especially the 'Welsh' theme with its falling third, which he introduced on a solo viola, as he had the *canto popolare* in *In the South*. He completed the work on 13 February 1905, shortly after receiving an honorary doctorate of music at Oxford, where Parry was professor. He conducted the first performance at an LSO concert in London on 8 March. Staying with Schuster, he had violent headaches a few days beforehand. Alice's diary says: '*Very* porsley. In evening so poorly we had a Dr Sinclair about 10.15.' The programme included the première of the third *Pomp and Circumstance* march, with the Variations and the *Grania and Diarmid* music. The *Introduction and Allegro* was under-rehearsed and coolly received. Several years were to pass before it was recognised as one of the greatest of works for strings, to be followed five years later by Vaughan Williams's Tallis Fantasia. Elgar's blending and contrasting of a solo quartet with the larger body of strings is masterly and the work's ideally proportioned combination of exuberance and lyricism ('smiling with a sigh' was his own phrase, borrowed from *Cymbeline*) has made it a favourite even with those whose response to his music is cool. Oddly, he never recorded it.

On 16 March he went to Birmingham to deliver his inaugural lecture, 'A Future for English Music', characteristically left until the last moment to prepare. Unfortunately he gave voice to his prejudices against academic musicians and extolled those who, like himself, had taken 'an active part in music . . . such as playing in orchestras'. He repeated Strauss's Düsseldorf strictures about English composers apart from Elgar himself and twisted the knife in Stanford, the composer of Irish rhapsodies, even further with his remarks that 'to rhapsodise is one thing Englishmen cannot do'. The audience grew restless and Rosa Burley described the occasion as 'one of the most embarrassing failures to which it has ever been my misfortune to listen . . . As the evening wore on and point after point missed its mark, feet were shuffled, a cross-fire of coughs set in and one gradually realised that the day was hopelessly lost.'[2]

Back in London at Schuster's for dinner at Buckingham Palace and to conduct a second LSO concert, the headaches returned ('E. dreffuly badly'). He cancelled a *Gerontius* in Leeds but rehearsed and conducted *The Apostles* in Leeds and *King Olaf* in Morecambe. But still the headaches persisted. Presumably these were migraines and perhaps associated with the chronic depression from which he had always suffered and which appeared to be growing worse. In 1904 he had met Samuel Sanford, professor of piano at Yale University, and this led to an invitation to the United States to receive an honorary doctorate at Yale. He sailed with Alice on 9 June 1905 when Elgar was 'rather badsley, headache &c – E. very mis.' On board the liner they met Sanford's wealthy friend Mrs Julia Worthington. The weather in New York and at New Haven, where Sanford lived, was unbearably hot and humid and Elgar was ill most of the time. The heat was still suffocating for two days in Boston and back in New York, where Elgar told a newspaper reporter: 'Your national anthem is worse than England's.'[3] Relief came at Mrs Worthington's home at Irvington-on-Hudson, which had electric fans, but he was glad to sail for Liverpool on 11 July. At Plas Gwyn during the rest of the summer, he contemplated setting Matthew Arnold's *Empedocles on Etna* and wrote a part-song (*Evening Scene*). In September he conducted *The Apostles* and the *Introduction and Allegro* at the Worcester Festival. To the usual festival house-party guests – Schuster, Jaeger, Canon Gorton – were added Sanford and Julia Worthington. On the opening day, the Freedom of Worcester was bestowed on Elgar by the city's first Roman Catholic mayor, Hubert Leicester. Processing from the Guildhall to the cathedral, Elgar (wearing his Yale hood and gown) saluted his eighty-three-year-old father, now very frail, who was watching from an upper room in 10 High Street.

As soon as the festival ended, Elgar and Schuster went to Brindisi and from there to Patras, where they boarded HMS *Surprise*. They had been

13  Frank Schuster aboard HMS *Surprise* in the Mediterranean, 1905

invited to cruise for a fortnight in the Mediterranean by Lady Charles
Beresford, whose husband had just become commander in chief of
the Mediterranean fleet. Other guests included Lady Maud Warrender
and her husband Sir George, who commanded the *Carnarvon*. Elgar
watched the fleet exercises and went ashore at Lemnos. Because of in-
ternational tension the fleet would not visit Turkish waters, so Elgar and
other guests boarded an Austrian vessel to visit the Bosphorus and Constantinople, which Elgar found 'insanely beautiful'. The Austrian ship
sank an unlit boat in darkness, killing all aboard, and in Constantinople
a bomb went off at a hotel near where they were staying. Elgar dined at
the embassy in Teraphia, where Lady Maud sang 'In Haven' and 'Where
corals lie' from *Sea Pictures* to his accompaniment, rejoined the *Surprise*
in Smyrna and visited the bazaar, where he saw hundreds of camels
and watched dancing dervishes. He wrote a piano piece, *In Smyrna*, and
played it on the ship's piano. They returned to Dover on 12 October
and next day he was in Norwich to rehearse *The Apostles*. He also read
an interview Fritz Kreisler had given to the *Hereford Times* in which he

described Elgar as 'the greatest living composer ... on an equal footing with Beethoven and Brahms' and expressed a wish that he would 'write something for the violin'. Elgar at once sketched some themes. One of them, in B minor, was to become the opening theme of his concerto a few years later, but not now. Another theme written at this time was marked 'Hans himself!' and that too had to wait a few more years to find its place in the finale of the Second Symphony. More pressing was the need to start work on the rest of The Apostles for Birmingham in October 1906. But this was interrupted by preparation of the second Birmingham lecture, 'English Composers', and a tour in which he conducted the LSO in works by Brahms, Schumann, Dvořák and himself in Cheltenham, Birmingham, Manchester, Sheffield, Glasgow, Edinburgh, Newcastle upon Tyne and Bradford. He needed the money, but he grew 'frightfully sick' of the tour.

Before Christmas other lectures had to be given – 'English Composers', 'English Executants', 'Brahms's Third Symphony', 'Critics' and 'Retrospect'. Each subject stirred up a hornet's nest. Stanford wrote to The Times. Alice complained of 'misleading quotations' in the press. Elgar must surely have agreed with the writer in the Musical News who said: 'Sir Edward Elgar must really be beginning to feel sorry that he accepted the Birmingham professorship, seeing that now he cannot open his mouth apparently without finding himself embroiled in some more or less lively controversy.'

At the beginning of January 1906 he composed the Prelude to The Kingdom, as the next part of The Apostles was to be called. He had written the great soprano solo 'The sun goeth down' five weeks earlier. But composition was difficult for him. He locked himself in his room without food for hours on end. Carice was sent to stay with the Littletons in London. (At home she had a room at the top of the house near the servants' quarters. She now went daily to Hereford Girls' High School.) Clearly Elgar went through some emotional or spiritual crisis at this time. Whenever he began to compose, the headaches returned. Alice's diary for 29 January: 'E. very porsely, altered & corrected Scene of choosing Matthias ... E. not well & thinking cd. not finish his work ... Very bad night.' 30 January: 'E. still very porsely . . . not able for anything & very depressed. A. dreadfully worried.' He was well behind schedule and after this work there was the third oratorio on the Last Judgement. Also he had fixed to go to America for eight weeks in April and May for an Elgar festival in Cincinnati. Best to give up. But Alice went to see Littleton to ask him to persuade Birmingham to take half – up to the Lord's Prayer – of what had been planned. The festival committee accepted this provided it was kept secret. By 18 February Alice could write: 'E. all well . . . played some new Apostle music to Troyte – much impressed.'

By the time Alice and Edward left for the United States on 6 April over half of *The Kingdom* was written. In Cincinnati they stayed at the Country Club. Scattered extracts from Alice's diary tell the story: 'Very hot & close – girls & ladies come and play bridge in the afternoon & shriek & make a wretched noise . . . Parish priest called, E. argued hotly with him . . . The evening was most unpleasant, noisy rowdy-sounding people . . . E. cd. not write . . . E. expressed himself forcibly about the noise &c, we were disgusted . . . E. works with bad headache . . . E. hard at work orchestrating.' On the opening day of the festival, Elgar learned that his father had died two days earlier. The following evening he conducted *The Apostles*, and was irritated by the applause after each scene, and the next evening *Gerontius*. Ten days in New York were filled with social activities including dinner at the home of Andrew Carnegie – 'very commonplace dinner & ugly dinner table' was Alice's verdict.

Depression descended again back at Plas Gwyn. 'Each day E. so unwell & quite unfit for his work.' 'Drefful headache.' Alice took him to New Radnor for a short holiday, and there he started a heavy cold. But slowly he conquered his creative block and on 23 July she could write: 'E. really finished the composing of his beautiful work – most thankful.' He completed the orchestration between 28 July and 6 August, sixty-eight pages in ten days, remarkably quick. At the Birmingham Festival on 2 October he conducted *The Apostles* and the following morning *The Kingdom*. The hall was full and a special train had come from London. 'E. looked most booful', Alice wrote. The orchestra and chorus saw that tears often streamed down his face. The critics were enthusiastic without being ecstatic. The Kingdom was less complex and more consistent in style than The Apostles. Its greatest glory is the orchestration and the choral writing. One does not have to agree with Schuster that 'Gerontius is the work of a raw amateur beside The Kingdom' to decide that the latter is a great work. The Kingdom has a melancholy sweetness about it and a vulnerability which perhaps reflect the mental anguish in which it was composed. When Elgar heard a performance in King's College, Cambridge, in June 1907, he told A. C. Benson that the music was 'so far behind what he had dreamed of – it only caused him shame and sorrow . . . He seemed all strung on wires & confessed that he petitioned for a seat close to the door that he might rush out if overcome.'4

Ernest Newman wrote in the Birmingham Post that 'a good deal of the music must frankly be called dull in itself, but Elgar is now so consummate a master of effect . . . that he can often almost persuade us against our own judgment that the actual tissue of the music is better than it really is'. Returning to the subject five months later, Newman described the scheme for the trilogy of oratorios as 'unwieldy' and 'impossible'. He went on:

> Until that scheme is done with and Elgar seeks inspiration in a subject of another type, the most sanguine of us cannot expect much from him in the way of fresh or really vital music. The wisest thing for him to do now is to abandon the idea of a third oratorio on the subject and turn his mind to other themes. These may bring him new inspiration and a new idiom; at present he is simply riding post-haste along the road that leads to nowhere.

It was harsh advice, but Elgar took it.

# 9 Symphony

The year 1906 ended with two more in the series of Birmingham lectures, on orchestration and Mozart's G minor symphony. He did not enjoy them and gave no more. His eyes were still giving him trouble – gout in the eyelids, he described the ailment – and Alice insisted on a return to Italy. They arrived in Naples on 6 January 1907 before going to Capri and finally to Rome. While there he wrote long and charmingly affectionate letters to Carice:

> The parrot here is a most amusing beast . . . There is another abandoned beast up the street who talks both languages & nothing decent in either: a bad bird, my child, & no fit company for Peter [her rabbit]. I hope Peter is well. I often think of him & wonder if he has any dried clover for a change: do get him some if he wants it. I know all the pen straw must be gone by now . . . Good night ducksie. I tiss bofe paws & 2 eyes.

At the beginning of March, leaving Alice at home, he went to the United States. In New York he conducted *The Apostles* and the American première of *The Kingdom* and refused to lead prayers that New York might be saved from a performance of Strauss's *Salome*. ('Strauss is the greatest genius of the age', he declared.)[1] Recalling this incident in a letter to Delius in December 1933 he described it as 'so staggering and screamingly absurd that I don't think I have recovered from the shock

14   Elgar and his daughter Carice, c.1906

even now'. In Chicago he conducted the Variations and *In the South* and
in Pittsburgh received an honorary degree from the new Carnegie Insti-
tute, later complaining that Carnegie, 'the old fibber', had defrauded
him in the matter of expenses. Again he was glad to leave for home.

On his fiftieth birthday, Sunday 2 June, while Alice, Carice and May
Grafton went to church, he wrote a part-song, *Love*, which he dedicated

'to C. A. E.'. Five days later he completed the fourth *Pomp and Circum-stance* march and, prompted by the nostalgia of his half-century, he looked out the music he had written for the play he and his siblings had performed when they were children. Some of it had become *Dream Children* a few years earlier. Now he orchestrated two suites called *The Wand of Youth*, music that epitomises the two sides of Elgar: the play-ful, exuberant lover of japes and jokes and the lonely, wistful dreamer, the sad child listening to what the reeds were saying. Then on 27 June Alice's diary entry is: 'E. much music. Playing great beautiful tune.' Nothing more was heard of it then. Summer and early autumn were taken up with conducting the two oratorios at Gloucester and else-where and with his passion for chemistry. He had his own laboratory and hoped to patent the 'Elgar Sulphuretted Hydrogen Machine'. Elgar wrote to the publisher of Arthur O'Shaughnessy's poem 'Ode' ('We are the music makers') for permission to set it, something he had told a reporter during the 1904 Elgar festival that he was working on. And in late October, on the day he was to attend a Brodsky Quartet concert in Malvern, he began a string quartet.

Elgar rented out Plas Gwyn and with Alice, Carice and May Grafton left for six months in Rome, arriving on 7 November. Two days later Alice's diary entry is 'E. with his quartet', and on 12 November, 'Writing his most beautiful IVt . . . wrote much of the Scherzo.' He also began to have French lessons. The quartet sketches are important because they contain much material that finally went into the First Symphony and *The Music Makers*. A section marked 'end of scherzo' contains the impetu-ous semiquavers of the symphony's second movement and that episode which Elgar described as 'like something we hear down by the river' and which Alice called 'the wind in the rushes' when she first heard the theme on the piano as early as August. The start of the quartet's Adagio is a slowing down of the Scherzo's semiquavers as in the symphony. Just when Elgar abandoned the quartet is unclear: the Brodsky Quartet were due to perform in Rome in April 1908 and he may have intended to give it to them for that occasion. But we know that he began to compose the symphony on 3 December, the day he wrote to Littleton telling him he had informed the Birmingham Festival that he had 'definitely and finally' given up the idea of a third oratorio for 1909. The symphony began with the march-like 'great beautiful tune' Alice had heard on 27 June, but progress on this first movement was soon interrupted when Elgar agreed to write some part-songs which Novello's had requested. 'I am trying to write music', he wrote to Schuster, 'but the bitterness is that it pays not at all & I must write & arrange what my soul loathes to permit me to write what *you* like & I like. So I curse the power that gave me gifts & loathe them now & ever.'

His soul might have loathed it but he never turned out shoddy trash. He sent off a part-song, How calmly the evening, on 2 December and followed it with A Christmas Greeting, to Alice's words, with accompaniment for piano and two violins, which he sent to Sinclair for the Hereford choristers. He followed this with Marching Song, which Littleton had wanted for the Worshipful Company of Musicians, and The Reveille (for male voices). Over Christmas he wrote the four masterly part-songs of his op. 53: There is sweet music, from Tennyson's 'The Lotos-Eaters', Deep in my soul (Byron), O wild west wind! (Shelley) and Owls (an Epitaph), to his own words. Owls, composed on 31 March 1907, is one of Elgar's most mysterious and chromatic compositions. 'It is only a fantasy & means nothing', he told Jaeger. 'It is in a wood at night evidently & the recurring "Nothing" is only an *owlish* sound.' But is it?

> What is that? Nothing:
> The leaves must fall and, falling, rustle;
> That is all:
> They are dead
> As they fall, –
> Dead at the foot of the tree;
> All that can be is said.
> What is it? Nothing.

While the first three of op. 53 were dedicated, respectively, to Canon Gorton, Julia Worthington and W. G. McNaught (of Novello's), Owls was dedicated 'to my friend Pietro d'Alba'. He was Carice's pet white rabbit Peter. Here was another Elgar enigma.

A. C. Benson called on the Elgars in Rome on 30 December:

> He said his eyes were weak & he cd. only work an hour a day. With all his pleasantness & some savoir-faire, one feels instinctively that he is always socially a little *uneasy* . . . Lady E. very kind but without charm & wholly conventional . . . Elgar's daughter about 16, a quiet, obedient, silent, contented sort of girl, interested in Rome.[2]

Early in the new year May Grafton had to return to England because her father, Will Grafton, was seriously ill. He died a few days later. Elgar was deeply upset. He had always liked Will and frequently cycled over to his and Pollie's home at Stoke Prior. A few days later Elgar developed influenza. This put paid to any further creative work. They went to Puccini operas, saw friends and spent a week in Florence. Elgar advised Hubert Leicester: 'If you have any religious feeling whatever, don't go to Rome – everything money.'[3]

They were back in England on 16 May. By 15 June Alice could write to Jaeger: 'E. sends his love . . . & he wants to say to you "the Sym. is A1" – it is gorgeous – steeped in beauty.'[4] He worked hard all summer, completing the Adagio on 23 August and celebrating by resigning his Birmingham professorship. (Peyton's comment to the university secretary was: 'The actual result & virtual waste of time has, I need not say, been a great disappointment to me.')[5] He took the finale to work on at The Hut, the riverside country house at Bray, near Maidenhead, where Schuster entertained friends with lavish hospitality. After the interruption of the Worcester Festival – where he conducted the first performance of *The Wand of Youth* suite no. 2 and there were empty seats for *Gerontius* and *The Kingdom* – the symphony was completed on 25 September and a week later he wrote the song *Pleading* for Lady Maud Warrender.

The symphony was dedicated 'to Hans Richter, Mus. Doc. True artist and true friend'. The great conductor, who was to conduct the first performance at a Hallé concert in Manchester, visited Plas Gwyn on

15   Elgar at The Hut

6 November to go through the score. On the morning of the first performance, 3 December, Elgar was 'so porsley' that it was doubtful until
the last minute if he would go to Manchester. That evening, fog seeped
into the Free Trade Hall and kept many of the audience at home. Robert
Buckley wrote in the *Birmingham Gazette* that 'the band scarcely seemed at
home with the music; the strings were rough, and other departments

failed to exhibit the perfection we expect from an orchestra of such reputation'. Nevertheless the audience insisted on Elgar appearing on the platform after the third movement (Adagio). 'The symphony is genuinely new Elgar', Newman wrote in the *Birmingham Post*; and Samuel Langford, in the *Manchester Guardian*, considered that Elgar had 'refertilised the symphonic form by infusing into it the best ideas that could be gathered from the practice of the writers of symphonic poems'. In London three days later, Richter opened the LSO rehearsal for the London première with the words: 'Gentlemen, let us now rehearse the greatest symphony of modern times written by the greatest modern composer, and not only in this country.'[6] Hundreds were turned away from Queen's Hall on the following evening. The ailing Jaeger was present and told 'Dorabella' how at the end 'the audience seemed to rise at E. when he appeared. I *never* heard such frantic applause after any novelty nor such shouting. Five times he had to appear before they were pacified. People stood up and even *on* their seats to get a view.'[7] He had seen the score beforehand and wrote to Elgar: 'My dear friend, that is not only one of the very greatest slow movements since Beethoven, but I consider it *worthy of that master* . . . The music was written by a good pure man.'[8] To his friend Sydney Loeb, Jaeger confessed to having difficulty with the first movement and found the coda 'ineffective' ('Elgar spoils *all* his codas (except in the Adagio in the symphony) by trying to be "unconventional" '). He also thought that the audience reaction was exaggerated and that the critics had gone 'slightly "dotty" '. The English, he wrote, 'are *now* proud of E. . . . the one man who is recognised abroad. Hence a charming but somewhat unmerited patriotism enters largely into the display of appreciation of a work which on the whole, is DIFFICULT to appreciate at a first hearing.'[9] But he went to the second London performance on 19 December and told Loeb that 'that puzzling first movement is now as clear as daylight to me, & *very* striking & dramatically beautiful it is . . . I like the Finale least until the peroration is reached . . . I fancy Nikisch or Elgar would give us a much more emotional & truly Elgarish reading than dear old Hans, though his performance is superb in its sanity, health, dignity & force.'[10] Elgar told Walford Davies: 'There is no programme beyond a wide experience of human life with a great charity (love) and a *massive* hope in the future.' To Schuster's sister Adela he wrote: 'The Symphony . . . is making a very wild career.' It continued to do so. In London it was soon repeated and during 1909 it had eighty-two performances throughout the world. Of those in Britain, twenty-two were given by Thomas Beecham's New Symphony Orchestra on a national tour. Beecham cut the first movement by half, trimmed the other three, and reduced the playing time from fifty-five to thirty-five minutes. It fared better under Nikisch.

On Christmas Day 1908 Elgar wrote a letter to a name that will now often recur. The recipient had sent a congratulatory telegram. He had met her several times at dinners at her London home and elsewhere, but formality was still the order of the day: 'Dear Mrs Stuart Wortley'. He had a cold, he told her, and was not doing any chemical experiments at the moment. Then: 'Alice & Carice & a friend have gone off to a far church in a car – I am worshipping several things by the fire – memories mostly of the New World geographically & musically – that Symphony is a new world, isn't it? Do say "yes".' On New Year's Day he conducted it (for the first time) in Queen's Hall and there again six days later. A critic wrote that under his baton 'the music was *sung*, and with infinite pathos'.[11] When he gave Novello's the work for publication, Elgar demanded a composer's fee for every performance, something they had never charged. Several organisations abandoned plans for a performance when confronted with Elgar's fee plus a fee for hire of the parts.

As always after a big work was launched, Elgar subsided into a depression. He wrote no music and spent no time in his laboratory (known as 'The Ark'). In April, he, Alice and Carice were invited by Julia Worthington to spend some weeks at her Villa Silli, at Careggi, near Florence. The weather was glorious, the air flower-scented. Elgar toyed with ideas for an opera, but found no subject congenial. He had with him the sketches for an E flat symphony and those for Kreisler's concerto. But again it was part-songs that paved the way for bigger things. He wrote *The Angelus* and dedicated it to Mrs Stuart Wortley.

16  Carice with her pet rabbit Peter ('Pietro d'Alba')

More ambitious was *Go, song of mine*, a D. G. Rossetti translation of
the Italian mediaeval poet Guido Cavalcanti. This is Elgar's greatest
part-song, containing intimations of the Violin Concerto and echoes
of Isolde's *Liebestod*. As he finished it he heard that Jaeger had died in
London on 18 May. Jaeger's wife Isabella wrote to inform him and he
replied saying he was 'overwhelmed with sorrow for the loss of my
dearest & truest friend'.

The holiday ended with visits to Pisa, Bologna and Venice. They returned home through their old haunts in Bavaria and called on Strauss, who had recently moved into his new house in Garmisch. There was a thunderstorm and they went up the passes to flowery meadows and heard the cowbells as the cattle went home. We might have had Elgar's Alpine Symphony! At Plas Gwyn he wrote the little *Elegy* for strings. In July a letter from the London Philharmonic Society asked if they could expect a new Elgar work for their 1910 concerts. A few weeks later, 'E. possessed with his music for the Violin Concerto'. But not for long. Festivals and conducting another LSO tour interrupted him, as did the request for an anthem (*They are at rest*, words by Cardinal Newman) to mark the tenth anniversary of Queen Victoria's death. Then Sir Gilbert Parker sent a volume of his poems and Elgar decided to use six of them for a song cycle with orchestra like *Sea Pictures*. He set the third, fifth and sixth, 'O soft was the song', 'Was it some golden star?' and 'Twilight'. All were nostalgic and intensely romantic, telling of unrequited love. He then turned to Elizabeth Barrett Browning for the text of *A Child Asleep*, a song completed on 21 December and dedicated to the year-old son of the mezzo-soprano Muriel Foster, who had sung so beautifully in *The Kingdom* and had retired (temporarily) when she was married. He did not return to the Parker poems but instead embarked on four solo songs to words of his own, of which only two were written. He said they were 'paraphrases' of eastern European folk songs and gave the author as 'my confidant and adviser Pietro d'Alba' – Carice's rabbit again. They were passionate songs, the first, *The Torch*, completed at Christmas 1909, the second, *The River*, completed on 19 February 1910. It was a gloomy 'festive season' during which he heard of the deaths of Basil Nevinson, Olga Ourousoff (the soprano and young wife of Henry Wood who had sung in his works) and, in America, Samuel Sanford, aged only sixty. But he had been happy at Christmas to receive the scores of the Beethoven quartets as a present from Edward Speyer and his wife. He told them in his reply that the scores took him back to his boyhood,

when the world of music was opening & one learnt fresh *great* works
every week – Haydn, Mozart and Beethoven. Nothing in later life can be
even a shadow of those 'learning' days: now, when one knows *all* the
music and all the mechanism of composition, the old mysterious
glamour is gone & the feeling of *entering* – shy, but welcomed – into the
world of the immortals & wandering in those vast works . . . is a holy
feeling & a sensation never to come again, unless our passage into the
next world shall be a greater & fuller experience of the same warm,
loving & *growing* trust – which I doubt.

# 10 Windflower

Alice Stuart Wortley was the second wife of Charles Stuart Wortley, Conservative MP for Sheffield (later its Hallam division) from 1880 until 1917. His first wife, Beatrice, had died in childbirth after a year of marriage. Music was his passion, after his family, and he could read a score as others would read a book. In 1886 he married Alice Sophie Caroline Millais, third daughter of the Pre-Raphaelite artist John Millais. She was born in 1862 and was a fine pianist. To her family and early friends she was known as 'Carrie' but was Alice to others. She and Charles had one child, Clare, born in 1889. Charles idolised his first wife's memory and Carrie felt she was always second best. This led to a soured relationship with Beatrice's daughter. Carrie had a small circle of intimate friends, chief among them Mina (Lady Charles Beresford), Claude Phillips, the art critic and first Keeper of the Wallace Collection, and Frank Schuster.

The Elgars first met the Stuart Wortleys at the Sheffield Festival in 1902. His first known letter to her, very formal, was when he sent her the score of a part-song. Occasionally Elgar wrote to Clare who was a year older than Carice. In mid-July 1906 the Elgars and the Stuart Wortleys were Schuster's guests at The Hut and Elgar played some of *The Kingdom* to them. At this period most of the letters were written by Alice Elgar to 'my dearest namesake' or 'my dearest Alice'. They all went to see Shaw's *Man and Superman* together and met often at Schuster's dinners.

In March 1909 Elgar addressed her as 'My dear Carrie', but she didn't like it and on 23 June it was 'My dear Alice', the name underlined. But he didn't like two Alices in his life and in a letter in November he told her: 'I have found no name for you yet.' So Alice it was for some months longer.

The correspondence between them stretches from 1902 to 1933 but begins in earnest in 1909. The published correspondence is chiefly of Elgar's letters to her, plus some to her from Alice Elgar and several from Elgar's sister Pollie.[1] Only one letter from Mrs Stuart Wortley is included. All the rest were destroyed, some by Elgar, later ones by an unknown hand, the most likely culprit being Clare Stuart Wortley, her daughter. It is likely that many of Elgar's letters were also destroyed. They devised a special method of correspondence. Some letters were written for general consumption. But often a letter would come at the same time which was for her (or his, as the case might be) eyes only. He bought a special box of stationery to write to her. In some of the extant letters, some passages have been cut away, scored over or otherwise eradicated. Mrs Stuart Wortley bequeathed her letters from Elgar to the Birthplace Museum. Carrying out this bequest, Clare wrote to Elgar's daughter in 1936:

> Being the soul of honour, he felt himself *under an obligation* [my italics] to her for giving him an impulse at a critical moment & he thought to discharge that obligation by giving her what she most liked, themes & MSS – dedicating two of the next themes to her & giving her a share in the final triumph, viz. the signed orchestral score. This I propose to write down and put with the MSS as it is the true explanation & honourable to all parties.[2]

Perhaps, one may feel, she protested too much.

Anyone who has been in love will recognise the symptoms in these letters, all the stronger because there was no likelihood of consummation. Nor do we know if Elgar's feelings were reciprocated, though we may suspect that they were. But as Jerrold Northrop Moore wisely

17  'Windflower': Alice Stuart Wortley, painted by her father, Sir John Millais

wrote in his introduction to the published correspondence: 'At the top
of the Edwardian tree may have been a gamesome aristocracy. But the
world of nocturnal country-house derring-do is not the world of these
letters, for all their affection and occasional extravagance.'

The year 1909 had opened with Elgar orchestrating the three Parker
songs for a concert to be held late in January in memory of Jaeger at

which Muriel Foster was to come out of retirement to sing them. Alice's
diary for 11 January also notes: 'E. very busy with Concerto & Bassoon
piece.' The bassoon piece – Romance – was for Edwin James, principal
bassoonist of the LSO, and shares the Violin Concerto's thematic mood.
Beginning to find Plas Gwyn noisy, Elgar took a London flat in Queen
Anne's Mansions so as to be able to concentrate on the concerto. He
had invented the first and second subjects of the first movement years
before, but could not find a bridge passage to join them satisfactorily
together, so he was working at the slow movement, the Andante. Elgar
conducted the new songs at the Jaeger concert on 24 January and Richter
the Variations. A week later Vassily Safonoff conducted the symphony
at the Queen's Hall. The Elgars and Stuart Wortleys were in the audience
and Elgar wrote to Alice Stuart Wortley: 'I am really alone in this music.'
At Schuster's a week later the Stuart Wortleys were guests again and
Elgar played the Andante of his concerto, with himself as pianist and
Sir Edgar Speyer's wife Leonora von Stosch (an Ysaÿe pupil) as violinist.
A letter next day to Alice Stuart Wortley introduced her to the depressive
Elgar:

> I do not think it [his visit to London] has been a success: it is too lonely
> & I cannot see how we are to 'take' a place big enough for us all . . . I
> think a decent obscurity in the country is all I can attain to – there is
> really no 'place' for me here as I do not conduct or in fact do anything & I
> am made to feel in many ways I am not wanted . . . I am not sure about
> the Andante & shall put it away for a long time before I decide its fate. I
> am glad you liked it.

It was not only Alice Stuart Wortley who liked it: her husband had
been so impressed he had asked to borrow the music and Elgar gave
him his short-score sketch. Alice Stuart Wortley was horrified that
the concerto might be abandoned and told him he *must* go on. That
evening, in Queen Anne's Mansions, he invented the theme which had
eluded him and bridged the two subjects in the first movement. He
inscribed the sketch: 'Feb. 7 1910 6-30 pm. This is going to be good!
"Where Love and Faith meet there will be Light".' This was the result
of her encouragement and thereafter they kept 7 February as a personal

anniversary. He called the two themes 'windflower' themes, after the white spring flower *anemone nemorosa*,[3] and he had found the name for the muse who had inspired him to go on with this work. The next letter was to 'Dear Windflower'.

Alice Elgar went flat-hunting in London later in the month and found 58 New Cavendish Street which they rented for three months. From there he went on 15 March to Covent Garden with Lady Maud Warrender to hear Strauss's *Elektra* conducted by Beecham. Elgar was 'much impressed', Alice confided to her diary, 'but kept on saying "The pity of it! The pity of it"'. At the end of March Elgar joined Schuster in Torquay, where Schuster was visiting his sister Adela. They then went by car to Tintagel where the Stuart Wortleys were staying, arriving on 3 April in bad weather. Elgar thought the village was '*awfully* dreary', but found Boscastle, which they visited in the afternoon of the next day, 'very quaint'. He preferred Falmouth ('the first place on this car tour which I really feel I want to see again') which Schuster and he visited after leaving Tintagel.

Back in London on 11 April, he found 'Dorabella' with Alice and Carice at New Cavendish Street and played them part of what was to become the slow movement of the Second Symphony. When the Stuart Wortleys returned, Elgar dined with them and took her to recitals. She went with the Elgars to Gluck's *Orfeo* and to the private view of the Royal Academy Exhibition. They went for afternoon drives together, and onto a sketch of a 'windflower' theme from the concerto which he gave her he pasted a cutting of a review by Claude Phillips of Titian's *Nymph and Piping Shepherd*, which Phillips described as 'the most wonderful love-poem of Venetian sixteenth-century art'.[4] The review contained the following passage:

> It . . . soon will be night with the lovers . . . The poetry of the early years has come back, intensified by something of added poignancy and of foreboding that is tinged, it may be, with remorse. The last passion has something that the earlier passion had not; in one sense it is nearer to earth and earthiness; in another it is infinitely higher and more far-reaching, more typical of the love that in its heights and depths, in

its tender light and sombre, fitfully illumined shadow, is truly that which to the end of all things must hold and possess Man.

This has been interpreted as meaning that Elgar had told 'Windflower' of his engagement to Helen Weaver and that this is a strong clue to Helen's being the 'soul' enshrined in the concerto. It could equally refer to his love for Alice Stuart Wortley – 'The poetry of the early years has come back . . . The last passion has something that the earlier passion had not.'

He was now working on the concerto and the symphony simultaneously. 'I am now ablaze with work', he told 'Windflower'. At a reception given by Sir Edgar Speyer for Strauss, Speyer, who was head of the Queen's Hall syndicate, had asked Elgar for a symphony to be premièred at a London Music Festival in May 1911 and Elgar had agreed. He was saddened on 3 May by the death of Carice's rabbit. 'It is terrible to think', he wrote to Mrs Sidney Colvin, 'how many human beings will be spared out of our little life's circle so much easier than my confidant & adviser Pietro d'Alba.' Three days later Edward VII died, 'that dear sweet-tempered King-Man' who was 'always so "pleasant" to me', as he told Schuster. A week later Elgar asked W. H. Reed to play through the sketches of the concerto and to advise him on bowings. Elgar pinned the sketches on the backs of chairs or put them on the mantelpiece ready for Reed to play. The lease on the flat expired and while Alice packed up their belongings there, he went to Lincoln to rehearse *Gerontius* and was joined for the performance on 9 June by 'Windflower'. Thence he went to The Hut to work on the concerto, 'so you had best invite its stepmother [Windflower] too', he told Schuster. Reed was also invited.

At The Hut he worked on the finale with its wonderful accompanied cadenza in which themes from the earlier movements are recalled. Back at Plas Gwyn, he wrote to 'Windflower' on 19 June: 'it took me a long time to "find myself" here, but the work goes on and the pathetic portion is really fixed'. He liked describing the cadenza. To Schuster he wrote of it as 'on a novel plan, I think – *accompanied* very softly by a few insts'. The strings' *pizzicato tremolando* was 'to be thrummed with the soft part of three or four fingers across the strings', he instructed in the full score. To Ernest Newman he wrote: 'The sound of a distant Aeolian harp flutters under and over the solo.' He heard the summer breeze activating the Aeolian harp fixed to his study window at Plas Gwyn. 'I have brought in the real inspired themes from the first movement', he told 'Windflower' on 16 June. 'The music sings of memories & hope.' Reed played it through at Plas Gwyn on 30 June, with Ivor Atkins accompanying, and Elgar was nearly moved to tears. Next day Elgar took the score to London to show Fritz Kreisler, who was delighted with it. On 17 July he wrote to 'Windflower': 'Our Concerto is fixed for Nov. 10 (& 30th) Kreisler – Philharmonic Society, Queen's Hall.' Five days later the Elgars and 'Windflower' returned to Plas Gwyn, where Reed joined them on the 26th to play the concerto 'through and through'.

Orchestration was completed in August. Kreisler wrote (in English) to Elgar on 5 August from Switzerland:

> I am studying most enthusiastically your wonderful work and shall do my utmost to set forth in my interpretation its grandeur and power. I would be very glad if you could see your way to not print it definitely until say Sept. 20 on which day I hope to be in London for the purpose of seeing you. On that occasion I would ask your permission to submit to you some trifling changes in one or two technical passages and decide definitely about bowing etc. . . . I am looking forward eagerly to the third movement.[5]

During the Three Choirs Festival at Gloucester in September, Kreisler played through the whole concerto to a private audience, as did Reed. Kreisler played it again in London on 15 October, making more revisions in the solo part. Alice Elgar turned the pages for him, 'Windflower' for Elgar. From Plas Gwyn on 25 October Elgar wrote to 'Windflower':

> I have been making a little progress with Symphony No. 2 & am sitting at my table weaving strange and wonderful memories into very poor music, I fear. What a wonderful year this has been! With all the sad

things in the great public life – the King's death downwards – the radiance in a poor, little man's private soul has been wonderful & new & the Concerto has come!

'Our Concerto.' 'The last passion has something that the earlier passion had not.' 'The radiance in a . . . man's private soul has been wonderful and new.' What further needs to be said about Elgar's feelings for Alice Stuart Wortley? In September he had written the inscription which heads the work's score – 'Aquí está encerrada el alma del . . . . .' 'Here is enshrined the soul of . . . . .' – on a sheet of notepaper. After leaving the Stuart Wortleys' house in Cheyne Walk he missed his train and wired 'Windflower' from Paddington: 'Missed train. Esta Encerrada El Alma.' The original quotation from Lesage's *Gil Blas* refers to 'el alma del licenciado Pedro Garcias'. Elgar was unsure if 'del' left the gender of the soul indeterminate and later made it 'de'. He told one of his biographers, Basil Maine, that the soul was feminine. Elgar gave Charles Sanford Terry a first proof of the full score to which Terry attached a note saying: 'I have never heard Elgar *speak* of the *personal* note in his music except in regard to the concerto and of it I heard him say more than once . . . "I *love* it".'[6] As the first performance drew near, Elgar wrote to 'Windflower' on 5 November: 'The piano arrgt. was published yesterday – how I hate its being made public.'

On the night of the first performance it 'poured in desperate torrents' (Alice's diary). Schuster gave a dinner party afterwards at which the guests included the Elgars, Stuart Wortleys, Lady Maud Warrender, Lord Northampton, Claude Phillips, the Kreislers and the twenty-one-year-old Adrian Boult. They were all uplifted by the fifteen-minute demonstration of 'pride and delight' with which the audience had greeted the concerto. Most of the critics agreed, although some found the solo part 'ungrateful' and Newman, in the *Birmingham Post*, felt that in the finale 'the thematic material is not so weighty nor the tissue so closely woven as in the earlier movements'. Samuel Langford, in the *Manchester Guardian*, shrewdly noted (after the work's first northern performance) Elgar's growing propensity for the constant juxtaposing of short melodic figures in place of long broad tunes. A sourer note was struck by the young Francis Toye in *Vanity Fair*, who mocked the 'ignorant, exaggerated, hysterical appreciation of Elgar' which greeted each new work. He called for a total abstention from 'velgarity'. There was a second London performance on 30 November. After the morning rehearsal Elgar wrote to 'Windflower' from the Athenaeum: 'The Concerto at 9 a.m. in the dark was divine – all the seats empty but a spirit hovering in block A' (where she was regularly seated).

The success of the concerto was widespread. It was played by Kreisler, with either Elgar or Henry Wood conducting, in all the major provincial cities. Kreisler played it throughout Europe and in St Petersburg and Eugène Ysaÿe in Berlin. Ysaÿe never played it in Britain, although he defied Novello's (with what seems to have been Elgar's tacit approval) on the matter of what he regarded as the excessive performing fee and performed it in Vienna and elsewhere, apparently extremely well. Kreisler's attitude to it is curious. After the First World War he seemed less interested in it. When he played it in the United States he cut it (as did Yehudi Menuhin) and he evaded all efforts to persuade him to record it. John Barbirolli, a conductor he greatly admired, tried in vain to arrange a performance with the New York Philharmonic in the 1940s and had to engage Heifetz instead. Fred Gaisberg, the guiding spirit of HMV, was ready to record the concerto with Kreisler in Berlin in 1930, but again Kreisler wriggled out of it and so Gaisberg turned to the sixteen-year-old Menuhin. The concerto's place among the very great works of its kind is secure. Elgar told Ivor Atkins that he would like the *nobilmente* theme of the slow movement (five bars after cue 53) to be inscribed on his tombstone. In that theme, we may feel, the soul of Edward Elgar is enshrined.

## 11 Second Symphony

Elgar returned to Plas Gwyn on 7 December and worked on the first two movements of the symphony. 'Windflower' came for Christmas. He told her to catch the 1.40 p.m. from Paddington. 'You will be met here [Hereford]. You pass thro' Worcester at 4 o'c & the guard (at Paddington) would telegraph for Tea to meet you at Worcester if you like it.' Those were the days! He played her the sketches of the symphony. She returned to London on Boxing Day, and next day Alice recorded: 'E. badsley headache went to bed very early.' He recovered to resume composing, drawing on abandoned sketches for Cockaigne no. 2, City of Dreadful Night, for the Larghetto. Sanford Terry stayed with them early in January 1911 and made some notes:

> In every movement its form, and above all its climax, were very clearly
> in his mind – indeed, as he has often told me, it is the climax which
> invariably he settles first. But withal there was a great mass of
> fluctuating material which might fit into the work as it developed in his
> mind to finality – for it had been created in the same 'oven' which had
> cast them all.[1]

Here surely is an explanation of short melodic figures. In no work does Elgar rely more on repetition of short phrases and sequences than in the Second Symphony.

He worked hard in spite of a patch of ill health. He had to. He had promised it for May and he had also agreed to go to America

in March. He had to finish it by then. He also had conducting engagements and was looking for a London house. He was especially
attracted by a Norman Shaw mansion, Kelston, in Netherhall Gardens,
Hampstead, which had been designed for the artist Edwin Long. He
and 'Windflower' found it in mid-January. It was on the market and
Alice went to see it on 1 February. The first movement of the symphony
was completed on 28 January and posted to Novello's. Elgar wrote to
'Windflower': 'I have recorded last year in the first movement . . . & I
must tell you this: I have worked at fever heat & the thing is tremendous in energy . . . I have written the most extraordinary passage I have
ever heard – a sort of malign influence wandering thro' the summer
night in the garden.' This remarkable passage he also described in a
letter to Ernest Newman as 'a love scene in a garden at night when
the ghost of some memories comes through it: – it makes me shiver'.
It occurs at cues 33 and 34 with the throbbing harps, muted horns
and yearning cellos and it does create a moment of mysterious, almost sinister tension in the midst of a movement notable for vernal
energy, restlessness and quixotry of mood. It is the climax of the de-
velopment, which begins at cue 24 with a passage Alice Elgar labelled
'Ghost'.

By 16 February the Larghetto and Rondo were completed. Next day
Elgar was approached to become principal conductor of the London
Symphony Orchestra when Richter retired in the spring. He agreed. He
wrote to 'Windflower': 'I have just put the last little dot to the IIIrd movement & very wild & headstrong it is with soothing pastoral strains in
between & very very brilliant.' The finale was completed on 28 February,
revised and taken to Novello's on 3 March. The whole fifty-five-minute
work had been composed and scored from sketches within two months.
Before he sailed (alone) for New York in the Mauretania, he sent
'Windflower' the sketches of 'the (your) symphony'. He conducted
Gerontius in Toronto with the Sheffield Choir, which was on a world
tour, and again in Buffalo and Cincinnati. A letter from 'Windflower'
awaited him in Cincinnati. She was in Tintagel and he replied: 'I am

selfish enough to be thankful that you can think of me there & you will not forget Frank's car taking us to Boscastle & you will not forget the road home – how lovely it was – a year ago!' He told her he loathed and detested every moment of his time in America and, in a later letter, said he had been asked how much he would want to settle there and conduct one of the big orchestras. 'Not 10 million dollars', he replied. 'This they do not understand.' He had asked Pollie to send her a windflower from her garden at Stoke Prior.

While in New York Elgar sent a more than usually detailed description of his own music to Alfred Littleton to be passed to Rosa Newmarch, who was to write the programme note for the symphony. He began by quoting the Shelley motto which heads the score – 'Rarely, rarely comest thou, Spirit of delight' – and continued:

> To get the mood of the symphony the whole of Shelley's poem must be read, but the music does not illustrate the whole of the poem, neither does the poem entirely elucidate the music. The germ of the work is in the opening bars [the Spirit of delight theme] – these in a modified form are heard for the last time in the closing bars of the last movement . . . The spirit of the whole work is intended to be high & pure joy: there are retrospective passages of sadness but the whole of the sorrow is smoothed out & ennobled in the last movement, which ends in a calm &, *I hope and intend*, elevated mood. (N.B. *private*. The second movement formed part of the original scheme – before the death of King Edward; – it is elegiac but has nothing to do with any funeral march & is a 'reflection' suggested by the poem.) The Rondo was sketched on the Piazza of S. Mark, Venice: I took down the rhythm of the opening bars from some itinerant musicians who seemed to take a grave satisfaction in the broken accent of the first four bars . . .
>
> Please note the new 'atmosphere' at [27] (suggested at [24]) with the added cello solo at [28] – remote and drawing someone else out of the everyday world): note the *feminine* voice of the oboe, answering or joining in, two bars before [30]. Note the happiness at [30] – real (remote) peace: note at [33] the atmosphere broken in upon & the dream 'shattered' by the inevitable march of the Trombone and

Tuba pp. In the 2nd movement at [79] the feminine voice laments over the broad manly 1st theme – and may not [87] be like a woman dropping a flower on a man's grave?

Elgar did not draw attention to the astonishing outburst towards the end of the Rondo when the 'malign influence' theme of the first movement returns above a steady pulsing on E flat and the percussion overwhelms the rest of the orchestra while the brass tears the heart out of the theme. The storm bursts upon us suddenly and as quietly subsides. Elgar likened it to lines from Tennyson's Maud, particularly

> The hoofs of the horses beat,
> Beat into my scalp and brain

and he told orchestras at rehearsal to imagine it as 'like that horrible throbbing in the head during some fever'. Was he thinking of Rodewald's death, an event which also inspired the slow movement? But the symphony is another set of 'friends pictured within' – 'Windflower', Richter, Rodewald, Edward VII (to whose memory it is dedicated), Alice Elgar and, of course, Elgar himself.

Elgar returned from New York to Liverpool, arriving on 9 May. He never went back to America. Writing to Ernest Newman a few days later he said that 'the "good-feeling" U.S. men & women . . . are wholly swamped by the blatant vulgarity of the mediocre crowd. America is getting worse – I see it in four years . . . The "Union" system makes wholly for mediocrity and the orchestras do not & can not improve under the system.' While he had been away Alice had taken a short lease of a house at 75 Gloucester Place (negotiations for the Hampstead mansion were making slow progress). He plunged into rehearsals of the symphony with the Queen's Hall orchestra. The first performance was on 24 May. The audience was the smallest of the festival week and although the critic of the Referee said 'the applause was loud and long', Elgar sensed a coolness compared with the reception given to the First Symphony and Violin Concerto and said to W. H. Reed, leader of the orchestra: 'What's the matter with them, Billy? They sit there like a lot of stuffed pigs.'[2] But other writers mentioned 'a warm reception'.

Three more London performances had been arranged. The audience on 1 June was smaller than that for the first performance, that for 8 June smaller still and on 15 June not much larger. The Elgar boom was over. Critical response to the work was divided. Newman was the only critic to remark that the music gave 'an infinite number of fine shades to the highly personal things he has been saying all his life'.[3]

Both symphonies are bound together by motto themes, broad and majestic in the First, short and restless in the Second. Both are marvellously orchestrated. Both have intimate secrets. The First's Adagio is Elgar at his most poignantly heart-easing, the Second's Larghetto is an expression of private and public mourning. The First ends in a kind of triumph, although the progress of the march theme is disrupted by syncopated off-beats. The Second ends in a calm resignation which still has echoes of discontent (and of Isolde's *Liebestod*). Both works are masterpieces of the Romantic symphony and could be described in the phrase Elgar applied to the Second – 'the passionate pilgrimage of a soul'. But Alice's entry in her diary on 28 February 1911, the day after Elgar finished the symphony, although obviously biased, is still as fine a summing-up of its qualities as one could find: 'It seems one of his very greatest works, vast in design, and supremely beautiful . . . it résumés our human life, delight, regrets, farewell, the saddest mood & then the strong man's triumph.'

Another of Elgar's tasks as soon as he returned from America was to orchestrate the march he had written (while in the States) for the coronation of King George V on 22 June. He also wrote an anthem, *O hearken Thou* (Psalm 5), for the Offertory part of the service. The march, still little known, is perhaps the finest of Elgar's 'laureate' works, over ten minutes long, almost symphonic in breadth with a heroic and tragic undercurrent and, in the trio, tenderness. The *maestoso* opening is a reworking of music intended for the Rabelais ballet of 1904. The trio replaced a projected second subject which later became the first Dream Interlude in *Falstaff*.

Five days before the coronation, Elgar was notified that he was appointed to the Order of Merit in the coronation honours. The Order is in the gift of the sovereign only and is limited to twenty-four members at a time. It is the highest and most exclusive honour of its kind, carrying no title. On 20 June he and Alice went to the rehearsal in Westminster Abbey of the music and the service, but he then announced that he would not go to the coronation and refused to allow Alice to go. What caused this strange and hurtful decision is not clear. One might have thought that he would have been buoyant because of the O.M., but instead a black depression descended. He was depressed because of the difficulties over buying the Hampstead house – Alice would have to break into a trust fund to use her inheritance from her mother – and he was devastated by the lack of enthusiasm for the new symphony. But was this enough to make him deprive Alice, never mind himself, of a memorable and historic occasion?

Worse followed. On 27 June he went to Novello's and discovered that few performances of the symphonies were booked. He thereupon wrote giving notice to end the 1904 agreement whereby Novello's paid him a 25 per cent royalty and had a near-exclusive contract to publish him. 'Everything of mine . . . dies a natural death . . . I may think of large works, but I shall not write them.' Thereafter Novello's had to bid for his work against other publishers. This break was immediately followed by the arguments with Ysaÿe over the Violin Concerto. On 17 July he took Rosa Burley, who had just returned from Portugal to live in London, to see the Hampstead house. Perceptive as ever, she noted his ambivalence. On the one hand he wanted to live in a grand house, with a music room and big staircase, as a symbol of his achievement and his status in the profession. But

> he wanted equally clearly to make me feel that his success meant nothing to him and that there was always some lovely thing in life which had completely eluded him . . . He also told me that the only part of his life that had ever been happy was the period of struggle at Malvern and that even now he never conducted his music without finding that his mind had slipped back to summer days on the Malvern Hills, to Birchwood, or to the drowsy peace of Longdon Marsh.[4]

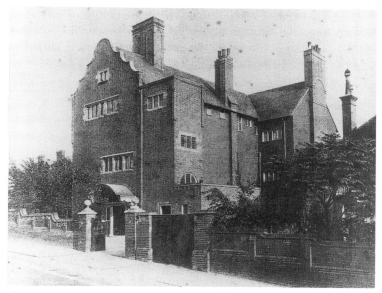

18  Severn House, Hampstead (now demolished)

He retreated to Plas Gwyn for almost the last time. Richter invited him to Bayreuth but he could not go. He went to The Hut alone, missing Carice's twenty-first birthday on 14 August. Alice wrote of her in her diary: 'Well again, I hope [Carice had had her tonsils out] & grown very helpful & wise & charming . . . Full of bright spirits – sorry not enough scope for those always.' At the Worcester Festival in September, Bach's St Matthew Passion was performed in the new edition ascribed to Elgar and Ivor Atkins although Atkins had done virtually all the work. In the autumn Elgar went to Turin to conduct performances of the Variations and the Introduction and Allegro. He also studied the scores of the works to be played at the six LSO concerts he was to conduct in London during the winter.

On New Year's Day, Alice having won her legal battle, they moved into what Elgar had named Severn House. Friends had given furnishings and Troyte Griffith had redesigned the library. Alice was determined that it should be a home worthy of a great composer. Elgar told one of the first visitors, Robin Legge of the *Daily Telegraph*, that he was at work on a setting of Arthur O'Shaughnessy's ode 'We are the music makers', with Muriel Foster in mind as soloist. He had been thinking about this since 1904, if not earlier, as we have seen. But work on it was laid aside when Oswald Stoll offered him a large sum to write and conduct the music for an 'imperial masque', *The Crown of India*, to celebrate the Delhi durbar (coronation) of the new king and queen. W. H. Reed visited Severn House while Elgar was working on this, but it was the day the billiard table arrived – 'after that *The Crown of India* faded out'.[5] Elgar dipped into his sketchbooks for a medley of marches, songs, melodrama and interludes. The music was published by Enoch. He had not been well since moving into Severn House. He had been giddy and had fallen down. 'Gout in the head' was diagnosed, as he told 'Windflower', who paid her first visit on 5 February. But he had several conducting engagements outside London and the masque involved him in conducting two performances a day at the Coliseum from 11 March for the first fortnight of the run. He was enjoying the money this brought him. He wrote to Frances Colvin: 'When I write a big serious work e.g. *Gerontius* we have had to starve & go without fires for twelve months as a reward: this small effort allows me to buy scientific works I have yearned for & I spend my time between the Coliseum & the old bookshops.' He also liked the stage staff – 'so desperately respectable & so honest & straightforward – quite a refreshing world after Society – only don't say I said so . . . God bless the Music Halls!' *The Crown of India* is in fact a large and by no means negligible score for soloists, chorus and orchestra which has never been performed in its original form (the orchestra is far bigger than the small pit band at the Coliseum). Elgar ruthlessly cut the libretto by Henry Hamilton. For the exciting prelude he returned to Sinclair's visitors' book for a theme from April 1903 describing 'the sinful youth of Dan', and elsewhere he quotes the main theme from his 1905 piano piece *In Smyrna*. Hamilton hymned India's cities, and a reference to Lucknow at the time of the Mutiny, when the Indian army commander was Sir Colin Campbell, and to the 'far, faint echo of thy bagpipes' skirl' brought from Elgar a hint of 'The Campbells are coming'. Later, a reference to England as 'dear Land that hath no like' evoked a two-bar quotation of 'Land of hope and glory'. Frances Colvin wrote to Elgar: 'Your music is gorgeous & and gave one just the right thrill. I longed to stop those women shrieking & just have the music.'[6]

The giddiness returned and on 28 March Elgar was 'very uneasy about noise in ear'. Another doctor diagnosed Menière's disease, which could lead to total deafness. He was ordered complete rest and undertook no more work on *The Music Makers* until early in May. He completed it on 18 July 1912 and went for a walk on Hampstead Heath in unseasonal cold weather. He wrote to 'Windflower': 'I . . . loathed the world – came back to the house – empty & cold – how I hated having written anything: so I wandered out again & shivered & longed to destroy the work of my hands – all wasted – & this was to have been the one real day in my artistic life – sympathy and the end of work.' In late July he made a suite from *The Crown of India*, orchestrated *The Torch* and *The River*, which Muriel Foster was to sing at Hereford, and also orchestrated *The Wind at Dawn*, the setting of Alice's words he had made in 1888. Orchestration of *The Music Makers* was completed on 20 August. 'Windflower' had been in Bayreuth, where she showed the vocal score proofs to Richter (and heard him conduct *Die Meistersinger*). Elgar wrote to her: 'The end of my work is as dreary as that awful day when I finished the composition & perished with cold on the heath.' A few days later: 'I have lost all interest in it. I have written out my soul in the Concerto, Sym. II & the Ode & you know it & my vitality seems in them now – & I am happy it is so – in these three works I have shewn myself.' They were the three works inspired by his love for her.

*The Music Makers* had its first performance at the Birmingham Festival on 1 October in the same programme as the British première of Sibelius's Fourth Symphony, each being conducted by its composer. Whether they met is not known, nor is there any comment on the symphony in Alice's diary. 'E. conducted magnificently. Had a great reception', she recorded, but the critics were not enthusiastic, Robin

Legge opining that the subject – the responsibility of artists 'to renew the world as of yore' – was 'greater than the composer could translate into terms of music'. Long dismissed as second-rate Elgar, The Music Makers is now appreciated as one of his most poignant and tragic works, overcoming the occasional triteness of the poem. He wanted to call it 'The Dreamers'; he was always at his best when dreaming of a world beyond his reach. It is a very personal work, almost a requiem for himself. Its second subject is unequalled in his music as an expression of yearning. This is intensified by his use throughout of self-quotation: the Enigma theme, 'because it expressed when written (1898) my sense of the loneliness of the artist';[7] 'Nimrod', at the words 'on one man's soul it hath broken, a light that doth not depart' as a tribute to Jaeger; snatches of both symphonies, the Violin Concerto, The Apostles, Gerontius and Sea Pictures. All were woven into the choral and orchestral tapestry with moving effect, quotations not for a 'hero's life' but for 'a sad man', as he described himself to 'Windflower'.[8] To Newman he wrote: 'All true art is to a great extent egotism & I have written several things which are still alive.'[9]

He was still not well – 'noises in the ear' – and at a performance of Verdi's Requiem two days later refused to shake hands with the Finnish soprano Aino Ackté, who had sung badly, and loudly declared it to have been the worst performance of the work he had heard. At this time, too, he was so irritated by the suggestion from 'Dorabella' that the 'hidden theme' in the Variations might be 'Auld Lang Syne' that he ended their friendship. Although Novello's arranged fifteen performances of The Music Makers in Britain in its first months of existence, promises by several German conductors, including Buths, Steinbach and Nikisch, to programme it came to nothing. This all contributed to his misanthropy, and it was becoming clear that he was disenchanted with Severn House even though Alice had lavished money and energy on making it as beautiful as she could. But all he was doing in the autumn of 1912 was revising and orchestrating, as Cantique, one of the wind quintet intermezzos of 1879 (he had recently borrowed back his 'Shed' books from Hubert Leicester). He complained of other ailments but, as Carice recalled, 'it is really impossible to say that there was anything definite wrong with him . . . if something favourable happened digestion was forgotten . . . He would complain of a terrible headache but if one could find something to interest him or something exciting happened, the headache would be quickly forgotten.'[10] He had sold his Gagliano violin to pay for the billiard table. Alice even agreed to have a dog, but the first wet the carpets and was sent back, while the second ran away and was never found.

In January 1913 the Elgars went to Naples and Rome, but his depression did not lift. The weather was bad and news came from New York that Julia Worthington was dying of cancer. On return, he knew he had to get down to work. He had promised the 1913 Leeds Festival a new work, about Falstaff, and had agreed to be the festival's joint conductor with Nikisch now that Stanford had departed. This was a subject he had toyed with and made sketches for since 1901. Basing his 'symphonic study' on the *Henry IV* plays, he began composing in March in London and continued while staying with Pollie. Progress on the composition can be followed in his letters to 'Windflower'. On 17 April he gave her a sketch from the Shallow's Orchard interlude (cue 103). He took time off to show two of Pollie's three daughters round London (the British Museum, the Zoo and the play *The Yellow Jacket* which he saw six times) but he missed the Royal Academy Banquet. 'I went in', he told 'Windflower', 'found they had omitted my O.M. & put me with a crowd of nobodies in the lowest place of all – the bottom table – I see no reason why I should *endure* insults. I can understand their being offered! to me . . . I left at once and came here [the Athenaeum] & had a herring.' Not for the first time, one regrets that her replies to letters like this have not survived. On 27 May he sent the Prince Hal melody (cue 5) to her; on 10 June, the day after conducting the second London performance of *The Music Makers*, he sent a two-bar *Falstaff* sketch and 'this original sketch – the very first thought [of *The Music Makers*] for you'.

A further cause of depression was the termination of his conductorship of the LSO. They wanted a 'bigger draw' and a conductor with better health. Next day, his royalties account from Novello's did nothing to lighten the gloom. Towards the end of June he played some of *Falstaff* to 'Windflower' and on 8 July sent her part of the tavern scene (cue 66). On the 11th Alice took the first part of the score to Novello's and he wrote to 'Windflower' on the 21st: 'I have just sent off 80 pages of *your* score to the printers.' He did not work in the evenings and often went to the theatre or the opera. This summer he went to *Tosca* and to Debussy's *Pelléas et Mélisande*, which he 'liked much', perhaps unexpectedly. Chaliapin asked him to compose *King Lear* for him and Sidney Colvin brought a message from Thomas Hardy that he was keen to collaborate on an opera, suggesting *A Pair of Blue Eyes*. After a weekend at The Hut where 'Windflower' was a fellow guest, Elgar continued to work on his score and gave her the short score of the Shallow's Orchard episode inscribed '(Farewell to The Hut) July 1913 written on Tuesday after you left and now Good Night'. Another fragment (cue 19) was sent on 3 August. He and Alice were due to go on holiday to Penmaenmawr in North Wales on 5 August. Elgar finished the score that morning by starting work at 4 a.m. 'A. made him tea &c &c and he finished his great work *Falstaff*', the diary says.

Elgar had read extensively many of the scholarly commentaries on Falstaff's character, finding him 'a knight, a gentleman and a soldier'. But there was also a large element of self-portraiture in the music, a Falstaff in C minor. A scrap of manuscript paper in the miniature score he gave to 'Windflower' is headed 'Falstaff (tragedy)'. He wrote to Ernest Newman: '*Falstaff* is the name but Shakespeare – the whole of human life – is the theme . . . I have made a larger canvas & over it all runs, even in the tavern, the undercurrent of our failings and sorrows.' Newman later wrote perceptively that '*Falstaff* is really the mad, pathetic mixture of contrarieties in us all, and the sense of something vast and inscrutable above us.'[11] Elgar told the journalist 'Gerald Cumberland' (pseudonym of Charles F. Kenyon) that he had enjoyed writing *Falstaff* 'more than any other music I have ever composed and perhaps for that reason it may prove to be among my best efforts. All I have striven to do is to paint a musical portrait – or, rather, a sketch portrait.'[12] Yet he insisted *Falstaff* was not programme music like Strauss's *Don Quixote*. Composers were still very touchy about this genre, which was considered by many critics to be inferior to 'abstract' music. Having made his denial, Elgar wrote a profusely detailed analysis of the work while at Penmaenmawr, first published in the *Musical Times*.

Elgar rehearsed *Falstaff* in London on 22 and 23 September and in Leeds on the 30th. He opened the festival on 1 October, conducting Beethoven's *Leonora* no. 3, *Gerontius* (its first Leeds Festival performance), Parry's *Ode to Music* and Brahms's Alto Rhapsody (Muriel Foster) and Symphony no. 3!! Next day Elgar and 'Windflower' took her daughter Clare and Carice to Fountains Abbey, missing Nikisch's afternoon concert which contained the first performance of George Butterworth's rhapsody *A Shropshire Lad*, and in the evening Elgar conducted the Prologue to Boito's *Mefistofele*, Bantock's new *Dante and Beatrice*, Mozart's Symphony no. 40 and *Falstaff*. Hamilton Harty conducted his own *The Mystic Trumpeter* and there were operatic arias. *Falstaff* baffled the critics except for Newman, who had long urged Elgar to write in a one-movement form. Robin Legge said it was a masterpiece but wanted five minutes cut out of it. He wished a greater conductor had expounded its complications. Unusually, Elgar revised the scoring of several passages after the performance.

Landon Ronald, to whom *Falstaff* is dedicated, conducted the London première on 3 November. The audience was pitifully small. Not many more attended another performance, which Ronald put on at his own expense, on 28 November and it was played at the Albert Hall on 14 December. It was to make its way in the world slowly until it became widely regarded as among his greatest works. The reservations I had about it when I wrote *Portrait of Elgar* have long vanished. Its humour, rumbustiousness, nobility and the heart-breaking poetry of the Dream Interlude stamp it through and through as *echt*-Elgar. Its scoring is masterly in every detail.

Elgar tried to ward off his depression over *Falstaff* by immediately returning to a setting of part of Matthew Arnold's *Empedocles on Etna* for Muriel Foster but soon abandoned it again. In the rest of the autumn he spent many days on excursions to places such as Hadley, north of London, with 'Windflower'. They lunched and dined together and went to plays, sometimes just together, sometimes with Alice. Then in December a new interest arose. Landon Ronald was music adviser to the gramophone company His Master's Voice, which also employed Muriel Foster's brother-in-law Jeffrey Stephens. With the publisher W. W. Elkin, Stephens asked Elgar to a lunch at which a contract was agreed for two short pieces, at 100 guineas and a royalty plus 'two thirds of net royalties received in respect of mechanical reproduction'. The pieces were first to be recorded, then published. The first of them, *Carissima*, was written immediately and Elgar conducted its first performance in the recording studio at Hayes on 21 January 1914. The second piece, however, turned out to be not so light. 'Soupir d'amour' it was called in the contract, 'Absence' in a sketch. It was published under the Italian title *Sospiri* (*Sighs*) for strings, harp and organ. It is Elgar at his saddest, a profound, almost Mahlerian expression of his inner unhappiness. He fulfilled his promise for a second light piece with *Rosemary* ('That's for Remembrance') in 1915, an orchestration of the 1882 piano piece *Douce pensée*. Some have claimed this as proof that he was still thinking of Helen Weaver, but there is nothing to show that his 1882 'sweet thought' was of Helen.

Novello's asked him for more part-songs. He set two poems by the seventeenth-century poet Henry Vaughan, *The Shower* and *The Fountain*. At the end of the settings he wrote the place names Totteridge and Mill Hill respectively, then country towns outside London which he had visited with 'Windflower' (he also liked going to Hendon with her to watch early aircraft flying). He wrote three other part-songs to Rosa Newmarch's translations of Russian poets, *Death on the Hills* ('one of the biggest things I have done', he told 'Windflower'), *Love's Tempest* and *Serenade*. For these he demanded 125 guineas and an immediate 25 per cent royalty. This drew a comment from Augustus Littleton, younger brother of Alfred. Agreeing to the terms, he added: 'I don't want any more Elgar symphonies or concertos, but am ready to take as many part-songs as he can produce even at extortionate rates.' Boosey paid Elgar 100 guineas and a royalty for *Chariots of the Lord* for Clara Butt. Other 'potboilers' were the song *Arabian Serenade*, four children's songs, the harvest anthem *Fear not, O Land* and a larger anthem, *Give unto the Lord*. These were the price of running Severn House.

On 19 June Elgar conducted *The Apostles* in Canterbury cathedral, also for a very high fee paid by Henry Embleton, patron and secretary of the Leeds Choral Union which took part. He had known Elgar and championed his music since 1896. It was a fine performance, with Elgar's closest friends all there. Embleton struck while the iron was hot, called at Severn House on 30 June and persuaded Elgar to compose the third part of *The Apostles* for him. On 19 July Elgar, Alice and Carice went to Scotland for a holiday. They were at the Gairloch Hotel, Ross-shire, on 4 August when Britain declared war on Germany.

## 12 'For the Fallen'

Isolated in the north-west of Scotland, the Elgars heard no news of the outbreak of war until telegrams from 'Windflower' arrived. They could not leave until 10 August because all public transport had been cancelled for troop movements. Stopping off in Leeds, Elgar missed the first performance of *Sospiri* at Queen's Hall on 15 August, but Alice, who was there, noted 'wonderful effect of Land of Hope and Glory'. Strauss's *Don Juan* was to have been in the same programme, but was removed. Carice was working for the Red Cross and on the 17th her father enrolled as a staff inspector in the Hampstead branch of the Special Constabulary, a corps formed to replace called-up policemen. Eight days later he wrote to Frank Schuster:

> Concerning the war I say nothing – the only thing that wrings my heart & soul is the thought of the horses – oh! my beloved animals – the men – and women – can go to hell – but my horses; – I walk round & round this room cursing God for allowing dumb brutes to be tortured – let Him kill His human beings but – how CAN HE? Oh, my horses.

To 'Windflower' he wrote about his police work: 'I am a fool & look a fool but I am doing what I can! Your letters have been very – no word of yourself & how you are – if better & if the massage has done you good – in fact nothing I really wanted to know: my heart is heavy & will remain so until – we shall see.'

One of his first musical tasks was to ask A. C. Benson for new words for 'Land of hope and glory'. These were supplied but never caught on. As the Germans conquered Belgium, war fever in Britain intensified. The Three Choirs Festival at Worcester was cancelled; Jaeger's widow changed her name to Hunter (the English translation of Jaeger); the conductor Basil Hindenburg became Basil Cameron; Prince Louis of Battenberg resigned as First Sea Lord; Muriel Foster's husband Ludovic Goetz became Foster by deed poll; Gustav von Holst dropped the 'von'; Hans Richter (under pressure) renounced his honorary doctorate, as did Max Bruch; Sir Edgar Speyer had to resign from the Queen's Hall management and eventually to leave Britain for alleged collaboration with the enemy (sending food parcels to hungry German relatives). Thomas Beecham, asked where were Elgar's friends, replied: 'They're all interned.' The Germans had been Elgar's friends and supporters; now he was being asked to hate them because of their reported atrocities. He went in September to stay with Pollie, but returned after three days.

Having first refused to contribute to *King Albert's Book*, an anthology organised by Hall Caine in aid of the Belgian Fund, Elgar remembered reading in the *Observer* a poem by the Belgian writer Emile Cammaerts called 'Après Anvers' about the ruined bell towers of Flanders. Cammaerts's wife Tita Brand Cammaerts, daughter of Marie Brema, the first Angel in *Gerontius*, had translated the poem into English and Elgar asked her if he could set it. He decided that the poem, which he called *Carillon*, should be recited and he provided an orchestral prelude and entr'acte as background. He conducted the first performance on 7 December, with Tita Brand Cammaerts as reciter. It swept the country. The actor Henry Ainley recorded a cut version with Elgar early in 1915 and Elgar took the work on a tour of northern cities with the LSO. 'Poem and music have the dignity of a noble grief and all the exultation of heroism' was the *Daily Telegraph*'s verdict. Everywhere *Carillon* caused intense patriotic fervour and sympathy for 'brave little Belgium'. The music, in piano score, was published in *King Albert's Book* just before Christmas 1914. Debussy's *Berceuse héroïque* was also included.

Rather more distinguished poetry than *Carillon* had been published in the first months of the war by Laurence Binyon, who had succeeded Sidney Colvin as Keeper of Prints and Drawings at the British Museum, under the title *The Winnowing Fan*. Colvin suggested to Elgar on 10 January 1915 that he should write 'a wonderful Requiem for the slain – something in the spirit of Binyon's "For the Fallen"'.[1] Elgar agreed and sketched settings of three of the poems for chorus and orchestra – 'For the Fallen', 'To Women' and 'The Fourth of August'. But he learned in March from Novello's that the Cambridge composer C. B. Rootham, a pupil of Stanford, was setting 'For the Fallen' for Novello's. Elgar immediately offered to withdraw and met Rootham to tell him so. As he told Binyon on 24 March: 'His utter disappointment, not expressed but shewn unconsciously, has upset me & I must decide against completing "For the Fallen" . . . The sight of the other man comes sadly between me & my music.' Binyon could not understand why both settings could not be published, but Elgar was firm: 'There is only one publisher for choral music in England: Mr Rootham was in touch with Novello first – my proposal made his manuscript waste paper and I could not go on.' Novello's did agree to publish both, but Elgar now said the public did not want his music, his usual tiresome excuse when he was upset and depressed. Colvin would have none of this: 'What has the poor British public done now which it had not done a month ago when you were full of the project?'[2] That did the trick. Elgar resumed composition next day, 14 April.

Elgar had resigned from the Special Constabulary in February 1915 and joined the Hampstead Special Reserve which involved him in drill and firing a rifle. He also promised the conductor Emil Mlynarski that he would write something for Poland as he had for Belgium. The result was *Polonia*, a symphonic prelude dedicated to Paderewski, in which three Polish national tunes (chosen by Mlynarski) and quotations from works by Chopin (chosen by Elgar) and Paderewski (chosen by 'Windflower') were blended together. Elgar conducted the LSO in the first performance on 6 July 1915 during a poorly attended concert in aid of the Polish Victims Relief Fund. He had also been persuaded by Cammaerts to compose another recitation. *Une voix dans le désert* was completed on 17 July. The poem describes a ruined house near to the battle front. A girl's voice sings of the coming of spring. This song, 'Quand nos bourgeons se rouvriront' ('When the spring comes round again'), makes a poignant effect and curiously anticipates Vaughan Williams's use of a solo soprano (wordless) in the finale of *A Pastoral Symphony* (1921). The finest of Elgar's three recitations – the third, *Le drapeau belge*, is of little account – *Une voix dans le désert* was first performed (conducted by Elgar) on 29 January 1916 at the Shaftesbury Theatre, London, as an intermezzo in costume between *Cavalleria rusticana* and *Pagliacci*.

Throughout the first months of 1915 Elgar worked fitfully on the Binyon settings, to which he had given the title *The Spirit of England*. He conducted often – *Carillon* twice a day for two weeks in August at the Coliseum. But whenever he could he escaped to Worcestershire to stay with Pollie. Her housemaid Ellen recalled in 1966 that she never remembered hearing Lady Elgar or Carice mentioned in conversations.[3] She once asked Pollie why Sir Edward's wife never came with him. 'Mrs Grafton hesitated, frowned and said "She does not care for travel".' But Pollie knew all about 'Windflower' and often picked the anemones for Elgar to send to her. She also wrote to her.

All three Binyon settings were sketched by spring 1915 except for one stanza in 'The Fourth of August'. This was a verse which described the enemy as 'inhuman' and Elgar was loath to pillory the Germans in this way. He told Ernest Newman later (in July 1917) that he had held this stanza over 'hoping that some trace of manly spirit would show itself in the direction of German affairs'. After the August *Carillon* performances, the Elgars had a fortnight's holiday in Sussex, near Midhurst. This enjoyable interlude was to prove significant. They then joined the Stuart Wortleys in the Lake District, and later in the autumn, after he had conducted more performances of *Carillon* with his friend Lalla Vandervelde, wife of the exiled Belgian politician Emile Vandervelde, as reciter, Elgar took Carice, who was now working in the censorship department in London, to Stratford-upon-Avon, where

the Stuart Wortleys were staying. Elgar's letters to 'Windflower' at this
time ache with suppressed love, almost every line containing a hidden, unspoken meaning. And these are only the letters that have survived. Whenever he could, he took her for lunch or to the theatre. It
was after an evening on 11 November when the Elgars shared a box
at the Kingsway Theatre with 'Windflower' that Alice wrote in her
diary:

> Alice S. W. with us. Enjoyed *Iris Intervenes* extremely. Lena [Ashwell]
> wonderfully clever in it. The only play or novel in which a woman has the
> sense to say 'nothing wd. make me believe it' (tale about her Husband).
> 'Even if it were absolutely proved I'd not believe it'. A. [herself] clapped
> & was joined by someone.

It requires little insight to read between those lines.

Lena Ashwell was an actress and producer who owned the Kingsway
Theatre. The day before the above-mentioned theatre visit she took
Elgar the script of a play that Algernon Blackwood and Violet Pearn had
adapted from Blackwood's novel *A Prisoner in Fairyland*. It was called *The
Starlight Express*. A plan by Basil Dean to produce it in 1914, for which
Clive Carey had written the music, had fallen through. The play was a
whimsical affair about an English family living in the Jura mountains
who suffer from misunderstandings because of a lack of sympathy. The
children believe that while they are asleep their spirits play among the
stars. They collect stardust (sympathy) and by sprinkling it produce
the desired changes of attitude. Elgar was immediately attracted to
it because of its superficial resemblance to the *Wand of Youth* play of
his childhood. Besides, he was depressed by the war news and this
offered a form of escape. His frequent visits to Worcestershire had
also intensified his nostalgia, as had meetings in London with W. M.
Baker and Hew Steuart-Powell of the Variations. Drawing on some of
his *Wand of Youth* music, he wrote within a month a 300-page score
containing fifty items, with enchanting songs such as those for the
Organ Grinder, who presents the play and appears before the curtain
of each act. It is one of Elgar's most attractive scores, with echoes of

the Violin Concerto and even of *Gerontius*, the dreamer of dreams at his most tenderly poignant.

Lena Ashwell chose the two singers, the soprano Clytie Hine and the baritone Charles Mott (whom Elgar had already recommended for *Gerontius*). The young conductor was to be Julius Harrison. But then matters went awry. Blackwood and Elgar detested the designs by Henry Wilson, and Violet Pearn told Clive Carey she was 'bored to tears' by Elgar's music. Carey, who was in the army, was peeved that Ashwell had not used his music, but she was under no obligation to do so. Carey bore no grudge against Elgar and Elgar, luckily, did not know about Carey's music or he would have felt he was in another Rootham situation. Personal problems also intervened. On 21 December, eight days before the scheduled première, Elgar's nephew William, elder son of Frank, died in Worcester from tuberculosis at the age of twenty-five, and on the 27th Alice was involved in a taxicab accident. She was concussed and stayed in bed for ten days. It was enough for Elgar to refuse to conduct on the first night and even to attend. He later relented and went, but it closed after three weeks on 19 January 1916. On 18 February, however, he recorded eight sides of extracts, with Mott and Agnes Nicholls, which HMV issued shortly afterwards.

In February Elgar completed the orchestration of 'To Women' and 'For the Fallen'. Rootham's setting of the latter had by now been published, but he was still not reconciled to Elgar's setting and continued to protest about it. (He never was reconciled. On the day in 1934 when Elgar's death was announced, he began a Cambridge lecture with the words 'Well, gentlemen, I see that a would-be English country gentleman has died', whereupon the whole class walked out.)[4] In March Elgar conducted the LSO on a tour of northern England and Scotland and returned with influenza, which Alice had too. Planning to convalesce at Stoke Prior (because of fuel shortages Severn House was bitterly cold), he set off by train on 8 April but was taken ill at Oxford and driven to a nursing home where he spent three days until Carice fetched him home. Still far from well, he insisted on conducting Embleton's Leeds Choral Union in Leeds on 4 May in the first

performance of 'To Women' and 'For the Fallen' (followed by Gerontius) with another performance the following night in Bradford. The
soprano soloist was Agnes Nicholls. The first London performances
were on the six days 8–13 May at Queen's Hall, when they preceded performances of Gerontius which Clara Butt had organised to benefit the Red
Cross. Agnes Nicholls sang in the Binyon settings; the Gerontius soloists
were Butt, Gervase Elwes and Charles Mott. The king and queen went
to the afternoon performance on 10 May. Alice's diary recorded that
George V 'seemed fidgety and un-King-like in demeanour . . . The King
was said to be much affected by "For the Fallen" but Gerontius was evidently too long for him. They seemed to have no music &c. So different
from King Edward.'

The Spirit of England, though still lacking the third part, received high
critical praise. 'Here in truth is the very voice of England', Newman
wrote in the Musical Times, while Percy Scholes wrote that 'if this country had a "Musician Laureate" it would be to Elgar that the laurel
would be offered. For he, of all musicians, is the one to whom we
turn in times of national feeling to provide us with the musical expression for which our spirits crave.'[5] That is still true today. The Spirit of
England distils anew the emotional power of the Second Symphony
and Gerontius.

This was the worst period of the war – Verdun, the third battle of
Ypres, the Battle of Jutland, the start of the Somme offensive on 1 July
with 60,000 British casualties. It depressed Elgar, already weakened by
ill health. He was exhausted after the Queen's Hall performances and
went to Eastbourne for a week. Then, while Alice went to Broadway,
he went to Stoke Prior, then to The Hut and on 15 July back to Stoke
Prior where on the 24th 'Windflower' came over from Stratford and he
met her train at Droitwich and drove her to Pollie's house. Alice joined
him and they went to the Lake District where he was soaked to the skin
walking on the Kirkstone Pass and developed a sore throat. On return
to London, his throat was cauterised on 29 August. Two days later he
wrote to 'Windflower': 'I feel that everything has come to an end & am
very unhappy.' In September he and Alice visited the Berkeley family at

Spetchley Park, another journey back to his childhood. 'Lovely place', he told 'Windflower', 'but I am very sad & cannot rest even here.' Lunches and theatre-going with 'Windflower' resumed in October and one day at Severn House she played him the sketches of his piano concerto, but he did not respond. He had several conducting engagements, including the Second Symphony, which he had conducted several times during the war. But this one on 27 November was to a sparse audience and was poorly played. 'I am very unwell indeed', he wrote to 'Windflower' on 11 December, 'and do not know what to make of it – I suppose it is the old thing [Menière's].' But on the 16th he recorded an abridged version of the Violin Concerto with Marie Hall for which he had written a harp part to accompany the cadenza. Afterwards he was ill again. Just before Christmas Charles Stuart Wortley was raised to the peerage and on the 20th Elgar wrote to the new Lady Stuart of Wortley to send love and congratulations and to say 'you are still the Windflower I think & hope'. He then added:

> Everything pleasant & promising in my life is dead – I have the happiness of my friends to console me as I had fifty years ago. I feel that life has gone back so far when I was alone & there was no one to stand between me & disaster – health or finance – now that has come back & I feel more alone & the prey of circumstances than ever before.

What was the cause of this outburst? 'Fifty years ago' seems odd: he was nine then. Did he mean thirty years ago? Brian Trowell thinks so, assuming that he was referring to 1886 and the break with Helen Weaver.[6] Trowell believes that Elgar would have known that Helen had had two children, Kenneth and Joyce, because he would have been told by Helen's brother Frank in Worcester. Kenneth joined the New Zealand army in 1914, was wounded at Gallipoli and was in England at military hospitals from August 1915 to January 1916. He was killed on the Somme on 8 July and his name was in the casualty lists in the Daily Telegraph on 12 July. On that day Alice's diary says: 'E. out a good deal and wishing for country.' This, Trowell maintains, was why Elgar felt that 'everything has come to an end' and he believes Elgar may even have met Kenneth in Worcester during one of his visits to Stoke Prior. It is a tempting theory but Trowell's article is entirely speculative, as must be any other attempted explanation of Elgar's more than usually black depression at this time. He ended 1916 with visits to the theatre with Alice and 'Windflower' and with a visit from Jaeger's widow and her children.

The year 1917 began with the delayed news of Hans Richter's death on the 5th of the previous month – 'my dear old friend', Elgar called him in a letter of condolence to the conductor's son-in-law Sydney Loeb. It also began with reviews of a new History of Music by Stanford and Cecil Forsyth in which Elgar was dismissed thus: 'Cut off from his contemporaries by the circumstances of his religion and his want of regular academic training, he was lucky enough to enter the field and find the preliminary ploughing already done.' On 5 January, Elgar's throat was again cauterised. Then on 9 February came news of the death at fifty-three of the Hereford organist George Sinclair. He had dined with the Elgars only a week earlier and had written on 5 February to tell Elgar of 'a wonderful viola player' called Lionel Tertis. Elgar told Ivor Atkins: 'I am overwhelmed & sorrowful & quite unable to see things as they are.'

But he was beginning to compose again. Lena Ashwell ran 'Concerts at the Front' and the dancer Ina Lowther, whom Elgar had known as a girl in Malvern, was one of a committee, which included 'Windflower', organising a matinée revue called Chelsea on Tip-Toe in aid of Ashwell's venture. She went to see Elgar on 7 February to ask him to write a short ballet. She had written its scenario, based on a lady's fan designed in sanguine by the artist Charles Conder (1868–1909). It was an escapist story, involving the classical mythology figures of Pan and Echo and young couples dressed in Louis XV costumes. The music for The Sanguine Fan, in Elgar's lightest and most fanciful vein, was written and orchestrated within a month during which Elgar heard of the death of his old Uncle Henry. He conducted The Spirit of England in Leeds on 7 March and in Worcester cathedral on the 15th, feeling unwell both times. While working on the ballet score, Elgar had written to

'Windflower' on 8 February: 'I wanted to tell you the theme & *every note* must be approved by you (bless you!) before anything can be done. Oh! why are you so far away & so difficult to get at??'

The ballet had its first – and only intended – performance, conducted by Elgar, at Wyndham's Theatre on 20 March. Rehearsals had been fraught and had annoyed Alice – 'other scenes vulgar, in bad taste & wretched', but E.'s ballet was 'exquisite & enchanting'. The dancers included Ina Lowther, Fay Compton and Ernest Thesiger, with Gerald Du Maurier as Pan. A second performance was arranged for 22 May, for which Elgar added a shepherd's dance. Elgar recorded some extracts in 1920, otherwise the music lay unperformed until Sir Adrian Boult recorded the complete score with the London Philharmonic Orchestra in 1973 and later conducted several performances of the ballet.

By 25 March Elgar was orchestrating some songs. These were four settings of poems Rudyard Kipling had published in a pamphlet called *The Fringes of the Fleet*. Elgar's friend Admiral Lord Charles Beresford had asked him to set them in January 1916 but Kipling had objected. Now it seemed he had relented. The war was going badly. French troops had mutinied, the U-boats were sinking more merchant ships, the Russian Revolution began. But on 6 April America entered the war. News of atrocities by the Germans finally impelled Elgar to set the anti-German stanza in 'The Fourth of August' and he returned to the score on 30 March, setting the lines about 'a lust to enslave or kill' to the Demons' Chorus from *Gerontius*. As he later told Ernest Newman:

> The Hun is branded as less than a beast for very many generations: so I wd. not invent anything low & bestial enough to illustrate the one stanza; the Cardinal invented . . . the particular hell in *Gerontius* where the great intellects gibber & snarl, *knowing they have fallen*. This is exactly the case with the Germans now . . . And this ends, as far as I can see, my contribution to war music.

The last sentence was not quite accurate. He conducted his third Cammaerts recitation, *Le drapeau belge*, on 14 April. Six days later he was

ill again and cancelled a visit to Stoke Prior. On the 23rd he decided to
go there but turned back at Paddington. Two days later he completed
the journey, sending 'Windflower' some anemones ('your prototypes')
on arrival. While he was away Alice searched for a country retreat where
he would be quiet and able to work. She was coming to realise that the
move to London had been a mistake. On 2 May she and Carice found
an isolated thatched cottage, Brinkwells, near Fittleworth in Sussex.
They rented it. On 11 May Elgar finished orchestrating 'The Fourth of
August' and on 25 May they moved into Brinkwells in glorious weather.
Next day Alice wrote to 'Windflower': 'I am delighted to tell you that
Edward's first exclamation was "This is too lovely for words".' He loved
the view of the Downs, the woods and their paths, the birdsong – and
the carpenter's bench at the cottage.

The Fringes of the Fleet songs were to be performed as part of a variety
at the Coliseum. Set in what Elgar called 'a broad salt-water style',
they were about the small peacetime coastal vessels which had been
equipped with guns for Channel and North Sea patrols. They were for
four baritones (one of them was Charles Mott) and the stage setting put
them, in fishing boots and sou'westers, sitting round a table outside
a village inn. Mott was due to be called up and his availability was due
to the influence of Lord Charles Beresford. Elgar conducted the first
performance on 11 June. Two performances a day followed until the end
of July. On 27 June Elgar added a fifth poem, Gilbert Parker's 'Inside
the Bar' (Novello's rejected it for publication), and on 4 July the Kipling
songs were recorded, the Parker following later. Elgar was exhausted
at the end of the run. He went to Stoke Prior for a rest before taking the
songs on a long provincial tour, returning to the Coliseum in October.
Mott was called up when the first Coliseum run ended. Elgar wrote to
'Windflower': 'Yes, Mott has gone with the rest of the heroes, while
those who can afford to pay are let off. Why does not someone, not a
musician, interfere?' Mott died on 22 May 1918 of wounds received two
days earlier. On 11 May he had written to Elgar: 'There is something
still very much wrong with a world that still sanctions war . . . There
is one thing that "puts the wind up me" very badly & that is of my

19 Brinkwells, Elgar's Sussex cottage

being wiped out & thus miss the dear harmonies of your wonderful works.'[7]

Elgar's health still gave concern. He went to Brinkwells for a few days before a week of conducting *Fringes* at Chiswick in September, when he told 'Windflower' that his head had 'quite gone giddy, alas! Yes, everything good & nice & clean & fresh & sweet is far away – never to return.' At Chatham some performances were cancelled because of Zeppelin raids on naval installations. Elgar told 'Windflower': 'The place is so noisy & I do not sleep – the guns are the quietest things here. I long for the country and Stoke. I think all the time of it – & you.' Earlier in the summer he had written to her: 'I am glad you "feel" Stoke – that is a place where I see & *hear* (yes!) you. A. has not been there since 1888 & does not care to go & no one of my friends has ever been but you.' She sent the children at The Elms a box of clothes.

At last a complete performance of *The Spirit of England* was arranged and was given in Birmingham on 4 October 1917. Appleby Matthews conducted and the soloist was Rosina Buckman. Elgar was at Stoke Prior but did not attend and made no reference to it in any letters. Another puzzle. He conducted it in Leeds on 31 October. There were two soloists, Agnes Nicholls and Gervase Elwes, even though the score specifies only soprano *or* tenor. Nicholls sang in 'The Fourth of August' and 'For the Fallen', Elwes in 'To Women'. But on the night Elwes lost his voice and 'whispered a few phrases & spoke it – just like praying'.[8] Another performance followed at Huddersfield on 2 November. He then spent ten days at The Elms before returning to London on 18 November. He was too ill to take a choral rehearsal for the London première of *The Spirit of England* but, the diary tells us, 'A. S. of W. to tea & talk to him.' He conducted the performance at the Albert Hall on 24 November, again with Nicholls and Elwes. Parry, whose *Chivalry of the Sea* was also performed, thought the Elgar was 'very poor stuff for the most part'. But Elwes told Rosa Burley that he did not know how they had all got through such a harrowing experience – 'the war casualties at that time were heartrending and almost every member of the choir must have lost a close relative or a friend'.[9] From 26 November to 1 December

Elgar conducted the last run of The Fringes of the Fleet at the Coliseum. Kipling had finally succeeded in stopping performances. Elgar was ill throughout the week and continued to be unwell for all of December. A second specialist said there was 'no organic trouble'. He perked up in February to go for walks, lunches and the theatre with 'Windflower' but Alice's diary continually mentions 'E. not very well.' During February, the young conductor Adrian Boult went to Severn House to go through In the South which he was conducting at a series of LSO concerts he was promoting.

Elgar had a relapse in March and a third specialist urged removal of his tonsils. This was done at a nursing home in Dorset Square on 15 March. Alice was shown the worst tonsil – 'all over abscess matter & a black stone, pea size, in it'. Elgar returned to Severn House on 22 March and that night wrote a theme in 9/8 which was eventually to be the principal subject of the first movement of the Cello Concerto. Three days later Alice recorded: 'E. began a delightful quartet. A remote lovely 1st subject. May he soon finish it – wrote all day.' He sent the 9/8 theme to 'Windflower' as a thank-offering 'arranged for a good pianist' and a week later wrote: 'It was wrong of me to put that inscription on the poor little MS – all is yours, not only that bit. I have written the continuation now – which is strange & good.'

In the long term the operation was a success. Tonsillectomy is not a cure for Menière's disease, but the fact remains that Elgar was not afflicted by deafness during the remaining sixteen years of his life.[10]

## 13 Brinkwells

Elgar was often in pain after his operation. But on 12 April he was well enough to be driven to The Hut for a fortnight. His fellow guests were Lalla Vandervelde, the poet Robert Nichols and Adrian Boult. Alice's plan was to get him to Brinkwells for the summer. They went there on 2 May. Elgar threw himself into carpentry, making footstools and doorstops, and he fixed the sundial from Plas Gwyn in the garden. At the Ministry of Food's request he set a Kipling poem, 'Big Steamers'. Alice commented: 'Very magnanimous to set anything more of R. Kipling's but he said "Anything for the cause".' He killed a snake, caught fish and after hearing the nightingale wrote to 'Windflower': 'Their song is really the most lovely thing in nature. Except one other thing which had a lovely tea in the Strand.' She sent him a pocket compass for his walks in the woods. She planned a visit in mid-May but was ill and put it off until 24 May. He wrote to her: 'The woods are still carpeted with bluebells . . . I have been down the wood & told them YOU are coming & asked them to remain for your loved visit.' Alice noted in her diary that the other Alice was 'delighted with everything, enjoying herself like a baby child'. She stayed four days. Before Carice went for a weekend in June, 'Windflower' met her at Victoria and sent a hamper of lobster, plaice, jam, teas, chocolate, dates and biscuits. Other visitors included Lalla Vandervelde. Frances and Sidney Colvin lived not far away. 'Windflower' visited again in August, just before Elgar helped with the harvest, and sent an adjustable blind for the garden studio – 'your room', Elgar told her. He also had a piano delivered on 19 August and next day began to compose a violin sonata.

On the 24th Alice noted: 'E. writing wonderful new music, different from anything of his. A. called it wood magic. So elusive & delicate.' This was the beginning of the sonata's slow movement, Romance. When two days later he heard that 'Windflower' had broken her leg at Tintagel, he wrote a long *dolcissimo* melody which became the movement's central section. He sent her 'the pencil notes as made at that sad moment' (when he received her telegram). Next day, the 27th, he played the sonata as far as it had gone to Landon Ronald and the 9/8 theme. The latter he 'loved & wants dreadfully', Alice noted, calling it 'the mysterious orch. piece', 'mysterious' only because as yet it had no provenance. On the 29th W. H. Reed played through the sonata, which now had the start of its finale. On 6 September Elgar wrote to offer the dedication to Marie Joshua, an old friend of his and Richter's. 'I fear it does not carry us any further but it is full of golden sounds and I like it, but you must not expect anything violently chromatic or cubist.' She was 'overwhelmed' but did not think she ought to accept, perhaps because of her part-German origin. A few days later she died. Elgar recalled the sonata's *dolcissimo* melody from the slow movement to become a nostalgic lament before the coda of the finale. He completed it on 15 September and began a piano quintet on the same day. 'Wonderful weird beginning. Same atmosphere as "Owls"', Alice wrote. Elgar later described the first movement to Ernest Newman as 'ghostly stuff', thus showing that Alice was on the right track. There can be little doubt that the agonies of the war are the inspiration behind the first movement. The fugato 'goes wild again – as man does' he told Newman. A 'cut-and-thrust dialogue of ferocity new to Elgar's music' is heard there by Jerrold Northrop Moore. But Elgar suddenly reverted from the quintet to the quartet. On 27 September Alice heard 'wonderful new music – real wood sounds & another lament wh. shd.

be in a War Symphony'. She wanted to return to Severn House and this brought Elgar's illness back. 'I have had – at the thought of town life – a recurrence of the old feelings & have been just as limp as before the nursing-home episode', he wrote to 'Windflower' on 10 October. He continued work on the quartet and said to Alice: 'I feel all right again.'

They returned to London on the 11th and five days later he and Reed played the sonata to friends including Schuster, the Colvins, Muriel Foster and Landon Ronald. 'It did not seem right to do it without you', he told 'Windflower', who could not yet manage stairs. On the 16th he attended Parry's funeral in St Paul's Cathedral. Alice had developed a wen (cyst) on her forehead and this was removed by surgery on the 29th. Two days later he and Reed played the sonata to 'Windflower' at her home in Cheyne Walk. The war was drawing to its end and Binyon tried to interest Elgar in setting his ode 'Peace'. Elgar wrote to him on 5 November:

> I do not feel drawn to write peace music somehow . . . The whole atmosphere is too full of complexities for me to feel music to it: not the atmosphere of the poem but of the time, I mean . . . I regret the appeal [in the poem] to the Heavenly Spirit which is cruelly obtuse to the individual sorrow and sacrifice – a cruelty I resent bitterly & disappointedly.

On the morning of 11 November, Armistice Day, Elgar put up a flag on Severn House and in the afternoon returned to Brinkwells. He composed the slow movement of the quartet, described by Alice as 'captured sunshine'. Elgar later said this movement had 'something in it that has never been done before'.[1] While composing these chamber works Elgar was intellectually keyed up more than usual. When Alice had her operation, he complained to 'Windflower' that his 'writing new stuff' had been held up and it had been 'a tragedy for my music'. He talked of 'broken threads'. And when Alice's worsening cough kept her in bed at Brinkwells and necessitated a return to London to see a doctor, he wrote to Schuster:

it means another interruption & the future is *dark* as A. poor dear is not well &, of course, is bored to death here while I am in the seventh heaven of delight . . . If I have to live again at Hampstead composition is 'off' – not the house or the place but London – *telephone* etc. *all day and* night drive me mad!

To 'Windflower' he wrote: 'I *wish* you were here. The studio is not too cold in the early morn. How I remember it all.' Reed went to Brinkwells on 3 December when Elgar played through the orchestral sketch of the 9/8 theme and told him it was to be part of a cello concerto.

In London the doctor found nothing amiss with Alice's lungs. She was well enough to go to hear Landon Ronald conduct *Falstaff* on 5 December, its first performance for over four years and the first time it was a success with an audience. 'Windflower', on crutches, and her husband were there. The Elgars returned to Brinkwells and composition on 7 December: 'E. gradually finding his broken threads.' He wrote the finale of the quartet. Alice returned alone to London on the 17th after news that Severn House had been burgled, with silver, clothes and whisky stolen. He finished the quartet on Christmas Eve, dedicating it to the Brodsky Quartet who had asked for it nearly twenty years earlier, and left Brinkwells after Christmas, going to stay with the Speyers in Hertfordshire while Alice packed up at the cottage and opened up Severn House. Elgar wanted another play-through of the new works and Alice, under much stress, arranged for Reed's quartet to play the quartet. Reed and Elgar played the sonata and Elgar was pianist in the first movement of the quintet. The Elgarian faithful made up the audience. He composed the quintet's slow movement and was able to play in it at another play-through at the Beresfords' house on 19 January 1919. The finale was written in time for yet another play-through at Severn House on 7 March, where a twenty-seven-year-old former Guards officer, Arthur Bliss, who had met the Elgars in 1916, turned the pages for Elgar in the sonata. He wrote years later that he had felt that 'the musical substance had little in common with the genius of his earlier masterpieces'.[2] Also present were Bernard Shaw and his

20  Elgar at Severn House, 1919

wife. Elgar had met Shaw a few days earlier at a lunch given by Lalla
Vandervelde.

The sonata was played by Reed and Anthony Bernard for the British
Music Society on 13 March. Its public première was given by Reed and
Landon Ronald at the Aeolian Hall on 21 March. At the rehearsal Elgar
had not liked his own music but Alice had persuaded him to go to the

concert. The hall was half empty, as it was for the Birmingham première a fortnight later. At Schuster's London house on 26 April the
quartet, the sonata's Romance and the quintet were played by Albert
Sammons, Reed, Raymond Jeremy (violin), Felix Salmond (cello) and
William Murdoch (piano). The same performers played all three works
(the quartet and quintet for the first time in public) at the Wigmore
Hall on 21 May. The critic of *The Times*, H. C. Colles, thought the
first movement of the quintet showed Elgar as 'still a force among
the many currents of the musical tide', but his review was a portent of
things to come. The immediate effect of listening to the three works, he
wrote,

> is to give one a new sympathy with the modern revolt against beauty of
> line and colour. A stab of crude ugliness would be a relief from that
> overwhelming sense of beauty . . . It is not really ugliness, and still less
> vulgarity, that one craves as an antidote to the Elgarian type of beauty.
> It is the contrast of a more virile mind . . . What has he to say now,
> and have the years stamped their meaning on him in any profound
> way?

Elgar now turned to the Cello Concerto, just the instrument to con-
vey the loneliness, disillusion and sense of belonging to a dying era that
underlies much of the music of the concerto, though not all of it, because, as he told Sidney Colvin, it was 'a real large work & I think *good* &
alive'. At Severn House on 10 June, with 'Windflower' turning the pages
for him, he played through the sketches with Felix Salmond. He worked
on it at Brinkwells for three weeks, ready for another Hampstead try-
out on 5 July. Back in Sussex he revised the quintet for publication and
orchestrated the concerto. Salmond arrived at Brinkwells on 31 July
to go through the work and on 2 August Elgar asked him to give the
first performance. Next day he wrote to 'Windflower': 'I want to finish
or rather commence the Piano Concerto which *must* be windflowerish', but he never did. The Cello Concerto was sent to the printer on
8 August. 'Windflower' spent three days at Brinkwells from 20 August.

In September Charles Beresford died and the Elgars went to his funeral in St Paul's. 'I feel very much depressed by it all', he wrote to 'Windflower' from Brinkwells on 22 September. 'Here we are, very cold & I want to get away – strange: but the Studio is sad sad & I feel I have destroyed the best thing I ever wrote & that it had to be so [what did he mean?]. I am not well & worried in many ways . . . The world is a changed place & I am awfully tired of it.' Almost symbolically, he spent much time at Brinkwells chopping wood and burning it. 'Fires of rubbish, great flames shooting up', Alice wrote.

The concerto's première was on 27 October at a London Symphony Orchestra concert conducted by Albert Coates except for the new work. It was his first season as the LSO's principal conductor and he was anxious to make an impression. He had appropriated over an hour of Elgar's rehearsal time on 26 October. 'Wretched hurried rehearsal', Alice wrote. 'An insult to E. from that brutal, selfish, ill-mannered bounder A. Coates.' The same thing happened next morning and the orchestra stayed on half an hour beyond their time for the Elgar. 'A. wanted to withdraw, but he did not for Felix S's sake.' Predictably, the performance was dreadful. 'Never, in all probability, has so great an orchestra made so lamentable a public exhibition of itself', Newman wrote in the *Observer*. He called the work 'the realisation in tone of a fine spirit's lifelong wistful brooding upon the loveliness of the earth'. Elgar called it 'a man's attitude to life'.[3] The hall was far from full.

The concerto recovered from its unfortunate launch. Young cellists such as Beatrice Harrison (who made the first recording, with Elgar, in December 1919) and John Barbirolli (who had played in the orchestra at the first performance) took it up. It held its place in the repertory and eventually attracted foreign soloists of the quality of Casals, Piatigorsky and Tortelier. In the last quarter of the twentieth century it achieved mass popularity in Britain, outstripping the Violin Concerto. Its melancholy and yearning (never, in Elgar, erotic yearning) and its sense of mourning for a lost ideal, wonderfully expressed in the brief Adagio, captured the hearts of millions of listeners. It is the musical equivalent of words he

21  Alice Elgar

wrote to 'Windflower': 'Well, I have put it all in my music & also much more that has never happened.'[4]

Alice now seemed to have a persistent cold and cough. While Elgar was in Brussels and Amsterdam conducting in November, she spent most of the two weeks he was away in bed. A small woman anyway, she seemed to W. H. Reed to be getting smaller and Rosa Burley was shocked to find her 'shrunken and terribly depressed'. In January Elgar worked on an abridgement (eighteen bars) of 'For the Fallen' for the dedication of the war memorial Cenotaph in Whitehall planned for 11 November 1920. He called it *With proud thanksgiving* and scored it for military band. But on 22 January he told 'Windflower': 'I fear (*private*) the Cenotaph affair will not include me – the *present* proposals

are vulgar & commonplace to the *last degree*. I really cannot appear in
it.' It was not performed until 7 May 1921, rescored for full orchestra,
at the jubilee concert of the Royal Choral Society.

Alice was told by her doctor that nothing was wrong with her. She
accompanied Elgar to the Queen's Hall on 16 March when the Second
Symphony had what was probably its first really fine performance. It
was conducted by Adrian Boult. Her diary recorded:

> Wonderful performance . . . From the beginning it seemed to absolutely
> penetrate the audience's mind & heart. After 1st movement great
> applause & *shouts*, rarely heard till end, & great applause all through.
> Adrian was wonderful – At end frantic enthusiasm & they dragged out E.
> who looked very nervous, hand in hand with Adrian at least 3 times – E.
> was so happy & pleased.

She wrote to the conductor the next day. Carice, who had been on
holiday in Mürren, Switzerland, since November returned with the
news that she had met an Englishman older than herself who was
interested in her. (A wartime friendship with an army captain had ended
when he was killed.) Alice did not accompany Elgar when he went to
conduct in Leeds but went with Carice to a concert of the three chamber
works. Elgar returned on 26 March to find her 'very unwell' in bed. He
wrote in his diary: 'Thoughts of the 30 (weary fighting) years of her help
and devotion.' Muriel Foster called to see her on the 27th. On 6 April
he wrote: 'My darling in great distress – cd. not understand her words.'
Next day the last rites were administered. She died, aged seventy-two,
from undetected lung cancer, in Elgar's arms at 6.10 p.m.

## 14 Post mortem

Elgar was devastated by Alice's death, so withdrawn into himself that Rosa Burley told him to pull himself together. She also tactlessly said that she now stood as Carice's mother – Carice was twenty-nine – and would take over the running of the Elgar household. Elgar never saw or spoke to her again. Alice was buried at Little Malvern and Elgar placed his ceremonial sword in her coffin. A string quartet – Reed, Albert Sammons, Lionel Tertis and Felix Salmond – played the slow movement of Elgar's quartet, the expenses being borne by Frank Schuster and 'Windflower' (who was in Tintagel). Elgar then stayed for a fortnight with Pollie at Stoke Prior, but he had a cold and 'giddiness' from his ear returned. Also he discovered that part of Alice's money now reverted to her family. 'Ancient hate & prejudice', he called it in a letter to Schuster. 'I feel just now rather evil that . . . Carice should be penalised by a wretched lot of old incompetents simply because I was – well – I.' What he felt about Alice was best summed up in a letter to Ivor Atkins in December 1922 referring to *King Olaf*:

> It seems strange that the strong (it is *that*) characteristic stuff shd. have been conceived & written (by a poor wretch teaching all day) with a splitting headache after dinner at odd sustained moments – but the spirit & will was there in spite of the malevolence of the Creator of all things. But thro' it all shines the radiant mind & soul of my dearest departed one: she travelled to London (I was grinding at the High

School) & became bound for one hundred pounds so that my work might be printed – bless her! You, who like some of my work, must thank her for all of it, not me. I shd. have destroyed it all & joined Job's wife in the congenial task of cursing God.

But music had to go on. He conducted the Embleton Choral Union in *The Apostles* in Newcastle upon Tyne on 8 May (and Embleton lent him £500 to write Part 3) and the Second Symphony at the end of the month in Cardiff 'to an audience of a handful of persons lost in an array of empty chairs', as the *South Wales News* reported. He and Carice spent the summer after mid-June at Brinkwells. He had seen 'Windflower' in London and wrote to her from Sussex describing himself as 'to all intents and purposes an invalid – you see, the stronger I get (& I am fairly well) the worse my *ear* is – if I am low in health and unable to get about, my ear is less troublesome: so there it is – in a vicious circle'. Visits to Schuster at The Hut – where he first met the war poet Siegfried Sassoon – and to the Speyers at Ridgehurst were disillusioning: 'I cannot say', he told 'Windflower', 'that I appreciate the influx of *Germans* . . . – *also* some extraordinary females, friends of the youth whom F. introduces as his "*Nephew*" – are we all mad? After this, *what*? And at Ridgehurst we had a German lady & her daughter – who sang to the Germans in Brussels!!!' But a fortnight later he asked Adrian Boult, who was to conduct the Second Symphony in Munich, to 'give my warm greetings to Strauss' and 'assure him of my continued admiration &, if he will, friendship'. When Kreisler returned to London in May 1921, Elgar left a note of welcome at his hotel.

In the summer of 1920 'Windflower' had picked wild roses from what she thought was the hedge at his cottage birthplace at Broadheath, but he told her she had not found it. 'It is nearer the clump of Scotch firs – I can smell them now – in the hot sun. Oh! how cruel that I was not there – there's *nothing between* that infancy & *now* and I want to see it.' She went to the first post-war Three Choirs Festival at Worcester where he conducted 'For the Fallen', *The Music Makers* and *Gerontius*. He conducted in Brussels and Amsterdam in October and at the end of

November heard Jascha Heifetz play his concerto at Queen's Hall. So did 'Windflower'. 'Yes, it was a tremendous display', he wrote to her, 'not exactly our own Concerto.' He insisted that music meant nothing to him any longer. 'I have "gone out" – & like it', was his pronouncement. On another occasion, 'there is nothing in it all somehow'. He told her: 'I like to think of the Worcester days & you & the flowers & the fruit & the warm sun & my cathedral & the music: but it is lonely.'[1]

He spent Christmas 1920 at Stoke Prior and went to Stratford-upon-Avon where he was horrified to find short-skirted waitresses and a jazz band for dancing in his favourite hotel. Soon the Graftons were having to leave Stoke Prior and by the summer of 1921 they were at Perryfield House, near Bromsgrove. It seemed that nothing in his life was the same. He and Alice had put up Severn House for sale in 1919 but there were still no offers for it, while Brinkwells would not be available after the summer of 1921. In March Carice became engaged to the farmer Samuel Blake whom she had met in Switzerland. And when Elgar suggested to Novello's that they might like to buy the copyrights on his smaller works and arrangements, they paid him £500 for the lot. He wished they could buy him out entirely – 'I never really belonged to the musical world – I detest my slightest necessary connection with it & should be glad to have done with it and get back to my (deceased) dogs and horses!'

The first creative task Elgar undertook after Alice's death was to reorchestrate *With proud thanksgiving* for an Albert Hall concert on 7 May. This he did in March; and in April he orchestrated Bach's Fugue in C minor for organ (BWV 537). Novello's paid him 100 guineas for the copyright. He had once discussed Bach transcriptions with Strauss, who favoured a restrained approach in contrast to Elgar's preference for use of the full orchestra. He hoped Strauss would orchestrate the preceding Fantasia, but nothing was forthcoming. Elgar orchestrated it himself in 1922. At Severn House he spent most of his time peering into microscopes. He resumed theatre-going and now there was the cinema. After the Hereford Festival, he moved into a flat at 37 St James's Place while Severn House and much of its furniture were put up for auction.

But the house still found no bidder. The flat was near his clubs: he was now a member of Brooks's, the Savile and the Garrick, as well as the Athenaeum. Elgar confessed to 'Windflower' that 'until a few weeks ago' he had believed that 'my dear A. would be sure to come back & take charge of things . . . Now I feel the desolation and hopelessness of it all.' On 27 October Eugene Goossens ('a great conductor') conducted the first performance of the Bach Fugue orchestration, which was encored. 'Windflower' was there, and they all went to Boult concerts and to the Diaghilev ballet during the autumn and, of course, to Queen's Hall on 6 December when Kreisler played the concerto. Elgar went to Bromsgrove for Christmas and 'Windflower' sent Pollie a ham. 'We love our new little nest and have no wish to be back in The Elms', she wrote to 'Windflower', evidently not sharing her brother's nostalgia for what has been.

Carice was married on 16 January 1922. Next day Elgar went with 'Windflower' and her husband to the first concert Strauss conducted in London after the war and six days later gave a lunch so that Strauss could meet young British musicians – Boult, John Ireland, Bliss, Arnold Bax, Goossens and Rutland Boughton. He also invited Bernard Shaw. He had written to 'Windflower' after the concert: 'How glorious the music was after the empty rot we have now.' He had little if any sympathy for the music of Stravinsky, Bartók, Hindemith and Schoenberg. As far as modernism was concerned, Strauss was as far as he went. Music had 'all gone ugly', he remarked to 'Windflower'. The three chamber works and the Cello Concerto could all have been written any time in the previous forty years. He knew his own music was out of tune with the times. His bold and colourful, almost garish, orchestrations of Bach and Handel were a protest against what he called 'cubist' music. In June 1922 Shaw complained in the *Daily News* that Queen's Hall was sparsely filled for *The Apostles*. Even so devoted an Elgarian as Adrian Boult cooled off (albeit temporarily). Talking to Siegfried Sassoon at the Three Choirs Festival in 1925 he said that he was 'losing faith in all Elgar's works except *The Kingdom*, the Second Symphony, the Enigma Variations and the fiddle concerto. "I thought *The Apostles* sounded awful last night!" '² There had, in any case, been a coolness between Boult and Elgar since October 1924, when Boult, just appointed conductor of the City of Birmingham Orchestra, told him that he was having to perform Gerontius with reduced woodwind because of the high cost. Elgar was furious and they barely spoke for the next seven years until April 1931 when Elgar thawed and explained:

> I have never had a real success in life – commercially never; so all I had (& have now) was the feeling that I had written one score which satisfied R. Strauss, Richter and many others; it was the discovery that no one in that very wealthy city – which always pretended to be proud of the production of Gerontius – cared a straw whether the work was presented as I wrote it or not.

In fact, Boult had engaged the extra players and paid them himself.

Although Elgar might have been regarded as an Establishment figure by this time, he was in reality an outsider. More than ever before he deliberately cultivated the image of himself as a country squire with philistine views who professed to know nothing about music. It was a tiresome pose, but it was a kind of refuge. For the rest of his life his musical epicentre, apart from the recording studio, was the Three Choirs Festival where his works formed the centrepiece of the programmes year by year and he would sometimes conduct them rather ridiculously attired in court dress. But then he was holding court, surrounded by admirers, like a king. Even so there were several occasions, there and elsewhere, when he lost interest in the performance because a mistake was made or he felt a lack of sympathy with the music. Then he would sulk or be rude. Even in the recording studio (where he was generously paid) he was often at first stiffly reserved and conducted with a minimum of interest. Gradually he would thaw and unbend.

His friends must sometimes have wearied of receiving letters in which he bemoaned the lack of appreciation of his music ('I regret everything good I have ever done' was a constant refrain). One of them, Lord Northampton, rebuked him: 'You must realise that you have in you a special power of bringing upon others the strongest influence for good.'[3] Yet Elgar sometimes seems to have regarded his musical gift as a curse rather than a blessing and this led to his curmudgeonly behaviour to those with whom he was always on the defensive, especially after Alice's death. Sassoon in his diaries has left several descriptions of Elgar as a club bore 'on the look-out for affronts'. Yet once at The Hut Elgar played him Mozart, Bach, Schubert and Elgar on the piano 'glowing with delight' and made him forget 'the other Elgar . . . At lunch, regaling us with long-winded anecdotes (about himself), he was a different man. The real Elgar was left in the music-room.'[4] Or perhaps the real Elgar was the one Pollie described in a letter to 'Windflower': 'I need not say what a consolation and help the frequent visits of that *dear big brother of mine* have been, coming so bright and doing all he can to cheer us up with his bright happy smile and consoling words' (Pollie's son had been ill).

At the end of 1922 he fitfully worked on sketches of the third oratorio and the piano concerto but soon abandoned them. But in January 1923 he allowed Laurence Binyon to persuade him into writing music for his play *Arthur*. The subject appealed (Tintagel?). He looked out old ideas in sketchbooks and wrote 'one or two windflowerish bits', as he told her, and completed the score at the end of February. He conducted the first performance (by a band of ten musicians) at the Old Vic on 12 March, telling Jane Bacon, who played Elaine, that if he had seen her earlier in her white dress he would have written more beautiful music. Only Schuster and the Stuart Wortleys were there. Poor 'Windflower' was recipient of the usual moan: 'My barren honours are dust. Not a single friend has shewn any sign of life, except your house, for years.' In April he took a six-month lease of Napleton Grange near Kempsey in Worcestershire where his niece Madge Grafton acted as hostess. He made an orchestration of a Handel overture and wrote two part-songs, *The Wanderer* and *Zut! Zut! Zut!* (the latter to his own words under the pseudonym Richard Mardon), which he offered to Novello's at 100 guineas for the two. They refused, Elgar told them to tear them up, they refused to do so and he accepted fifty guineas. He conducted at the

Worcester Festival. Schuster and 'Windflower' were there, but he didn't see them. He wrote to her about his own works: 'I think I deserve *my peerage* now, when these are compared with the new works!!!' This was the beginning of a new obsession, which she encouraged. Six months later he wrote to her: 'Tell me what you do about the Peerage!' This was when all peerages were hereditary. Life peerages were several decades into the future.

Seeking a holiday away from everyone, he sailed from Liverpool on 15 November 1923 in the *Hildebrand* on a voyage up the Amazon to Manaus in Brazil, where he was impressed by the opera house the 'rubber barons' had built in 1896. He returned on 30 December and settled down to write songs and a march for the British Empire Exhibition due to open at Wembley on 23 April. Most of his score was not used because of rehearsal difficulties. The whole affair, at which he conducted the massed bands and choirs in a popular programme, caused him disgruntlement, as he told 'Windflower':

> The K. insists on Land of Hope & there were some ludicrous suggestions of which I will tell you – if we ever meet . . . I was standing alone (criticising) in the middle of the enormous stadium in the sun: all the ridiculous Court programme, soldiers, awnings etc: 17,000 men hammering, loudspeaker, amplifiers – four aeroplanes circling over etc etc – all mechanical and horrible – no soul & no romance & no imagination. Here had been played the great football match [the first Wembley Cup Final] – even the turf, which is good, was not there as turf but for football – but at my feet I saw a group of real *daisies*. Something wet rolled down my cheek – & I am not ashamed of it: I had recovered my equanimity when the aides came to learn my views – Damn everything except the daisy – I was back in something sure, wholesome & GENTLEMANLY – but only for two minutes.

Well, one may exclaim, what did he expect?

His mind was on another matter. On 27 March Sir Walter Parratt, who had been Master of the King's Music since 1893, died. Next day Elgar wrote to Lord Stamfordham, the king's private secretary: 'If there

22   Elgar conducting at the Wembley Empire Exhibition, 1924

is to be a new appointment may I suggest, without presumption, that I should feel it to be the greatest honour if I might be allowed to hold the position?' Stamfordham passed this to Sir Frederick Ponsonby, Keeper of the Privy Purse, who told Elgar that the king was thinking of abolishing the post. Elgar replied that this would 'have a very deterrent effect on the prestige and progress of British music, especially abroad'. Ponsonby took soundings in the royal household. He wrote to the Earl of Shaftesbury, Lord Steward, that it was 'difficult to resist' Elgar's claims but that 'it is generally thought that Vaughan Williams is the most representative of British music, Elgar having always adopted German methods. Elgar, however, is much better known to the British public than Vaughan Williams.'⁵ Shaftesbury plumped for Elgar. The applicant was keeping 'Windflower' informed:

> As far as I can make out the three (?) depts. simply quarrel over those things: no grit, no imagination – no *music*, no nothing except boxing, football & racing . . . I believe the matter is to drop tacitly . . . Everything seems so hopelessly & irredeemably *vulgar* at Court . . . I fear the matter of the 'Master' is dead. As to any peerage I fear it is hopeless but it wd. please me.

The matter was not dead. He was offered the post on 25 April and it was made public on 5 May.

In June he conducted *Gerontius* and the Second Symphony in Paris and then went to The Hut. Elgar now referred to Schuster as 'poor dear old Frank' and found him changed. He told 'Windflower':

> Frank called . . . Bankrupt he says & very vague: this afternoon [16 April 1924] he was sitting in the back of a smart car – the young man was driving with an *odd looking* – I hate to say it – '*bit of fluff*'!! in flamboyant PINK on the front seat, all laughing loudly; they did not see me & I was glad for I shd. have been thoroughly ashamed.

This is the Elgar who resigned from the Athenaeum in 1924 when the first Labour prime minister, Ramsay MacDonald, was offered ex-officio membership. At The Hut in July 1924 Sassoon remarked that Elgar 'smoked innumerable pipes of fragrantly strong tobacco. His eyes blink a lot and look small and weak.' Schuster had engineered a meeting with the artist Walter Sickert:

Elgar wears sleeve-links given him by Edward VII. Sickert couldn't possibly be imagined doing so. Sickert 'knows nothing about music', which makes Elgar want to tell him about it. If S. were knowledgeable about music Elgar wouldn't want to discuss it. Both like telling stories. E's are long-winded and trivial. S's terse and witty.[6]

Old friends – Nicholas Kilburn, Frances Colvin and Claude Phillips – died. But in Worcestershire he had acquired a car (Lea Francis) and two dogs, a spaniel, Marco, and a cairn, Mina. Since Alice's death he had enjoyed the company of Pollie's dog Juno and Carice's Aberdeen terrier Meg. He did not drive, but engaged a chauffeur and valet, Richard Mountford, with his wife as cook and her sister as maid. He engaged Mary Clifford as his secretary. Away from London more than usual, he saw less of 'Windflower', but the letters continued: 'I am only old-fashioned in loving you' and, from Pollie's home, 'They send love from here – or at least such of them as dare.' She went with him to the rehearsal and concert in December when Bruno Walter conducted the First Symphony. 'I felt I liked some of the Symphony & really deserve *some* recognition (Your *peerless* idea – not mine. However, I like it) for having written it!' – the obsession continued.

The lease of Napleton Grange was extended and he spent most of 1925 there. He was usually in the most cheerful mood when he had visits from Ivor Atkins with his son Wulstan, then in his early twenties, who was Elgar's godson. Wulstan shared Elgar's love of his microscope and enjoyed looking at slides of insects and fossils. They would take the dogs for walks in the countryside, Elgar with lumps of sugar in his pocket to give to horses, and make excursions to Pershore, where Elgar had found a shop which sold delicious pork pies. He also enjoyed discussing horse-racing with Ivor Atkins's wife Katharine, who was equally inexpert at picking winners. Yet even Atkins experienced Elgar's cranky side, as when he suggested including *Sospiri* in a Three Choirs programme only to be told: 'I have not the remotest notion of what

*Sospiri* is, was, or will be.' When *Dream Children* was suggested instead, the reply was: 'I have no recollection of them – or it. But I do not want them or it done.'[7] Atkins programmed them, but Elgar refused to conduct.

Only two part-songs, *The Herald* and *The Prince of Sleep*, were written in 1925. Elgar worked fitfully on the piano concerto inspired by the playing of 'Windflower', but no real progress was made. The same applied to the third part of *The Apostles*. He still fulfilled conducting engagements and was thrilled to conduct for broadcasting for the first time. But it took little to send him back to Worcestershire: 'My beloved Marco is ill . . . He is now the only thing left in the world to me – & he's ill & looking for me everywhere.' He was with his eldest sister, Lucy Pipe, when she died in October. On 19 November, the Royal Philharmonic Society belatedly presented him with its Gold Medal at an Elgar concert which he conducted.[8] 'A *dreadful* evening', he wrote to 'Windflower':

Such a sparse audience. I *was* glad when it was over. Then we had a supper. B.[runo] Walter was there & made an excellent speech . . . I could not help looking round at you [in Queen's Hall] at some of the windflower passages! . . . I cd. not help thinking of your scheme of aggrandisement of the undersigned when some of the big, brilliant passages resounded. However I have the medal!

On Christmas Eve he had an operation for haemorrhoids. Pollie wrote to 'Windflower' to report 'everything going on all right' when he returned to Napleton Grange. She added: 'I should like you to know I conveyed your message *quite privately* to E. when in the [nursing] Home, I felt you would like it so.' How much did Pollie know? After the operation Elgar saw a consultant physician, Dr (later Sir) Arthur Thomson, in Birmingham. Thomson told Jerrold Northrop Moore, Elgar's biographer, in 1976 that he had found Elgar a neurotic who most of all wanted reassurance . . . He told me there was only one thing he really loved in life. That was the Golden Valley of the River Teme, especially a place 500 to 800 yards below the Knightsford Bridge down the right bank near the Ankerdine Hills. He used to sit on the banks and said he composed much of *Gerontius* there.[9]

On 24 April 1926 Charles Stuart Wortley died. The next time Elgar conducted his own music in Queen's Hall he wrote to 'Windflower': 'It was a great ordeal & I missed something too great to express – I looked at the familiar seats & my eyes filled.' She went to Switzerland for a long rest until September. On return she heard him conduct the Violin Concerto on 25 November and in his letter afterwards he reverted to the idea of a peerage:

> I wanted to ask you about the subject which you had (very much) in mind long ago; the last time we spoke of it you said I was to do something. Can you tell me *who* knows or has known anything of the idea? . . . I should like to know if 'it' is entirely dead – my birthday (70) next June is to be 'recognised' by concerts in the musical world & I do not want this or these & shall *squash* them unless the other thing turns up.

He did not know the prime minister, Stanley Baldwin, even though they were fellow Worcestershire men. She told him she would talk to Schuster.

His seventieth birthday was widely celebrated. Parts of the *Gerontius* performance which he conducted in February 1927 were recorded and issued by HMV, as were parts of *Gerontius* and *The Music Makers* when he conducted them at Hereford in September. He rerecorded the Second Symphony in the new electric process[10] and on the actual birthday, 2 June, conducted an Elgar concert with the BBC Wireless Orchestra and Chorus, speaking into the microphone at the end to say: 'Good night everybody. Good night Marco.' On 26 June Schuster organised a concert of the chamber music at The Hut. During the war Schuster had met a young New Zealand officer, Leslie ('Anzy') Wylde, who had lost a leg at Gallipoli. From 1920 'Anzy' and his fiancée, later wife,

23  Elgar with John Coates, his favourite Gerontius, 1925

Wendela played an increasingly large part in the running of The Hut,
including the building of an annexe where they could live after their
marriage (they were the couple Elgar had seen with Schuster in his car).
It was their arrival that caused Elgar to write so often to 'Windflower'
of the changed atmosphere at The Hut. In about 1926 its occupancy

passed to the Wyldes, who renamed it The Long White Cloud (the Maori name for New Zealand). Schuster borrowed back the house for the Elgar occasion. 'Windflower' was not well enough to be there. 'The Hut atmosphere has gone never to return', Elgar told her. 'Dear old Frank was radiant &, as usual, a perfect host . . . I *wish* you could have heard the things which seem to me to be of my best & the Quintet is not of this world; but you know more of this than I do.' Among the guests was Osbert Sitwell, who wrote of seeing:

> the plump wraith of Sir Edward Elgar who, with his grey moustache, grey hair, grey top hat and frock-coat looked every inch a personification of Colonel Bogey . . . In the main the audience was drawn from the famous composer's passionately devout but to me anonymous partisans here gathered for the last time . . . One could almost hear, through the music, the whirr of the wings of the Angel of Death.[II]

Sitwell's words were prophetic. On 17 December Schuster wrote to tell Elgar how impressed he had been by John Barbirolli's conducting of the Second Symphony at a concert he and 'Windflower' had attended. Nine days later he died after a short illness. Because of heavy snow, neither Elgar nor 'Windflower' could go to the funeral on the 30th at Putney Vale. He wrote to her: 'The radiant happy & sunny Frank I have before me as I write & the small temporary little irritations, which worried one at the time, are gone & forgotten forever.' In his will Schuster left Elgar £7,000 (over £200,000 at today's values) for saving Britain 'from the reproach of having produced no composer worthy to rank with the Great Masters'.

Schuster's death overshadowed the announcement of the New Year Honours. There was no peerage for Elgar. 'I am very sorry to tell you that H. M. has offered me the wretched *K.C.V.O.* (!!!) Which awful thing I must accept!', he told 'Windflower'. Just before Christmas he moved into Battenhall Manor, just outside Worcester. This was only for the winter and in the spring he rented Tiddington House on the river near Stratford-upon-Avon. At the end of October 1928 he wrote a carol, *I sing the birth*, and incidental music, again drawn from old sketchbooks, for a play by Bertram P. Matthews called *Beau Brummel*. He conducted the small pit orchestra at the Theatre Royal, Birmingham, on 5 November. He told Ivor Atkins he was thinking of setting Shelley's 'The Daemon of the World' and 'Adonais' for Worcester, but the dean thought the texts were 'unsuitable'.

He knew his music was out of fashion. It was often broadcast (Delius's wife Jelka had written to Philip Heseltine in September 1926 complaining of 'the Elgar-clique' at the BBC),[12] there were plenty of performances and he was busy recording many of his own works for HMV (he kept urging 'Windflower' to buy a gramophone and the records of 'your own symphony'). But audiences were often small and when he conducted *Gerontius* with the Hallé in Manchester, many of the audience walked out, 'passing along the base of the platform even while Sir Edward was conducting the ineffably lovely strains that herald the close', Neville Cardus reported in the *Manchester Guardian* in January 1929. At a dinner in July 1929 Elgar said: 'The character of English people musically is extremely bad; they do not care for music in the least. They follow a man for a time and then drop him.' Elgar had little interest in younger composers. As had happened with Coleridge-Taylor, he grew jealous if they succeeded financially. Arthur Bliss was one who felt the chill for this reason. Vaughan Williams suffered because of his academic connections. 'I am surprised you come to hear vulgar music like this', Elgar said to him at a performance of the Cello Concerto in Hereford. But during the mid-1920s they grew friendly and Elgar would write to 'My dear Ralph'. He was generous in his praise of *Sancta civitas*, which he heard at Worcester in 1929.

Writing to 'Windflower' to thank her for her annual gift of food at Christmas, Pollie again gave her a very different picture of Elgar from the morose self-portrait he painted in his letters: 'He . . . is so full of fun and easy – just like a boy, it does us good to have him . . . Last Wednesday we had great fun. E. took us all but Clare to the Worcester Pantomime.' It was only in such surroundings, or with orchestral players, that he could overcome his chronic insecurity. His passion for his dogs kept him from London. This meant he saw less of 'Windflower' and there are fewer letters over the next four years (there was another reason for that, as we shall see). She was moving from Cheyne Walk into a smaller house and was not always well. He invited her to Stratford: 'you wd. love it & must come sometime. I think I answered all your beautiful notes – so if anything has gone wrong it's mine! Rest assured that you know all about my music. The windflowers will soon bloom. Love. E. E.'

# 15  Vera

Old friendships persisted. He saw much of Troyte Griffith and when he helped to collect photographs of the 'friends pictured within' to illustrate a booklet about the Variations, he re-established contact with 'Ysobel' Fitton. He still wrote to Charles Buck in Yorkshire and had much affection for Ivor Atkins and the other Three Choirs organists, Herbert (John) Sumsion, who had succeeded Herbert Brewer at Gloucester in 1928, and Percy Hull, Sinclair's successor at Hereford. In his London clubs he enjoyed the company of actors, particularly Norman Forbes, brother of Sir Johnston Forbes-Robertson, and he often corresponded with Ernest Newman. But the friendship he revelled in, somewhat surprisingly, was that with Shaw, with whom he joined in a successful battle to defeat a proposed copyright law which would have drastically reduced royalties.

For the 1929 Worcester Festival he rented a house in Worcester, on Rainbow Hill, called Marl Bank, then decided to buy it. 'Windflower' went to lunch there during the festival after hearing his new orchestral accompaniment for Purcell's *Jehova, quam multi sunt hostes mei*. The only other work from 1929 was a four-part carol, *Good Morrow*, written to celebrate George V's recovery from a serious illness. This was the last work of his to be published by Novello's, with whom his relationship was now formal and frigid. He moved into Marl Bank in foul weather on 5 December, a task undertaken and supervised by Carice (some

24  Elgar with Percy Hull at a Three Choirs Festival

furniture from Severn House had been in storage for nearly ten years), and also gave up his London flat. On his first Christmas card from his new home he quoted lines by Walt Whitman beginning: 'I think I could turn and live with animals.'

Another death opened 1930. Henry Embleton of the Leeds Choral Union died on 7 February, still hoping for the third oratorio. His executors immediately demanded repayment of the £500 loan made in 1921. Coincidentally Herbert Whiteley, an editor of brass band music, offered Elgar generous terms for a piece for the twenty-fifth annual brass bands competition festival at Crystal Palace. Elgar accepted, went to old scores such as the 1878 wind quintets and produced the five-movement *Severn Suite*. He wrote a full band score but the suite as played in September 1930 was the work of a brass band expert, Henry Geehl, who orchestrated a skeleton score Elgar provided. They argued and clashed. Geehl's work was often careless. However, Elgar made no public complaint and dedicated the work to a delighted Shaw. He did not attend the competition because of pain attributed to sciatica. His health had not been good again. A few months earlier he had told 'Windflower' that 'my *ear* has failed (& is painful) after threatening for years!'

Driving in Worcestershire in June 1929 he suddenly asked his chauffeur Dick Mountford for paper. All that could be found was an Ordnance Survey map, in the margin of which Elgar pencilled a theme he had sketched fifty years earlier for the Powick asylum. He converted it into his fifth *Pomp and Circumstance* march and in May 1930 sent it to Boosey, who grudgingly offered £75 and a royalty. He ended his contract with them and next month signed up with Keith Prowse on a retainer of £250 a year for three years with no royalties provided he submitted no fewer than three songs each year. He was in pain with 'sciatica' while conducting at the Hereford Festival but went to London on 18 September to conduct the first performance of the new march in the recording studio. But he did not stay for the first public performance two days later.

Looking through old sketchbooks also gave him ideas when an HMV executive suggested that the birth in August of Princess Margaret Rose

25 First sketch of Pomp and Circumstance march no. 5, scribbled on an Ordnance Survey map, 27 June 1929

to the Duke and Duchess of York might make a subject for a new work. The result was the *Nursery Suite* of eight delightful movements, contrasts of sadness and merriment, which ranks alongside *The Wand of Youth*, with 'The Waggon Passes' as perhaps the finest movement in any of the suites and an 'Envoy' in which a solo violin recalls nostalgically earlier themes in the manner of his concerto. He dedicated it to the Duchess of York (later Queen Elizabeth the Queen Mother) and the Princesses Elizabeth and Margaret Rose. He conducted the first performance, again as an HMV recording, in the Kingsway Hall on 23 May 1931 with an extra session on 4 June which was attended by the duke and duchess with Princess Elizabeth, as well as by Shaw, Sir Landon Ronald and some of Elgar's actor friends. In between the two sessions the Birthday Honours on 2 June (his birthday, as it happened) included a baronetcy for him. He chose the title 'of Broadheath'.

Elgar would have been pleased that a young composer, C. W. Orr, wrote in 1931 that 'he, who has never worried about nationalism, is the most *national* of all our composers'. But the year was clouded by the publicity given to the entry on modern English music in the second edition of the German *Handbuch der Musikgeschichte*, in which E. J. Dent claimed that for English ears Elgar's music was 'too emotional and not quite free from vulgarity', described the chamber music as 'dry and academic' and said that Elgar 'possessed little of the literary culture of Parry and Stanford'. This drew a letter of protest to the newspapers with eighteen signatories including Shaw, Augustus John, Philip Heseltine and William Walton; and when he conducted the new BBC Symphony Orchestra in the Second Symphony in London on 2 October, the hall was full and the applause at the end overwhelming. It wiped out an old memory – 'oh, that awful first performance', he wrote to 'Windflower'. In the audience was the sixteen-year-old Benjamin Britten, who wrote in his diary: 'Elgar 2nd Symphony dreadful (nobilmente sempre) – I come out after 3rd movement – *so* bored. He conducts – ovation beforehand!!!!!!!!!'

Although the 'sciatica' abated, he developed urticaria (persistent nettle rash, an allergy) to the extent that he needed a morphine injection at 5 a.m. on one occasion. But he conducted the public première of the *Nursery Suite* at the Promenade Concerts in August and at the Gloucester Festival the following month. There was an evening at Marl Bank when his former violin pupil Frank Webb, to whom he had dedicated *Virelai* in 1883, took his son Alan and daughter-in-law for a visit. Alan, who became a distinguished curator of the Elgar Birthplace Museum, left a vivid account, written the next day:

> The maid goes to announce us and my straining ears catch the sound of his voice – jovial, and so English. He is talking to, or about, Marco . . . then Miss Grafton, his niece . . . comes down the hall to greet us, and he is following, with the familiar slow, hunch-shouldered stride . . . The forehead, with the silky white hair growing far back over it, is veined and intensely sensitive in appearance. The nose, mouth and chin are so heavy as to be almost coarse, and yet the general effect is one of outstanding distinction and refinement. It is the abrupt downward break in the curve of the nose which seems to give the whole face its character. The eyes are not big, and of no particular striking colour, and yet they are astonishingly expressive and light up now with a merry twinkle, now with a beautiful happiness at the sound of well-loved music. And they look at you directly. He blinks slightly as he talks . . . Sometimes he chuckles rather thickly behind his moustache when talking . . . He gives the impression of being intensely occupied with his own thoughts and feelings and his voice seems to come from some inner life of thought . . .[1]

On 12 November 1931 Elgar officially opened the new HMV studios in Abbey Road, St John's Wood. Pathé Pictures filmed him conducting the London Symphony Orchestra in 'Land of hope and glory'. He then continued the recording of *Falstaff* which he had begun the previous day. During the year he had revised an 1889 Sonatina for piano for his niece May Grafton. He took immense care with it, making it more subtle. It made up his first year's delivery to Keith Prowse, along with the *Nursery Suite* and a song, *It isnae me*, written for a young soprano, Joan Elwes, who had caught his fancy. His susceptibility to attractive young women was widely known. One of his household called him 'a naughty old man'. There were stories of his chasing Lalla Vandervelde round the table at The Hut and of his groping the violinist Jelly d'Arányi in a taxi. The pianist Harriet Cohen was another beautiful and vivacious woman who attracted not only Elgar but other composers. Five days before the Abbey Road occasion, Elgar had gone to Croydon, where W. H. Reed lived, to conduct a rehearsal of *Gerontius* and other works with the LSO and the excellent Croydon Philharmonic Choir, which had been trained to a high standard for over forty years by a dedicated amateur, Alan Kirby, a City stockbroker.

On the second desk of the first violins was Vera Rebecca Hockman, a dark-haired young Jewish woman, in her thirties, married to but separated from a rabbi. She played regularly in Reed's Croydon Philharmonic Orchestra and each year in the Leith Hill Festival orchestra conducted by Vaughan Williams, with whom she was on affectionate terms. She was good enough to join the LSO as a freelance at the Croydon festivals organised by its leader, Reed. Again and again at rehearsal of *Gerontius* on 7 November Elgar caught her eye and he asked to meet her afterwards. The performance was on the 10th. At the reception that followed he recounted his life story to her and said he must see her again. He wrote to her, sent her a score of his quartet and on a visit to London took her to lunch. On 3 December she went to Worcester, they played his sonata, fussed the dogs and listened to a recording of Verdi's Requiem. On the 7th they met at Vera's aunt's home at Carlton Hill. There he gave her his mother's copy of *Hyperion* and told her about Alice's attitude to Carice – 'Carice', he said, 'who is so clever but alas is buried alive in a Sussex village where there is no scope for her brains and energy, but one can do nothing for her!'[2] He decreed that the 7th of each month should be a 'mensiversary' of their first meeting because he didn't expect to live long enough for anniversaries. It was like a repetition of the anniversary he had shared with 'Windflower' of the day (also the 7th of a month) she 'saved' the Violin Concerto. Already, according to Vera's somewhat breathless account, he was calling her 'my mother, my child, my lover and my friend'. Gradually he introduced her to his friends, including Frank Schuster's

26  Vera Hockman in 1945

elderly sister Adela, but not, it seems, to 'Windflower'. She wrote down snatches of his conversation: 'I prefer good Delibes to bad Brahms, but of course you have a Royal College mind and think all light music is bad music.' Writing to her on return to Worcester on 10 December, he began his letter 'Sweetest and Dearest' and next day sent her 'all the existing sketches of your Sonata', adding after his signature on the last page: 'who only now knows why this was written'. He also built a happy friendship with Vera's schoolgirl daughter Dulcie, writing her amusing letters as he had done to Carice years before.[3]

It might have been regarded as just 'a little flutter' by those who knew Elgar's susceptibilities, but little flutters soon pass, and Vera did not. She became a close and valued friend of Carice who often picked up Vera in her car to drive to meet Elgar in London or elsewhere. She was often in Worcester and spent the whole of the Worcester Festival of 1932 at Marl Bank. She met Troyte Griffith, Ivor Atkins and other friends and was driven to see the Broadheath cottage. Friends noticed how sprightly Elgar seemed and soon there were signs that he was returning to creative life. Oddly, Vera is airbrushed out of Wulstan Atkins's book, *The Elgar–Atkins Friendship*, where she is never mentioned as a house guest at the 1932 and 1933 Three Choirs Festivals. But she was very much a member of the family party, as the home movies taken at the time and now available on video and DVD testify.

Towards the end of 1931 Elgar was approached to become associated with the new Shakespeare Memorial Theatre at Stratford-upon-Avon which was due to open in 1932. William Bridges-Adams, director of the theatre company, had met Elgar during the time he lived at Stratford. He now suggested that Elgar should write a new Falstaff overture for the opening. All went smoothly until Elgar went on 15 February 1932 to see the new theatre, designed by Elisabeth Scott. He was appalled and at once telegraphed Bridges-Adams to announce his withdrawal from the proposed festival: 'Have today seen the theatre and amazed at the abominable ugliness. It is an insult to human intelligence. I shall never visit Stratford-upon-Avon again.' He followed this with a letter describing the building as 'distressing, vulgar and abominable', and added: 'I can conceive no crime that deserves the punishment inflicted on poor Stratford and us by that awful female [Elisabeth Scott].' It is tempting to believe that Elgar used his dislike of the building as a way of withdrawing from writing a piece to which he had agreed in a moment of weakness.[4]

Some time in 1931 Shaw had lent Elgar £1,000 to help him out of financial difficulty, probably caused by the expense of repair and upkeep of Marl Bank. Although Elgar was always complaining of having no money, he lived in some style, with servants, secretary and chauffeur, and enjoyed good cigars as well as spending a fair amount of money on his favourite hobby of horse-racing, at which his capacity for picking winners was low. He boasted to 'Windflower' of having 2,000 tulips in his garden, hardly an economy. There is no doubt what Shaw meant years later when he wrote to Sir John Reith, director general of the BBC, in 1948 telling him of the loan and adding: 'Immediately he bought a car for £800 and made a present of it to Miss Clifford, his very attractive secretary . . . What he did with your donation I don't know. Probably bought a Rolls-Royce with it.'[5] In January 1932, while on a cruise, Shaw had written to Elgar: 'Why don't you make the BBC order a new symphony? It can afford it.'[6] Talk of a third symphony had been in the air for some time. Something, even if in a flippant way, must have been said at the Gloucester Festival in September 1931, because on the 9th Vaughan Williams wrote him a letter, signed by himself and seven others including the Sumsions, W. H. Reed and the composer R. O. Morris, saying: 'You said last night that owing to the badness of the Woolworth pencils you could no longer write music. We all want that new symphony & the 3rd part of The Apostles. Will these pencils of varying softness help?'[7]

But Elgar's creative work in the winter of 1931 was to score the Severn Suite for orchestra, giving the movements names with Worcester connections, such as 'Cathedral' for the Fugue. He recorded it with the LSO in April 1932. At the end of June that year, the month of Elgar's seventy-fifth birthday, Shaw returned to the fray with a light-hearted postcard: 'Why not a Financial Symphony? Allegro: Impending Disaster. Lento mesto: Stony Broke. Scherzo: Light Heart & Empty Pocket. All° con brio: Clouds Clearing.'[8] Elgar sent Shaw's postcard to Fred Gaisberg and suggested HMV might wish to commission a symphony for £5,000 (well over £150,000 at today's values). Nothing materialised. But he had written three unison or two-part songs for children to words by Charles Mackay, and an ode to words by the Poet Laureate, John Masefield, So many true princesses who have gone, for the unveiling of a statue of Queen Alexandra at Marlborough House. Elgar conducted the first

27 Elgar and his gramophone, 1929

performance of the ode on 8 June, wearing his doctor's robes over court dress.

Apart from a dinner in London, the chief event to mark his birthday was the recording of the Violin Concerto with sixteen-year-old Yehudi Menuhin, yet another attempt to persuade Kreisler to record it in Berlin with Elgar having failed. The story has often been told of how the young virtuoso and the old composer met on 12 July to go through the concerto, with Ivor Newton playing the piano. Elgar was completely satisfied, went off to Newmarket and conducted the LSO at the recording sessions on 14 and 15 July. The result was a gramophone classic. After the recording Elgar wrote to Vera: 'I do not think there is anything *quite* like it [the concerto], and some day perhaps it will be understood how much soul went into the making of it.' Test pressings were available after a month and Elgar played them at Marl Bank on 2 September to the Shaws, T. E. Lawrence (who was in the RAF as Aircraftman T. E. Shaw), Carice, the Grafton nieces and Vera, who left this description:

> Here we all sat, spellbound at the glorious sounds, GBS with head bowed, sometimes softly singing with the music; Aircraftman Shaw serious and silent, looking straight ahead with those unforgettable blue eyes . . . After Menuhin had lovingly lingered over the last melting phrase of the slow movement, E. E. whispered: 'This is where two souls merge and melt into one another.'[9]

That lingering was to be criticised by Ernest Newman in the *Sunday Times* after Menuhin played the concerto in public in the Albert Hall on 20 November 1932 with Elgar and the LSO ('I have never felt such a reading as you gave it, with such a thrill of expression', Elgar wrote to Menuhin next day). Newman wrote that Menuhin played it too beautifully and sounded too rich and sensuous, robbing the work of its 'English reserve and austerity'. Elgar wrote to Neville Cardus, of the *Manchester Guardian*: 'This is how I heard the slow movement when I was composing it. Why does Ernest Newman object that Menuhin makes the second subject of the first movement lovely & luscious – it is a lovely and luscious theme, isn't it? Austerity be damned! I am not an austere man, am I?'[10] In a letter to Novello's a few days after the recording was made, Elgar described Menuhin as 'the most wonderful artist I have ever heard'.

At the 1932 Worcester Festival Elgar conducted *The Dream of Gerontius*, *The Music Makers*, 'For the Fallen', the First Symphony and the *Severn Suite*

28  Elgar with Yehudi Menuhin and Sir Thomas Beecham, 1932

(orchestral version). He also heard Walton's Viola Concerto and hated it (but he had earlier enjoyed and formed a high opinion of Constant Lambert's The Rio Grande, as he told its composer in a letter in October 1931). He was by now enthusiastic about composing an opera, The Spanish Lady, to be based on Ben Jonson's The Devil is an Ass, with Barry Jackson, director of the Malvern Festival and of Birmingham Repertory Theatre, as librettist. He raided old sketchbooks for ideas and was determined it was to be 'Grand Opera on the biggest scale'. W. H. Reed was drawn a plan of the stage, shown all the 'properties' and exactly where the characters were to stand, 'but', he wrote, 'if I am ever asked what it was all about, I shall have to confess that I have not the faintest idea and never had'.[11]

The opera project receded after 30 September 1932 when Shaw wrote to Sir John Reith urging him to commission the Third Symphony, adding: 'I know that he has the material for the first movement ready because he has played it to me on his piano.'[12] With Landon Ronald negotiating in the background, a contract was signed in December whereby Elgar was to receive £250 a quarter while the work was in progress, with a separate payment of £1,000 on completion. Elgar was still very cagey about the project, but he had made a start. He began to sketch the first movement, opening with a theme intended for the third oratorio, The Last Judgement, and the second subject was a new idea, a cantabile melody against which he wrote: 'V. H.'s own theme'. Earlier he would have called it 'windflowerish'. To mark Elgar's seventy-fifth birthday, the BBC gave three concerts of his music, conducted by Elgar and Boult, on 30 November and 7 and 14 December. At a Guildhall dinner after the final concert, Ronald announced the symphony commission. Elgar was not at the dinner, preferring to join Carice and Vera at Vera's home Robin Hill, at Pine Coombe, near Croydon. Next day Gaisberg wrote to suggest a recording 'immediately before or after' the first performance, which was scheduled for autumn 1933. At New Year Elgar sent Vera some sketches of the first movement with the message: 'First thought for Sym. III and last thought for V. H. Jany 1933. E. E. Or rather, 31st Dec. 1932.' On the first sketch of her own theme he wrote: 'Will never be finished!'

Reed went to Marl Bank in February to play through sketches. Elgar had written themes for the second movement, borrowed from *Arthur*, and for the Adagio and Finale, drawing on themes written for *The Last Judgement* and for the setting of Arnold's 'Callicles' which he had thought about in 1926. But Reed noted he was restless and ill at ease and would soon break off work to take the dogs for a walk. After receiving the first quarterly cheque, he told Reith he was satisfied with progress and that the symphony was 'the *strongest* thing I have put on paper'. But there was no Alice to organise his life so that his music took precedence over more tempting diversions.

His obsession with his dogs Marco and Mina dominated his life. A place was set for them at table. The diarist James Lees-Milne remembered a dinner at Brooks's club when Elgar was interrupted by 'an urgent telephone call'. The hall porter told him: 'They are on the line now, Sir Edward.' Lees-Milne could hear barking coming over the phone and Elgar saying: 'Don't bite the cushions.' At Christmas 1932 all his friends received a card containing an embarrassing fable he had written about the creation of a puppy by the 'Maker-of-All'.

He told Adela Schuster on 17 March 1933 that he was 'working hard at new things'. It was in this letter that he mentioned being

in a maze regarding events in Germany – what are they doing? In this morning's paper it is said that the greatest conductor Bruno Walter &, stranger even, Einstein are ostracised: are we all mad? The Jews have always been my best & kindest friends – the pain of these news is unbearable & I do not know what it really means.

On 21 April the BBC suggested 18 October for the first performance of the symphony, which meant that 'parts and score would have to be ready by the end of September at the latest'. Elgar took fright and the BBC fixed on May 1934 instead. He told them it was in C minor and listed the four movements, although he was not yet sure if the Adagio would

29  Elgar with Carice, Marco and Mina at Marl Bank

come second or third. On 25 April he had a kind of seizure and Carice
had to send for the doctor three times in the course of the evening. He
did not mention his illness in a letter to 'Windflower' on 27 April, the
last he was to write to her. She was not well and had been unable to go
to the Worcester Festival in 1932. His letter ends, poignantly: 'I could
not get out to gather windflowers and now they are over – I believe my
sister sent some: she can grow them in her garden & I cannot, alas!' But

a week later, when he was in London, he played 'Windflower' parts of the opera and symphony, conducted *The Apostles* in Croydon on 6 May and on the 11th wrote to Keith Prowse that he hoped to send portions of the full score of the symphony 'very shortly'. On 28 May he made his first flight, from Croydon to Paris where he was to conduct the Violin Concerto on the 31st with Menuhin. He had had 'another bad turn' the night before the flight, but soon recovered. He completed a crossword puzzle during the flight. The French president attended the performance, the concerto's first in France, but it was coolly received by French critics. During his visit, on 30 May, Elgar went to Grez-sur-Loing to visit the paralysed Frederick Delius. They discovered they had much more in common than they had thought. Elgar took him new recordings of Sibelius and of Hugo Wolf. He flew home on 2 June, his seventy-sixth birthday. In the next day's Honours List he was appointed G.C.V.O. but missed the investiture because of a chill and the decoration was sent to him.

Work on the symphony continued throughout the exceptionally hot summer of 1933. He played his sketches to visitors, including Basil Maine, whose two-volume biography was published that spring. Maine received little idea of the conception as a whole:

> He relied partly on the sketches (so disjointed and disordered as to
> be a kind of jigsaw puzzle), partly on memory, partly I imagine on
> extemporisation . . . The experience was so clouded and so fleeting that
> it could not possibly be recaptured by the means of the sketches alone. It
> is my conviction that . . . the last revealing light had not yet broken upon
> his mind. Or, if it had, it broke when he lacked the physical strength to
> set down the signs.[13]

He played parts of all four movements to Gaisberg on 27 August, who believed that scoring was 'well advanced'. Mary Clifford told Gaisberg that Elgar had recently preferred to work on the opera.

Elgar conducted the Second Symphony at the Proms on 17 August, seated in a chair. A critic who went to see him afterwards found his voice weak and his hands trembling. 'He had also lost a lot of weight . . . He

30  Elgar at Marl Bank, 1933

seemed to have shrunk to half the size.'¹⁴ On 29 August he recorded his Serenade for strings and *Elegy* in Kingsway Hall, and he conducted *Gerontius* at the Hereford Festival (he had also conducted it in Manchester the previous January). He entertained as usual at the festival, with Carice and Vera, the Shaws and Billy Reed part of the close circle. Carice thought he was full of vitality, but 'I felt so sure that we were doing things for the last time.'¹⁵ He had another bad attack of 'sciatic pain' in late September and on 8 October underwent an operation under local anaesthetic in South Bank nursing home in Worcester. This revealed inoperable cancer. He was not told, but he divined the truth. The consultant Arthur Thomson from Birmingham went to see him. 'After all his years of worrying over imagined troubles', Thomson wrote, 'he displayed magnificent courage . . . He told me that he had no faith whatever in an afterlife: "I believe there is nothing but complete oblivion".'¹⁶

In great pain, he still dictated letters. To his old friend Florence Norbury he wrote on 14 October: 'it is a miserable business – I lie here hour after hour thinking of our beloved Teme – surely the most beautiful river that ever was and it belongs to you too – I love it more than any other.' He told Carice that he wanted his ashes to be buried in unconsecrated ground at the confluence of the Teme and Severn.

Concerned about the symphony, some BBC officials asked Elgar's doctors if anything could be done to relieve his pain and yet leave his mind clear to compose. Cutting the spinal cord was one suggestion, but Elgar refused to contemplate such a procedure. He had a relapse in mid-November and Carice sent for Reed. It was then, according to Reed, that Elgar asked him not to let anyone 'tinker' with the symphony and that perhaps it would be better to burn it. Reed did not think that was necessary, but assured him 'no one shall ever tinker with it'.¹⁷ After a visit from Ernest Newman on 20 December, Elgar sent him the introductory bars of the slow movement, adding: 'I am fond enough to believe that the first two bars (with the F♯ in the bass) open some vast bronze doors into something strangely unfamiliar. I have added the four final bars of this movement. I think and hope you may like the unresolved *estinto* of the viola solo.'¹⁸

He had visits from Granville Bantock and Basil Maine. Delius wrote to him and sent him barley sugar made by nuns. Elgar wrote to Delius on Christmas Day 1933:

> It has been a matter of no small amusement to me that, as my name is indissolubly connected with 'sacred' music, some of your friends and mine have tried to make me believe that I am ill-disposed to the trend and sympathy of your great work. Nothing could be further from the real state of the case. I admire your work intensely and salute the genius displayed in it.

Gaisberg took him records of the three chamber works and Elgar played them again and again, weeping during the slow movement of the Piano Quintet. In December he asked Gaisberg to bring a photographer to the nursing home and four photographs were taken. 'Windflower' did not visit him; she was not well enough to travel, but Pollie Grafton and Carice kept her informed of his progress. We do not know if Vera visited him: Carice did not keep a diary while she nursed her father and all letters between Elgar and Vera were later destroyed.

On 3 January 1934 Elgar was taken home to Marl Bank. He was nursed by Kathleen Harrison, who had looked after him at the nursing home. He had frequent injections of morphine to deaden the pain. Gaisberg suggested that Elgar should supervise by telephone a recording session at Abbey Road of extracts from *Caractacus* conducted by Lawrance Collingwood. This was arranged for 22 January but in the morning Elgar was drowsy. In the afternoon he rallied, talked to the LSO, criticised the tempo of the Triumphal March and asked for the Woodland Interlude to be repeated twice – 'I want it very much lighter and a slower tempo.' The effort weakened him. Six days later Carice told Newman that he was 'very drowsy and muddled . . . he is greatly living in the most extraordinary dreams'. In a radio interview towards the end of her own life, Kathleen Harrison recalled how he would ask: 'What are they playing?' Told there was no music, he said: 'It's in this silly old head of mine, of course you can't hear it.' She added: 'He said

31 Elgar at South Bank nursing home, Worcester, 12 December 1933, with Carice and Fred Gaisberg

something about a little girl, but he didn't have a little girl, he only had Mrs Blake.'[19]

Newman visited him on 5 February, when, as he revealed twenty-one years later, 'he made a single short remark about himself which I have never disclosed to anyone and have no intention of ever disclosing'.[20] Carice wrote three days later to 'Windflower' that her father 'was very confused' and he and Newman 'had really no proper talk'. 'Windflower' had sent a diary at Christmas as usual. 'I do not think he has even realised it', Carice told her. On 8 February Pollie wrote to 'Windflower':

> My heart is broken. Our dearest Edward is oh so ill . . . Sometimes he knows them and sometimes not. I went on Sunday evening to see him and struck a good moment. I sat by the bed quietly, then he woke up and saw me & said 'Well Beak it is nice to see you again'. He always called me Beak, I don't know why; I sat and talked a bit and *held* and *stroked* his lovely hands and he was quite sensible who it was . . . I am broken down and am sure you will be. I wish you could see him lying there, for I know you love him.

Either at the nursing home or at Marl Bank, Father Valentine Elwes, son of the tenor Gervase Elwes, called to see him but on Elgar's orders was turned away. This Gerontius wanted no priest to tell him to go forth upon his journey. Hubert Leicester's son, Philip, a devout Catholic, was horrified to hear of Elgar's wish to be cremated and for his ashes to be scattered at the confluence of the Teme and Severn. Carice was commandeered to persuade Elgar that he should be buried beside Alice in Little Malvern. He wrote what he wanted to be added on her headstone: 'In memory of the above-named Edward Elgar.' Against the doctor's advice, Carice and the Leicesters summoned Father Reginald Gibb from St George's church, who 'ministered to him such sacraments as he could receive'.[21] Kathleen Harrison 'never knew that he was a Roman Catholic, although I nursed him for three months in South Bank'. She was with him when he died in the early morning of 23 February. 'He just died. He didn't say anything, he was unconscious with the drugs. I used to go every day and arrange the flowers in his room after he died.'

The cottage at Broadheath was bought by Worcester Corporation in May 1935 and opened as a permanent museum in 1938, with Carice as its first curator. She and Vera remained friends. In 1935 Vera began to live with a double bass player, C. H. ('Don') Cheeseman. (Her husband lived until 1942.) She developed Parkinson's disease soon after the Second World War and died in March 1968. 'Windflower' died on New Year's Day 1936, Pollie Grafton later in the same year. The windflowers bloomed unpicked.

NOTES

PROLOGUE

1. William Henry Reed, *Elgar as I Knew Him* (London, 1936), pp. 140–1.
2. Letter to Alice Stuart Wortley, 29 August 1912.
3. Peter J. Pirie, 'World's End', *Music Review* 18 (1957), p. 89.


1 'BOYHOOD'S DAZE'

1. Elgar to Mr and Mrs Alan Webb, 13 January 1931 (notes made afterwards by Alan Webb, now at Elgar Birthplace Museum).
2. Worcester Papers, no. 6, 18 September 1852 (MS at Elgar Birthplace Museum).
3. MS note by Philip Leicester of a conversation between Hubert Leicester and Fr Driscoll SJ, 28 November 1909. See Jerrold Northrop Moore, *Edward Elgar: A Creative Life* (Oxford, 1984), p. 17.
4. Lucy Elgar Pipe, 'Reflections', 1912 (MS at Hereford and Worcester Records Office, henceforward HWRO).
5. Letter from Elgar to Alice Stuart Wortley, 13 November 1914.
6. MS notes by Carice Elgar Blake, Elgar's daughter, c.1935 (HWRO).
7. William Henry Reed, *Elgar as I Knew Him* (London, 1936), p. 45.

8. Draft preface to a collection of children's piano pieces (MS at Elgar Birthplace Museum).

9. Typewritten notes by Carice Elgar Blake of a conversation with Hubert Leicester (Elgar Birthplace Museum).

10. 'Reflections'.

11. Hubert Leicester, newspaper article of 1934. See Moore, *A Creative Life*, p. 27.

12. MS notes by Carice Elgar Blake, *c*.1935 (HWRO).

13. Letter from Elgar to Sir Sidney Colvin, 13 December 1921.

14. Typewritten notes by Carice Elgar Blake of a conversation with Hubert Leicester (Elgar Birthplace Museum).

15. MS note by Philip Leicester of a conversation between Hubert Leicester and Fr Driscoll SJ, 28 November 1909. See Moore, *A Creative Life*, p. 39.

16. Robert J. Buckley, *Sir Edward Elgar* (London, 1905), pp. 12–13.

17. Edward Wulstan Atkins, *The Elgar–Atkins Friendship* (London, 1984), p. 471.

18. Article by Philip Leicester submitted to the *Musical Times* in 1921 (typescript at Elgar Birthplace Museum).

19. Reed, *Elgar as I Knew Him*, p. 86.

20. Elgar's draft notes for gramophone records of *The Wand of Youth*, 1929 (HWRO).

21. Draft programme note for *The Wand of Youth* suite no. 2 (in the possession of Jerrold Northrop Moore).

22. Atkins, *The Elgar–Atkins Friendship*, p. 474.

23. Elgar in interview in the *Strand Magazine*, May 1904, p. 540.

24. Atkins, *The Elgar–Atkins Friendship*, p. 472.

25. Compton Mackenzie broadcast talk, 'The Fifteenth Variation', 1957, in which he recalled a conversation with Elgar.

2 HELEN

1. Edward Wulstan Atkins, *The Elgar–Atkins Friendship* (London, 1984), pp. 474–5.

2. MS note by Philip Leicester of a conversation between Hubert Leicester and Fr Driscoll SJ, 28 November 1909. See Moore, *A Creative Life*, p. 71.
3. Interview in the *Strand Magazine*, May 1904, p. 540.
4. MS draft of a speech by Elgar at an HMV reception in London, 16 November 1927 (Elgar Birthplace Museum).
5. Edward Elgar, 'My Visit to Delius', *Daily Telegraph*, 1 July 1933.
6. Edward Elgar, 'The College Hall', *Three Pears Magazine*, 1931.
7. William Reginald Mitchell, *Mr Elgar and Dr Buck: A Musical Friendship* (Settle, Yorkshire, 1991), p. 9.
8. Letter to Charles Buck, 1 July 1883.
9. Atkins, *The Elgar–Atkins Friendship*, p. 478.
10. *Ibid.*, p. 477.
11. *Sunday Times*, 18 November 1956.
12. *Sunday Times*, 6 November 1955.
13. Elgar's notes for the Aeolian Company's 'Duo-Art' pianola rolls of the Variations (1929), reprinted in Elgar's *My Friends Pictured Within* (London, 1949).


3   ALICE

1. Elgar did not complete and publish the song until 1908.
2. Letter to F. G. Edwards, 19 September 1900.
3. Elgar's diaries are held at HWRO.
4. Edward Wulstan Atkins, *The Elgar–Atkins Friendship* (London, 1984), p. 26.
5. *Ibid.*
6. Mrs Richard C. Powell, *Edward Elgar: Memories of a Variation* (London, 1994), p. 125.
7. Joseph Macleod, *The Sisters d'Arányi* (London, 1969), p. 118.
8. Alice Elgar's diaries are held at the Barber Fine Art and Music Library, University of Birmingham.
9. Rosa Burley and Frank C. Carruthers, *Edward Elgar: The Record of a Friendship* (London, 1972).

10. *Ibid.*, p. 26.
11. *Ibid.*, p. 70.
12. *Ibid.*, p. 30.
13. Kevin Allen, *Elgar in Love* (Malvern, 2000), p. 39.
14. 'Dear Carice . . . Postcards from Edward Elgar to His Daughter' (Elgar Birthplace Museum).
15. Burley and Carruthers, *The Record of a Friendship*, p. 89.
16. Robert J. Buckley, *Sir Edward Elgar* (London, 1905), pp. 29–30.
17. Burley and Carruthers, *The Record of a Friendship*, pp. 87–8.
18. Reginald Nettel, *Ordeal by Music* (Oxford, 1945), pp. 11–12.
19. Letter of 31 October 1896 (HWRO).
20. Jerrold Northrop Moore, *Edward Elgar: A Creative Life* (Oxford, 1984), p. 218 and note.

### 4 CARACTACUS

1. Jerrold Northrop Moore, sleeve-note for EMI Classics CDM 5 65108 2 (1987).
2. An excellent detailed account of the Elgars' Bavarian holidays is Peter Greaves's *In the Bavarian Highlands: Edward Elgar's German Holidays in the 1890s* (Rickmansworth, 2000).
3. Sir Adrian Boult recalled that Manns every day for a week played a work 'which he variously called Rondo in F, Symphonic Sketch, etc. etc. by Richard Strauss. Finally, on the Saturday afternoon, he announced the first performance in London of Strauss's *Till Eulenspiegel*. That is one way of solving the rehearsal problem!' (*Proceedings of the Royal Musical Association*, session 49, 1923, pp. 50–1).
4. Florence Fidler, *Musical Standard*, 29 November 1902, p. 334.
5. Letter to Jaeger, 11 July 1900.
6. Lecture given at Birmingham University on 1 November 1906, reprinted in P. M. Young (ed.), *'A Future for English Music' and Other Lectures by Edward Elgar* (London, 1968), p. 243.
7. Simon Mundy, *Elgar* (London, 2001), pp. 59–60.

8. Mrs Gertrude Sutcliffe in a letter to Roger Fiske, dated 9 December 1948, published in the *Gramophone*, July 1957, p. 54.
9. Rosa Burley and Frank C. Carruthers, *Edward Elgar: The Record of a Friendship* (London, 1972), p. 115.

5  ENIGMA

1. James Aikman Forsyth, 'Edward Elgar: True Artist and True Friend', *Music Student* 12 (December 1932), p. 243, and Basil Maine, *Elgar, His Life and Works* (London, 1933), vol. II, p. 101.
2. Mrs Richard C. Powell, *Edward Elgar: Memories of a Variation* (London, 1994), pp. 23–4.
3. Programme note for the first performance on 19 June 1899 by C. A. Barry, quoted in Jerrold Northrop Moore, *Edward Elgar: A Creative Life* (Oxford, 1984), pp. 269–70.
4. Rolf Clark, *'Elgar and the Three Cathedral Organists' and Other Essays* (Oxford, 2002), p. 71.
5. Julian Rushton, *Elgar: 'Enigma' Variations* (Cambridge, 1999), p. 14.
6. Ibid., pp. 58–9.
7. Letter held in Novello's archives.
8. Barry's letters to Elgar are held at HWRO.
9. Moore, *A Creative Life*, pp. 269–70.
10. Elgar's notes for the Aeolian Company's 'Duo-Art' pianola rolls of the Variations (1929), reprinted in Elgar's *My Friends Pictured Within* (London, 1949).
11. The Variations were played at the end of the first half. The concert began with Dvořák's *Carnival* overture, Svendsen's *Legend* (*Zorahayda*) and the closing scene from *Götterdämmerung* sung by Marie Brema. After the interval came a suite from Rimsky-Korsakov's *The Snow Maiden* and Mozart's Symphony no. 38 (Prague).
12. Letter of 23 June [1899] (HWRO).
13. Edward Wulstan Atkins, *The Elgar–Atkins Friendship* (London, 1984), pp. 39–40.

14. Powell, *Memories of a Variation*, pp. 133–4.
15. William Henry Reed, *Elgar as I Knew Him* (London, 1936), p. 155.

### 6 'THE BEST OF ME'

1. Myrrha Bantock, *Granville Bantock: A Personal Portrait* (London, 1972), pp. 47–8.
2. Rosa Burley and Frank C. Carruthers, *Edward Elgar: The Record of a Friendship* (London, 1972), pp. 145–6.
3. Mrs Richard C. Powell, *Edward Elgar: Memories of a Variation* (London, 1994), pp. 35–7.
4. Jerrold Northrop Moore (ed.), *Edward Elgar: Letters of a Lifetime* (Oxford, 1990), pp. 91–2.
5. Letter held at HWRO.
6. Powell, *Memories of a Variation*, p. 47.
7. Henry Wood, *My Life of Music* (London, 1938), p. 154.
8. Omitting pp. 68–94, 112–55 and 163–4 of the vocal score.

### 7 DARKNESS AT NOON

1. Lewis Foreman (ed.), *'Farewell, My Youth' and Other Writings by Arnold Bax* (Aldershot, 1992), pp. 23–4.
2. *Sunday Times*, 30 October 1955.
3. It is often said that it was a lunch, but Alice, writing to Elgar's sister Dot on 21 May, says: 'Last evening there was a great Fest Supper, R. Strauss made a beautiful speech' (letter at HWRO).
4. *The Times*, 23 May 1902.
5. Elgar believed that the trouble was caused by the Reverend Edward Vine Hall, who had criticised the libretto of *The Light of Life* in 1896 and now wanted to stop *Gerontius*.
6. Rupert Hart-Davis (ed.), *Siegfried Sassoon Diaries 1920–1922* (London, 1981), pp. 293–4.
7. Mrs Richard C. Powell, *Edward Elgar: Memories of a Variation* (London, 1994), p. 73.

8. Maud Warrender, My First Sixty Years (London, 1933), p. 188.

9. Letter of 17 July 1903.

10. Letter of 22 October 1903 (Elgar Birthplace Museum).

11. Diana McVeagh, 'A Man's Attitude to Life', in Raymond Monk (ed.), Edward Elgar: Music and Literature (Aldershot, 1993), pp. 1–9.

12. Byron Adams, 'The "Dark Saying" of the Enigma: Homoeroticism and the Elgarian Paradox', Nineteenth-Century Music 23/3 (2000), pp. 218–35.

13. Interview with Miller Ular, Chicago Sunday Examiner, 7 April 1907.

14. Henry Wood, My Life of Music (London, 1938), p. 179.

8    THE LAST ORATORIO

1. Kevin Allen, August Jaeger: Portrait of Nimrod (Aldershot, 2000), p. 175.

2. Rosa Burley and Frank C. Carruthers, Edward Elgar: The Record of a Friendship (London, 1972), p. 183.

3. Jerrold Northrop Moore, Edward Elgar: A Creative Life (Oxford, 1984), p. 463.

4. Arthur Christopher Benson, MS diary at Magdalene College, Cambridge, quoted in Moore, A Creative Life, p. 513.

9    SYMPHONY

1. Interview in the Chicago Inter-Ocean, 7 April 1907.

2. Arthur Christopher Benson, MS diary at Magdalene College, Cambridge, quoted in Jerrold Northrop Moore, Edward Elgar: A Creative Life (Oxford, 1984), p. 526.

3. Jerrold Northrop Moore, Edward Elgar: A Creative Life (Oxford, 1984), p. 527.

4. Letter held at HWRO.

5. Letter to G. H. Morley, 28 August 1909 (HWRO).

6. William Henry Reed, Elgar (London, 1939), p. 97.

7. Kevin Allen, *August Jaeger: Portrait of Nimrod* (Aldershot, 2000), p. 256.
8. *Ibid.*, p. 253.
9. *Ibid.*, pp. 257–8.
10. *Ibid.*, p. 260.
11. *Musical Standard*, 9 January 1909.

### 10  WINDFLOWER

1. Jerrold Northrop Moore (ed.), *The Windflower Letters* (Oxford, 1989).
2. Letter in the author's possession.
3. 'Nemorosa' means 'of the wood'. Elgar later wrote a description of the flower (in the Birthplace Museum). Part of it reads: 'The little group of anemones commonly called windflowers are happily named, too, for when the east wind rasps over the ground in March and April they merely turn their backs and bow before the squall.' Every year Elgar picked the first windflowers he found growing and enclosed them in letters to Mrs Stuart Wortley. Their dried remains can poignantly still be found in some of the letters.
4. Moore (ed.), *The Windflower Letters*, p. 47.
5. Letter in the possession of Raymond Monk.
6. Sanford Terry MS notes held by the Athenaeum club.

### 11  SECOND SYMPHONY

1. Sanford Terry MS notes held by the Athenaeum club.
2. William Henry Reed, *Elgar* (London, 1939), p. 105.
3. *Musical Standard*, 27 May 1911.
4. Rosa Burley and Frank C. Carruthers, *Edward Elgar: The Record of a Friendship* (London, 1972), pp. 191–2.
5. William Henry Reed, *Elgar as I Knew Him* (London, 1936), p. 49.
6. Robert Anderson, *Elgar and Chivalry* (Rickmansworth, 2002), p. 311.

7. Introductory note sent to Ernest Newman at the time of the first performance (now at Elgar Birthplace Museum).
8. Letter of 18 October 1910 (in the author's possession).
9. Letter of 14 August 1912.
10. Percy M. Young, *Alice Elgar, Enigma of a Victorian Lady* (London, 1978), p. 171.
11. *Nation*, October 1913.
12. *Daily Citizen*, 18 July 1913.

### 12 'FOR THE FALLEN'

1. Jerrold Northrop Moore (ed.), *Edward Elgar: Letters of a Lifetime* (Oxford, 1990), p. 288.
2. Ibid., p. 290.
3. Jerrold Northrop Moore, *Edward Elgar: A Creative Life* (Oxford, 1984), pp. 685–6.
4. Brian Trowell, 'The Road to Brinkwells', in Lewis Foreman (ed.), *Oh My Horses! Elgar and the Great War* (Rickmansworth, 2001), p. 382.
5. *Music Student*, August 1916, p. 358.
6. Trowell, 'The Road to Brinkwells', pp. 355–61.
7. Moore (ed.), *Letters of a Lifetime*, p. 313.
8. Letter to 'Windflower', 1 November 1917.
9. Rosa Burley and Frank C. Carruthers, *Edward Elgar: The Record of a Friendship* (London, 1972), p. 199.
10. The most likely explanation is that the recurrent tonsillitis led to repeated inner ear infections, and that these were the cause of his temporary deafness, rather than Menière's disease.

### 13 BRINKWELLS

1. MS reminiscences of Elgar by Arthur Troyte Griffith (Elgar Birthplace Museum).
2. Arthur Bliss, *As I Remember* (London, 1970, rev. 1989), p. 24.
3. Percy M. Young, *Elgar O.M.* (London, 1950), p. 260.
4. Letter to 'Windflower', 5 March 1917.

## 14  POST MORTEM

1. Letter of 22 October 1920.
2. Rupert Hart-Davis (ed.), *Siegfried Sassoon Diaries 1923–1925* (London, 1985), p. 283.
3. Letter of 15 August 1904, quoted in Jerrold Northrop Moore (ed.), *Edward Elgar: Letters of a Lifetime* (Oxford, 1990), p. 155.
4. Hart-Davis (ed.), *Sassoon Diaries 1923–1925*, pp. 151–2.
5. Moore (ed.), *Letters of a Lifetime*, p. 383.
6. Hart-Davis (ed.), *Sassoon Diaries 1923–1925*, p. 153.
7. Edward Wulstan Atkins, *The Elgar–Atkins Friendship* (London, 1984), p. 393.
8. The programme was the Fantasia and Fugue (Bach, arr. Elgar), Enigma Variations, Cello Concerto (soloist Beatrice Harrison), *Falstaff* and *In the South*.
9. Jerrold Northrop Moore, *Edward Elgar: A Creative Life* (Oxford, 1984), p. 773.
10. These historic performances are available on CD in EMI's 'The Elgar Edition', vol. 1.
11. Osbert Sitwell, *Laughter in the Next Room* (London, 1949), pp. 196–7.
12. Lionel Carley, *Delius, a Life in Letters, 1909–1934* (London, 1988), p. 311.

## 15  VERA

1. MS dated 13 January 1931 (Elgar Birthplace Museum).
2. Vera Hockman, 'The Story of November 7th 1931', in Kevin Allen, *Elgar in Love* (Malvern, 2000), p. 41.
3. Allen, *Elgar in Love*, p. 75.
4. David Bury, *'Elgar and the Awful Female' and Other Essays* (Rickmansworth, 2003) gives a full account of this episode (p. 75).
5. Allen, *Elgar in Love*, p. 118.
6. Percy M. Young (ed.), *Letters of Edward Elgar and Other Writings* (London, 1956), p. 334.

7. Jerrold Northrop Moore (ed.), *Edward Elgar: Letters of a Lifetime* (Oxford, 1990), p. 440.

8. Jerrold Northrop Moore, *Edward Elgar: A Creative Life* (Oxford, 1984), p. 796.

9. Hockman, 'The Story of November 7th 1931', in Allen, *Elgar in Love*, p. 75.

10. Humphrey Burton, *Menuhin: A Life* (London, 2000), p. 134.

11. William Henry Reed, *Elgar as I Knew Him* (London, 1936), pp. 91–2.

12. Sir John Reith, *Into the Wind* (London, 1949), p. 163.

13. *World Radio*, 1934.

14. *Evening Standard*, 23 February 1934.

15. Letter to Clare Stuart Wortley, 16 March 1934 (Elgar Birthplace Museum).

16. Moore, *A Creative Life*, p. 818.

17. Reed, *Elgar as I Knew Him*, pp. 113–15.

18. After Elgar's death the sketches were placed in the British Museum (later Library) where they remained untouched for over fifty years until Anthony Payne reconstructed them to make a whole (first performed in February 1998) that is as convincingly Elgarian as anything could be without being completed by Elgar himself.

19. Kathleen Harrison, 'Memories of Elgar', transcribed in Allen, *Elgar in Love*, pp. 130–4.

20. In a letter to an unidentified correspondent ('Dear Madam') dated 12 August 1935 Newman answered the suggestion that he should write a book about 'the real Elgar' with the words: 'I saw a good deal of Elgar during his last illness and he was such a pathetic figure that I can only think with love about him and brood over him: the thought of treating him as a literary "subject" is abhorrent to me at present' (letter in the possession of Raymond Monk). At Elgar's suggestion, Newman had been approached before Basil Maine to write his biography but refused. He explained to Gerald Abraham some years later: 'I doubt whether the public has a right

to know certain things about the lives of great men . . . I turn an increasingly tolerant eye on the attempts of the inner circle to hide some things from the public gaze' (letter quoted in the *Listener*, 23 July 1959).

21. 'Fr. Reginald Gibb', in *Our Dead: Memories of the English Jesuits Who Died between June 1909 and December 1945* (n.p., 1947–8), p. 241.

The most comprehensive biography of Elgar is Jerrold Northrop Moore's *Edward Elgar: A Creative Life* (Oxford, 1984). It is the fruit of many years' research and covers every aspect of the composer's personal and public life. Moore has also edited all Elgar's letters in a series of volumes: *Elgar on Record* (London, 1974), *Elgar and His Publishers*, 2 vols. (Oxford, 1987), *The Windflower Letters* (Oxford, 1989) and *Edward Elgar: Letters of a Lifetime* (Oxford, 1990). He has also edited *Elgar: A Life in Pictures* (London, 1972) and has written an excellent shorter biography *Spirit of England: Edward Elgar in His World* (London, 1984). Other useful documentary volumes, all edited by Percy M. Young, are *Letters of Edward Elgar and Other Writings* (London, 1956), *Letters to Nimrod from Edward Elgar* (London, 1965) and *'A Future for English Music' and Other Lectures by Edward Elgar* (London, 1968). The last-named gives the texts and drafts of the 1905–6 Birmingham lectures.

Reminiscences by people who knew Elgar are W. H. Reed's *Elgar as I Knew Him* (London, 1936, 2nd edn 1978), Mrs Richard C. Powell's *Edward Elgar: Memories of a Variation* (London, 1937, 2nd edn 1947, 3rd edn 1979, rev. 1994), Rosa Burley and Frank C. Carruthers's *Edward Elgar: The Record of a Friendship* (London, 1972) and E. Wulstan Atkins's *The Elgar–Atkins Friendship* (London, 1984).

The earliest biographies, still worth reading, are Robert J. Buckley's *Sir Edward Elgar* (London, 1905) and Ernest Newman's *Elgar* (London,

1906). Also published in Elgar's lifetime was Basil Maine's Elgar: His Life and Works, 2 vols. (London, 1933, rev. 1973). Since his death biographical studies have included W. H. Reed's Elgar (London, 1939), Diana McVeagh's Edward Elgar: His Life and Music (London, 1955), Percy M. Young's Elgar O.M. (London, 1956, 2nd edn 1973), the present writer's Portrait of Elgar (Oxford, 1968, 2nd edn 1982, 3rd edn 1987), Michael Hurd's Elgar (London, 1969), Simon Mundy's Elgar (London, 1980, rev. 2001) and Robert Anderson's Elgar (London, 1993). Diana McVeagh wrote the entry on Elgar for the New Grove Dictionary of Music and Musicians, vol. VI (London, 1980 and 1981), and for the second edition, vol. VIII (London, 2001).

Of special interest are two books edited by Raymond Monk: Elgar Studies (Aldershot, 1990), with essays by eleven contributors, and Edward Elgar: Music and Literature (Aldershot, 1993), with essays by ten contributors. Robert Anderson's Elgar in Manuscript (London, 1990) examines the origins of the major works and his Elgar and Chivalry, published by Elgar Editions (Rickmansworth, 2002), looks in detail at the ceremonial works and incidental music. Two other volumes published by Elgar Editions are indispensable: The Best of Me: A Gerontius Centenary Companion, edited by Geoffrey Hodgkins (Rickmansworth, 1999), and Oh, My Horses! Elgar and the Great War, edited by Lewis Foreman (Rickmansworth, 2001).

A series of monographs, many of them inaugurated by the Elgar Society, others individual efforts, are well worth the researcher's attention and will give pleasure to the general reader. These include Elgar Country by Barry Collett (London, 1981), Elgar Lived Here by Pauline Collett (London, 1981), The Thirteenth Enigma? The Story of Elgar's Early Love by Cora Weaver (London, 1988), Mr Elgar and Dr Buck: A Musical Friendship by W. R. Mitchell (Settle, Yorkshire, 1991), In the Bavarian Highlands: Edward Elgar's German Holidays in the 1890s by Peter Greaves (Rickmansworth, 2000) and 'Elgar and the Awful Female' and Other Essays by David Bury (Rickmansworth, 2003). There is special illumination in Rolf Clark's 'Elgar and the Three Cathedral Organists' and Other Essays (Oxford, 2002).

One work, the Enigma Variations, has two books to itself: *Elgar: 'Enigma' Variations* by Julian Rushton (Cambridge, 1999) and *Elgar's 'Enigma' Variations: A Centenary Celebration* by Patrick Turner (London, 1999). Recommended reading on associated subjects is Kevin Allen's *August Jaeger: Portrait of Nimrod* (Aldershot, 2000) and his *Elgar in Love* (Malvern, 2000), an account of Elgar's infatuation with Vera Hockman. There is also Percy M. Young's *Alice Elgar, Enigma of a Victorian Lady* (London, 1978).

Issues of the *Elgar Society Journal* contain many scholarly contributions on Elgarian subjects.

# INDEX

Ackté, Aino, 134
Acworth, Harry Arbuthnot, 49, 50, 56
Adams, Byron, 93–4
Ainley, Henry, 141
Alder, Mary Beatrice, 41
Alexandra, Queen, 84, 89, 95–6, 188
Allen, William, 6, 9, 16
Arányi, Jelly d', 38, 185
Arnold, Richard Penrose, 40
Ashton, Sir Frederick, 63, 70
Ashwell, Lena, 144, 145, 148
Athenaeum club, London, 96, 124, 135, 166, 171
Atkins, Edward Wulstan, 13, 27, 29, 30, 37, 172, 187
Atkins, Sir Ivor, 29, 37, 55, 62, 66, 69, 85, 93, 94, 97, 122, 124, 131, 148, 163, 172, 173, 177, 179, 187
Atkins, Lady (Katharine), 172
Auber, Jacques, 14

Bach, Johann Sebastian, 18, 79, 98, 131, 165, 166, 168
Bacon, Jane, 168
Baker, Mary Frances (Minnie), 38, 39, 43
Baker, William Meath, 38, 39, 62, 63, 144
Baldwin, Stanley, 174
Balfour, Arthur James, 96
Bantock, Sir Granville, 72–3, 86, 137, 198

Bantock, Myrrha, 73
Barbirolli, Sir John, 124, 160, 176
Barrie, Sir James, 4
Barry, Charles A., 67
Bartók, Béla, 166
Bax, Sir Arnold, 83, 166
Bayreuth Festival, 39–40, 131, 133
BBC, see British Broadcasting
Corporation
BBC Symphony Orchestra, 183
Beauchamp, Earl, 30, 55, 68–9
Beecham, Sir Thomas, 112, 120, 141
Beethoven, Ludwig van, 8, 11, 13, 14, 17, 27, 39, 40, 59, 63, 92, 102, 111, 114, 115, 137
Bellini, Vincenzo, 14, 18
Bennett, Joseph, 57–8
Benson, Arthur Christopher, 84, 104, 109, 141
Beresford, Admiral Lord Charles, 87, 101, 149, 150, 157, 160
Beresford, Lady (Mina), 101, 116, 157
Berlioz, Hector, 23, 25, 74
Bernard, Anthony, 158
Binyon, Laurence, 142, 143, 146, 156, 168
Birmingham, 33, 59, 64, 74, 88, 89, 92, 97, 98, 99, 102, 103, 105, 109, 152, 159, 167, 173, 177, 192
Birmingham Festival, 25, 59, 63, 74, 79, 82, 87, 89, 103, 108, 133

Bizet, Georges, 35
Black, Andrew, 59
Blackwood, Algernon, 4, 144, 145
Blair, Hugh, 39, 40, 41, 44, 46–7, 55
Blake, Carice Elgar, 37, 40, 43, 44, 45,
    63, 77, 86, 88, 94, 95, 97, 102, 105,
    106, 107, 109, 112, 116, 120, 121, 131,
    134, 137, 139, 140, 143, 145, 150,
    154, 162, 163–4, 165, 166, 172, 179,
    185, 187, 190, 192, 194, 197, 198,
    200, 201
Blake, Samuel, 165
Bliss, Sir Arthur, 157, 166, 177
Boito, Arrigo, 137
Boosey & Co., 73, 81, 85, 138–9, 181
Boughton, Rutland, 166
Boult, Sir Adrian, 24, 123, 149, 153, 154,
    162, 164, 166–7, 192
Brahms, Johannes, 25, 27, 35, 36, 102,
    137, 186
Brand, Tita, 141
Breitkopf & Härtel, 40, 47
Brema, Marie, 79, 141
Brewer, Sir Herbert, 55, 58, 82, 179
Bridges-Adams, William, 187
British Broadcasting Corporation (BBC),
    193, 197
British Empire Exhibition, 169
British Medical Association, 24
Britten, Benjamin (Lord Britten of
    Aldeburgh), 183
Broadheath, 8, 9, 12–13, 14, 164, 187, 201
Brodsky Quartet, 107, 157
Browning, John, 59
Bruch, Max, 141
Bruckner, Anton, 33
Buck, Dr Charles, 24, 26, 27, 28, 32, 33,
    34, 39, 48, 62, 70, 179
Buckley, Robert J., 110
Buckman, Rosina, 152
Bülow, Hans von, 22
Burley, Rosa, 40, 42, 43, 44, 45, 46–7,
    49, 59, 61, 62, 77, 88, 94, 99–100,
    130, 152, 161, 163
Buths, Julius, 82, 85, 134
Butt, Dame Clara, 64, 66, 73–4, 84, 86,
    139, 146

Butterworth, George, 137
Byrd, William, 13

Caine, Sir T. H. Hall, 141
Caldicott, Alfred, 19, 24
Cameron, Basil, 141
Cammaerts, Emile, 141, 143, 149
Cammaerts, Tita, see Brand, Tita
Campbell, Sir Colin, 132
Capel-Cure, Rev. Edward, 47, 48
Cardus, Sir Neville, 177, 190
Carey, Clive, 144, 145
Carnegie, Andrew, 103, 106
Casals, Pablo, 160
Catel, Charles Simon, 13
Chaliapin, Feodor, 136
Cheeseman, C. H. ('Don'), 201
Cherubini, Luigi, 13
Chopin, Frédéric, 142
Clayton, Henry Reginald, 51
Clifford, Mary, 172, 188, 195
Coates, Albert, 160
Coates, John, 86
Cohen, Harriet, 185
Coleridge-Taylor, Samuel, 53, 58, 79, 177
Colles, Henry Cope, 159
Collingwood, Lawrance, 198
Colvin, Lady (Frances), 121, 132, 133,
    154, 156, 172
Colvin, Sir Sidney, 136, 142, 154, 156, 159
Compton, Fay, 149
Conder, Charles, 148
Corelli, Arcangelo, 10, 14
Covent Garden, 3, 35, 42, 84, 92, 94,
    95–6
Cowen, Sir Frederic, 33, 52, 57, 80
'Cumberland, Gerald', 136
Crystal Palace concerts, 21, 26, 27, 32,
    36, 49, 51, 52, 55, 75, 85, 181

Daily News, 166
Daily Telegraph, 57, 132, 141, 147
Dan (bulldog), 63, 70–1, 132
Davey, Alice, 42
Davies, Fanny, 82
Davies, Sir H. Walford, 111–12
Dean, Sir Basil, 144

Debussy, Achille-Claude, 136, 141
Delibes, Léo, 186
Delius, Frederick, 82, 105, 177, 195, 198
Dent, Edward Joseph, 183
Diaghilev, Serge, 166
Done, William, 11
'Dorabella', *see* Powell, Dora
Dudley, Earl of, 6, 18
Du Maurier, Sir Gerald, 149
Dvořák, Antonin, 27, 35, 79, 102

Edward VII, King, 1, 2, 84, 85, 89, 95,
    121, 123, 127, 128, 172
Edwards, Frederick George, 67
Einstein, Albert, 193
Elgar, Ann (*née* Greening) (mother), 8, 9,
    10, 23, 27, 37, 50, 53, 69, 80, 186
Elgar, Carice (daughter), *see* Blake,
    Carice Elgar
Elgar, Lady (Caroline Alice) (wife), 29,
    32, 33–4, 36, 37, 38, 40, 41, 42,
    43–4, 45, 46, 49, 51, 52, 53, 58, 61,
    62, 66, 69, 70, 71, 73, 75, 77, 80, 81,
    84, 85, 86, 88, 89, 92, 95, 96, 99,
    100, 102–3, 105, 106, 107, 109, 112,
    116, 117, 120, 121, 122, 126, 128, 129,
    130, 131, 134, 135, 136, 138, 139,
    140, 143, 144, 145, 146, 147, 148,
    149, 150, 152, 153, 154, 155, 156–7,
    158, 160, 161–2, 163–4, 165, 185
Elgar, Sir Edward William
    childhood and schooling, 8, 9, 10, 11,
        12, 13
    desire for peerage, 169, 171, 172, 174
    early music lessons, 13
    homes
        Avonmore Road, Kensington, 36
        Battenhall Manor, 176
        Birchwood, 43, 56, 57, 77, 83, 130
        Brinkwells, 150, 152, 154, 156, 157,
            159, 160, 164, 165
        Craeg Lea, 66, 74, 96
        Forli, 38–9, 62
        10 High Street, Worcester, 9, 23,
            50, 96, 100
        Marl Bank, 179, 184, 187, 188, 190,
            193, 198, 200

Marloes Road, Kensington, 34
Napleton Grange, 168, 172, 173
Plas Gwyn, 96, 97, 100, 103, 107,
    109, 114, 119, 121, 122, 125, 131,
    154
Severn House, 131, 132, 134, 139,
    145, 147, 153, 156, 157, 159, 165,
    181
Tiddington House, 176
honours
    Baronetcy, 183
    G.C.V.O., 195
    K.C.V.O., 176
    Knight Bachelor, 3, 96
    Master of the King's Music, 3, 169
    O.M., 129
    RPS Gold Medal, 173
illnesses, 45, 57, 73, 81, 99, 100, 103,
    105, 109, 132, 133, 134–5, 145, 146,
    147, 148, 150, 152, 153, 156, 163,
    164, 173–4, 181, 183–4, 194, 195, 197
relationships with
    Atkins, Sir Ivor, 37, 62, 93, 94
    Buck, Dr Charles, 24, 26, 27, 28, 34
    Burley, Rosa, 40, 42, 43, 44, 46–7,
        59, 62, 77, 130, 163
    Delius, Frederick, 195, 198
    Elgar, Ann, 50, 53, 69
    Elgar, Caroline Alice, 32, 33–4, 40,
        41, 42, 43–4, 58, 66, 73, 80, 84,
        88
    Elgar, William, 11–12
    Grafton, Susannah (Pollie), 23,
        168, 177, 200
    Hockman, Vera, 185–7, 190
    Jaeger, A. J., 53, 55, 56, 58, 59, 69,
        76, 93, 113
    Newman, Ernest, 30, 83–4, 104
    Novello's, 47–8, 50, 51, 52, 53, 63,
        72, 73, 81, 92, 108, 112, 130, 165,
        168, 179
    Reed, W. H., 14, 93
    Richter, Hans, 66, 69–70, 79, 81,
        92, 109
    Rodewald, Alfred, 80, 89, 92–3, 94
    Schuster, Frank, 87, 92, 95, 96, 100,
        108, 176

Elgar, Sir Edward William (*cont.*)
    Shaw, George Bernard, 179, 188
    Stuart Wortley, Alice
        ('Windflower'), 116–17, 119–21,
        122–3, 124, 126, 133, 135, 136,
        140, 144, 146, 152, 153, 154–5,
        156, 157, 164, 165, 172, 178,
        194
    Weaver, Helen, 25, 26, 27, 28, 31
    religion, 4, 42, 79, 115, 156
    WORKS
    arrangements
        Bach, J. S., Fantasia in C minor,
            165; Fugue in C minor (Elgar
            op. 86), 165, 166
        Beethoven, symphonies (Elgar
            Credo), 17
        *God Save the King*, 84
        Handel, Overture in D minor, 168
        Mozart, Violin Sonata in F (K. 547)
            (Elgar Gloria), 17
        Purcell, *Jehova, quam multi sunt hostes*
            *mei*, 179
        Wagner, *The Flying Dutchman*,
            Overture, 19; *Parsifal*, Good
            Friday Music, 45
    chamber
        *Capricieuse, La* (op. 17), 38
        *Chanson de matin* (op. 15, no. 2), 57,
            69
        *Chanson de nuit* (op. 15, no. 1), 55, 69
        *Idylle, Une* (op. 4, no. 1), 27
        Powick quadrilles, 22
        Quintet for piano and strings
            (op. 84), 155, 157–8, 159, 176,
            198
        *Reminiscences*, 19
        Romance for violin and piano
            (op. 1), 28
        *Salut d'amour* (*Liebesgrüss*) (op. 12),
            34
        Sonata for violin and piano
            (op. 82), 155, 157, 158, 159, 186
        String Quartet (op. 83), 155, 156,
            157, 159
        *Virelai* (op. 4, no. 3), 184
        Wind quintets, 19–21, 23, 134, 181

    choral
        *Apostles, The* (op. 49), 48, 74, 87, 88,
            89–92, 96, 97, 100, 101, 102,
            103–4, 105, 134, 139, 164, 166,
            195
        *Banner of St George, The* (op. 33), 51,
            52, 55, 59
        *Black Knight, The* (op. 25), 23, 36,
            39, 40, 41, 49
        *Caractacus* (op. 35), 41, 56–7, 58, 59,
            60, 69, 84, 198
        *Coronation Ode* (op. 44), 2, 60, 84–5,
            86, 87, 88, 89
        *Dream of Gerontius, The* (op. 38), 12,
            33, 48, 71, 74–7, 78–9, 80, 81,
            82, 85, 86, 88, 91, 95, 96, 100,
            103, 104, 109, 121, 126, 132, 134,
            137, 141, 145, 146, 149, 164, 167,
            171, 174, 177, 185, 190, 197
        *Kingdom, The* (op. 51), 91, 102,
            103–4, 105, 109, 114, 116, 166
        *Light of Life, The* (*Lux Christi*) (op. 29),
            47–8, 52, 73
        *Music Makers, The* (op. 69), 4, 5, 67,
            107, 132, 133–4, 135, 164, 174,
            190
        *Scenes from the Saga of King Olaf*
            (op. 30), 23, 45, 47–8, 49, 51, 52,
            56, 57, 71, 74, 100, 163
        *Spirit of England, The* (op. 80), 48, 71,
            143, 145, 146, 148, 152, 164, 190
        *With proud thanksgiving*, 161, 165
    church music
        *Christmas Greeting, A* (op. 52), 108
        Credo (Beethoven), 17
        *Fear not, O Land*, 139
        *Give unto the Lord* (op. 74), 139
        Litanies, 32
        *O hearken Thou* (op. 64), 129
        *Salve regina*, 19
        *Tantum ergo*, 19
        Te Deum and Benedictus (op. 34),
            52, 53
        *They are at rest*, 114
    dramatic
        *Arthur*, 168, 193
        *Beau Brummel*, 177

Carillon (op. 75), 141, 142, 143
Crown of India, The (op. 66), 71, 132–3
Drapeau belge, Le (op. 79), 143, 149
Grania and Diarmid (op. 42), 82, 99
Sanguine Fan, The (op. 81), 148–9
Starlight Express, The (op. 78), 144–5
Voix dans le désert, Une (op. 77), 143
orchestral
Air de ballet, 24
Cantique (op. 3), 23, 134
Carissima, 138
Cello Concerto in E minor (op. 85), 153, 159, 160–1, 166, 177
Cockaigne (In London Town) (op. 40), 66, 80–1
Coronation March (op. 65), 60, 129
Dream Children (op. 43), 84, 107, 173
Elegy (op. 58), 114, 197
Falstaff (op. 68), 129, 135, 136–7, 157, 184
Froissart (op. 19), 36–8, 39, 41, 49, 96
Imperial March (op. 32), 51, 55
Intermezzo: Sérénade mauresque (op. 10, no. 2), 26
In the South (Alassio) (op. 50), 71, 94–5, 97, 99, 106, 153
Introduction and Allegro for strings (op. 47), 99, 100, 131
Nursery Suite, 183, 184
Pas redoublé, 24
Polonia (op. 76), 142
Pomp and Circumstance marches (op. 39), 81–2, 97, 99, 107, 181
Romance for bassoon (op. 62), 119
Rosemary ('That's for Remembrance'), 24, 138
Salut d'amour (Liebesgrüss)(op. 12), 34, 36
Serenade for strings (op. 20), 39, 40, 197
Severn Suite (op. 87), 181, 188, 190
Sevillana (op. 17), 41, 51
Sospiri (op. 70), 138, 140, 172
Suite in D, 36
Sursum corda (op. 11), 45

Symphony no. 1 in A flat major (op. 55), 4, 81, 107, 108, 109–12, 128, 129, 172, 190
Symphony no. 2 in E flat major (op. 63), 2, 4, 5, 94, 102, 120, 122, 125, 126, 127–9, 146, 147, 162, 164, 166, 171, 174, 176, 183, 195
Three Bavarian Dances (op. 27), 46, 55
Three Characteristic Pieces (op. 10), 68
Three Pieces for strings, 33, 36, 37
Variations on an Original Theme ('Enigma') (op. 36), 21, 29, 30, 38, 39, 46, 60, 61–3, 66–71, 72, 73, 74, 76, 87, 96, 99, 106, 119, 131, 134, 144, 166, 179
Violin Concerto in B minor (op. 61), 4, 102, 113, 114, 119, 121–4, 128, 130, 134, 145, 147, 160, 165, 166, 174, 185, 189–90, 195
Wand of Youth, The (suites 1 and 2) (op. 1a and 1b), 3, 4, 14, 23, 39, 107, 109, 144, 183
organ
Eleven Vesper Voluntaries (op. 14), 36
Sonata in G (op. 28), 46, 47
part-songs, etc.
Angelus, The (op. 56), 112
Death on the Hills (op. 72), 138
Deep in my soul (op. 53, no. 2), 108
Evening Scene, 100
Five Part-Songs from the Greek Anthology (op. 45), 2, 87
Fly, Singing Bird (op. 26, no. 2), 45
Fountain, The (op. 71, no. 2), 138
From the Bavarian Highlands (op. 27), 46, 47, 88
Good Morrow, 179
Go, song of mine (op. 57), 113
Herald, The, 173
How calmly the evening, 108
I sing the birth, 176–7
Love (op. 18, no. 2), 106
Love's Tempest (op. 73, no. 1), 138
Marching Song, 108
My love dwelt in a northern land, 36

Elgar, Sir Edward William (cont.)
    O happy eyes (op. 18, no. 1), 36
    O wild west wind! (op. 53, no. 3), 108
    Owls (op. 53, no. 4), 108, 155
    Prince of Sleep, The, 173
    Reveille, The (op. 54), 108
    Serenade (op. 73, no. 2), 138
    Shower, The (op. 71, no. 1), 138
    Snow, The (op. 26, no. 1), 45
    So many true princesses who have gone
        (choral ode), 188
    Spanish Serenade (op. 23), 39, 41
    There is sweet music (op. 53, no. 1),
        108
    To her beneath whose steadfast star, 69
    Wanderer, The, 168
    Weary wind of the west, 87
    Zut! Zut! Zut!, 168
    piano solo
        Concert Allegro (op. 46), 82
        Douce pensée, 23, 24, 138
        In Smyrna, 101, 132
        Rosemary, 23, 24, 138
        Salut d'amour (Liebesgrüss)(op. 12),
            33, 34
        Sonatina, 184
    songs and song cycles
        Arabian Serenade, 139
        Big Steamers, 154
        Chariots of the Lord, 139
        Child Asleep, A, 114
        Fringes of the Fleet, The, 149, 150, 152,
            153
        'Inside the Bar', 150
        It isnae me, 184
        'Land of hope and glory', 60, 81,
            84–5, 86, 89, 140, 141, 169, 184
        Language of Flowers, The, 15
        Love alone will stay (Lute Song), 52, 66
        O, soft was the song (op. 59, no. 3),
            114
        Pipes of Pan, 69
        Pleading (op. 48), 109
        'Quand nos bourgeons se
            rouvriront' (Une voix dans le désert)
            (op. 77), 143
        River, The (op. 60, no. 2), 114, 133
    Sea Pictures (op. 37), 23, 66, 73–4,
        75, 114, 134
    There are seven that pull the thread
        (Grania and Diarmid), 82
    Three Songs with Orchestra
        (op. 59, nos. 3, 5 and 6), 114
    Through the long days, 33
    Torch, The (op. 60, no. 1), 114, 133
    Twilight (op. 59, no. 6), 114
    Was it some golden star? (op. 59,
        no. 5), 114
    'When the spring comes round
        again', see 'Quand nos bourgeons
        se rouvriront'
    Wind at Dawn, The, 33, 133
    unfinished or projected
        'Callicles' (Empedocles on Etna), 137,
            193
        Cockaigne no. 2 (City of Dreadful
            Night), 88, 125
        Gordon Symphony, 59–60, 63–4, 69,
            75
        Last Judgement, The, 168, 173, 188,
            192, 193
        Mottoes, 55–6
        Piano Concerto, 147, 159, 168, 173
        Rabelais (ballet-pantomime), 98,
            129
        Scottish Overture, 28
        Spanish Lady, The (opera, op. 89),
            23, 192
        Symphony no. 3 (op. 88, completed
            by Anthony Payne and first
            performed in 1998), 188, 192–3,
            195, 212
Elgar, Francis Thomas (Frank)
    (brother), 9, 19, 26, 145
Elgar, Frederick Joseph (Jo) (brother), 9,
    10–11, 12
Elgar, Helen Agnes (Dott or Dot)
    (sister), 9
Elgar, Henry (uncle), 9, 11, 13, 34, 148
Elgar, Henry John (Harry) (brother), 8,
    10, 12
Elgar, Lucy Ann (sister), see Pipe, Lucy
Elgar, Susannah Mary (Pollie) (sister),
    see Grafton, Susannah

Elgar, William (nephew), 145
Elgar, William Henry (father), 6, 9, 11,
    13, 16–17, 18, 26, 37, 100, 103
Elizabeth, Princess (Queen Elizabeth II),
    183
Elkin, W. W., 138
Elwes, Gervase, 96, 146, 152, 200
Elwes, Joan, 184
Elwes, Father Valentine, 200
Embleton, Henry, 139, 145, 164, 181
Enoch & Sons, 132
Exton, Frank, 19

Fauré, Gabriel, 59
Fitton, Harriet, 36
Fitton, Hilda, 36, 45
Fitton, Isabel ('Ysobel'), 36, 58, 63, 179
Forbes, Norman, 179
Forsyth, Cecil, 148
Forsyth, J. A., 61
Foster, Muriel, 85, 86, 97, 114, 119,
    132, 133, 137, 138, 141, 156, 162

Gaisberg, Fred, 124, 188, 192, 195,
    198
Geehl, Henry, 181
George V, King, 45, 60, 129, 132, 169,
    170, 179
German, Sir Edward, 63
Gibb, Father Reginald, 200
Gibbons, Orlando, 13
Gloucester Festival, 58, 82, 86, 107, 122,
    184, 188
Gluck, Christoph Willibald von, 120
Goossens, Sir Eugene, 166
Gordon, General Charles (of
    Khartoum), 33, 59, 75
Gordon, John Joseph, 75
Gorton, Canon Charles, 87, 91, 100,
    108
Gounod, Charles, 36
Grafton, Madge, 168, 190
Grafton, May, 97, 106, 107, 109, 184, 190
Grafton, Susannah (Pollie), 8, 9, 23, 25,
    34, 38, 97, 109, 117, 127, 135, 141,
    143, 146, 163, 165, 166, 168, 172,
    173, 177, 198, 200, 201

Grafton, William, 23, 34, 109
Grahame, Kenneth, 3
Grainger, Oswin, 19
Green, William, 86
Greene, Harry Plunket, 79, 86
Griffith, Arthur Troyte ('Troyte'), 3, 62,
    63, 131, 179, 187
Grove, Sir George, 46
Groveham, Edith, 25, 27

Hall, Rev. Edward Vine, 25, 33, 48
Hall, Marie, 147
Hallam, Arthur H., 93
Hallé Orchestra, 49, 81, 88, 92, 95, 109,
    110–11, 177
Hampton, Rev. J., 41
Handel, George Frideric, 13, 14, 17, 60,
    166, 168
Harding, Emily, 97
Hardy, Thomas, 136
Harrison, Beatrice, 160
Harrison, Julius, 145
Harrison, Kathleen, 198, 200
Harty, Sir Hamilton, 137
Haydn, Franz Joseph, 8, 13, 14, 115
Heap, Charles Swinnerton, 45, 47, 50,
    52, 79
Hedley, Percival, 74
Heifetz, Jascha, 124, 165
Henson, Medora, 59
Hereford Festival, 53, 79, 86, 165, 174,
    181, 197
Herefordshire Philharmonic, 41
Heseltine, Philip (Peter Warlock), 183
Hess, Willy, 49
Hewlett, Maurice, 82
Hindemith, Paul, 166
Hine, Clytie, 145
His Master's Voice (HMV), 124, 138, 145,
    174, 177, 181, 183, 184, 188
Hockman, Dulcie, 187
Hockman, Vera, 185–7, 190, 192–3, 197,
    198, 201
Holland, Vyvyan, 93
Holloway, Miss J., 22, 23
Holst, Gustav, 141
Hull, Sir Percy, 71, 179

Humperdinck, Engelbert, 55
Hut, The (Schuster's home), 109, 116,
    121, 131, 136, 146, 154, 164, 168,
    171, 174, 175, 176, 185
Hyde, Martina, 55

Ireland, John, 166

Jackson, Sir Barry, 192
Jaeger, August Johannes ('Nimrod'), 50,
    53, 55, 56, 58, 59, 61, 63, 66–7, 69,
    73, 74, 75–6, 77, 79, 80, 81, 84,
    85–6, 89, 93, 94, 97–8, 99, 100,
    108, 109, 111, 113, 118, 119, 134
Jaeger, Isabella, 113, 141, 148
James, Edwin F., 119
Jeremy, Raymond, 159
Joachim Quartet, 22
John, Augustus, 183
Johnstone, Arthur, 49, 85, 89
Johnstone, George Hope, 74–5, 88, 92
Jonson, Ben, 192
Joshua, Marie, 155

Kenyon, Charles F., see 'Cumberland,
    Gerald'
Kilburn, Nicholas, 52, 57, 59, 62, 75,
    172
Kipling, Rudyard, 2, 85, 149, 150, 153,
    154
Kirby, Alan, 185
Kozeluch, Leopold, 10
Kreisler, Fritz, 101–2, 112, 122, 123, 124,
    164, 166, 189

Lambert, Constant, 192
Lang, Andrew, 36
Langford, Samuel, 111, 123
Lawrence, T. E. (Lawrence of Arabia),
    190
Lees-Milne, James, 193
Legge, Robin, 132, 133, 137
Leicester, Charlotte, 8
Leicester, Sir Hubert, 11, 12, 13, 19, 21,
    62, 100, 109, 134, 200
Leicester, John, 6, 9

Leicester, Philip, 13, 200
Leicester, William, 8, 19
Leipzig, 16, 25, 26, 29
Levi, Hermann, 42
Liszt, Ferenc, 32, 85
Littleton, Alfred Henry, 73, 75, 89, 92,
    102, 103, 107, 108, 127, 138
Littleton, Augustus, 138
Liverpool Orchestral Society, 73
Lloyd, Charles Harford, 32
Lloyd, Edward, 48, 49, 59, 69, 79
Loeb, Sydney, 111, 148
London, 6, 19, 33, 34–5, 37, 38, 40, 51,
    55, 59, 66, 69, 74, 79, 80, 85, 87,
    88, 89, 96, 100, 111, 120, 124, 129,
    130, 135, 137, 143, 146, 150, 152,
    163, 164, 166, 172, 178, 183, 185,
    189, 195
London Philharmonic Orchestra (LPO),
    149
London Symphony Orchestra (LSO), 98,
    99, 100, 102, 111, 114, 119, 126, 131,
    135, 141, 142, 145, 153, 160, 184,
    185, 188, 190, 198
Longfellow, Henry Wadsworth, 25, 36,
    39, 45, 49, 87
Lowther, Ina, 148, 149
Lucas, Stanley, 33
Lygon, Lady Mary, 29, 30, 55, 58, 59,
    68–9, 70

MacDonald, Ramsay, 171
Mackenzie, Sir Alexander, 24, 57, 69
McNaught, William G., 108
McVeagh, Diana, 93
Mahler, Gustav, 41, 44, 72, 74
Maine, Basil, 61, 123, 195, 198
Malvern, 32, 33, 36, 40–1, 42, 45, 46, 49,
    66, 74, 80, 92, 95, 107, 130, 148,
    192
Manchester Guardian, 49, 85, 89, 111, 123,
    177, 190
Manns, Sir August, 21, 26, 36, 49, 51,
    52, 85
Marco and Mina (spaniels), 172, 173,
    174, 193

Margaret, Princess, 181, 183
Masefield, John, 188
Matthews, Appleby, 152
Matthews, Bertram P., 177
Mendelssohn, Felix Bartholdy, 18, 29, 36
Menuhin, Yehudi (Lord Menuhin of Stoke d'Abernon), 124, 189–90, 195
Messchaert, Johannes, 85, 89
Meyerbeer, Giacomo, 14
Millais, Sir John, 87, 116
Miller, Cyril, 52
Mlynarski, Emil, 142
Moore, George, 82
Moore, Jerrold Northrop, 29, 52, 117–18, 155, 173
Morris, Reginald Owen, 188
Mott, Charles, 145, 150–2
Mountford, Richard (Dick), 172, 181
Mozart, Wolfgang Amadeus, 8, 13, 14, 17, 18, 22, 35, 62, 105, 115, 137, 168
Mundy, Simon, 57
Munro, Helen, *see* Weaver, Helen Jessie
Munro, John, 29
Munro, Joyce, 29, 147
Munro, Kenneth, 29, 147–8
Murdoch, William, 159
*Musical Times*, 67, 69, 137

Nevinson, Basil, 36, 40, 59, 62, 63, 114
Newman, Ernest, 23, 30, 31, 44, 83–4, 86, 111, 122, 123–4, 126, 128, 134, 136, 137, 143, 146, 149, 155, 160, 179, 190, 197, 198, 200, 212–13
Newman, Cardinal John Henry, 33, 74–5, 86, 114
Newmarch, Rosa, 127, 138
Newton, Ivor, 190
Nicholls, Agnes, 145, 146, 152
Nichols, Robert, 154
Nikisch, Arthur, 111, 112, 134, 135, 137
'Nimrod', *see* Jaeger, August Johannes

Norbury, Florence, 58, 63, 197
Norbury, Winifred, 55, 58, 63
Northampton, fifth Marquess of (William George Spencer Scott), 89, 123, 167–8
Novello & Co., 37, 39, 40, 45, 47–8, 50, 51, 52, 53, 55, 58, 59, 63, 66, 67, 68, 72, 73, 78–9, 81, 82, 86, 88, 89, 92, 108, 124, 126, 134, 135, 136, 142, 150, 165, 190

Ogle, C. H., 19
Orléans, Charles, Duc d', 32
Orr, Charles Wilfred, 183
Orsborn & Tuckwood, 36
O'Shaughnessy, Arthur, 107, 132
Ourousoff, Olga (Mrs Henry Wood), 114

Paderewski, Ignace, 142
Parker, Sir Gilbert, 114, 118, 150
Parratt, Sir Walter, 84, 87, 169
Parry, Sir Charles Hubert, 24, 35, 59, 60, 62, 66, 79, 85, 96, 99, 137, 152, 156, 183
Payne, Anthony, 212
Pearn, Violet, 144, 145
Penny, Rev. Alfred, 38
Penny, Dora, *see* Powell, Dora
Percival, James Gates, 15
Peyton, Richard, 98, 109
Phillips, Sir Claude, 87, 116, 120, 123, 172
Piatigorsky, Grigor, 160
Pipe, Charles, 23, 25, 34
Pipe, Lucy, 8, 9, 11, 16, 23, 25, 34, 70, 173
Pirie, Peter J., 5
Pollitzer, Adolphe, 19, 21, 27
Ponsonby, Sir Frederick, 170, 171
Powell, Dora ('Dorabella'), 38, 58, 62, 63, 67, 71, 73, 77, 81, 88, 111, 120, 134
Powick (Worcs.) County Lunatic Asylum, 22, 23, 28, 181
Prowse, Keith, 181, 184, 195
Puccini, Giacomo, 109, 136
Purcell, Henry, 49, 57

Queen's Hall, London, 52, 59, 82, 111,
    112, 119, 121, 122, 128, 140, 141, 146,
    162, 165, 166, 173, 174

Radnor, Countess of, 95
Raikes, William, 36
Reed, William Henry, 10, 14, 71, 93, 121,
    122, 128, 132, 155, 156, 157, 158,
    159, 161, 163, 185, 188, 192, 193,
    197
Reeve, Francis, 12
Reeves, Sims, 13
Reicha, Anton, 13
Reith, Sir John, 188, 192, 193
Richter, Hans, 24, 27, 31, 33, 35, 66–7,
    69–70, 72, 73, 74, 79, 81, 88, 92,
    95, 96, 98, 111, 119, 126, 128, 131,
    133, 141, 148, 155, 167
Ricketts, Sarah, 10
Roberts, Caroline Alice, see Elgar, Lady
Roberts, Major General Sir Henry Gee,
    32
Roberts, Lady (Julia Maria), 33
Roberts, William, see Newman,
    Ernest
Rodewald, Alfred E., 72, 80, 82,
    83, 85, 86, 89, 92–3, 94,
    128
Ronald, Sir Landon, 137, 138, 155, 156,
    157, 158, 183, 192
Rootham, Cyril B., 142, 145
Rossini, Gioachino, 36
Royal Albert Hall, London, 86, 137, 152,
    165
Royal Philharmonic Society, 75, 80, 114,
    122, 173
Rubinstein, Anton, 25
Rushton, Julian, 63

Safonoff, Vassily, 119
Saint-Saëns, Camille, 23
Salmond, Felix, 159, 160, 163
Sammons, Albert, 159, 163
Sanford, Samuel Simons, 100, 114
Santley, Sir Charles, 13
Sassoon, Siegfried, 87, 93, 164, 166, 168,
    171

Schobert, Johann, 10
Schoenberg, Arnold, 166
Scholes, Percy, 146
Schott & Sons, 28, 34
Schubert, Franz, 14, 168
Schumann, Robert, 22, 25, 63, 102
Schuster, Adela, 112, 120, 186, 193
Schuster, Leo Francis (Frank), 74, 87,
    89, 92, 93, 95, 96, 100, 104, 109,
    116, 119, 120, 121, 123, 140, 156,
    159, 163, 164, 168, 169, 171, 174,
    175, 176
Scott, Elisabeth, 187
Shaftesbury, Earl of, 171
Shaw, George Bernard, 157–8, 166, 181,
    183, 187–8, 190, 192, 197
Sibelius, Jean, 133, 195
Sickert, Walter, 171–2
Siloti, Alexander, 72
Sinclair, George Robertson, 37, 52, 53,
    55, 59, 63, 70, 71, 94, 108, 132, 148,
    179
Sitwell, Sir Osbert, 176
Slingsby-Bethell, Henry, 42, 47, 53
Slingsby-Bethell, Sarah, 42, 47, 53
Speyer, Sir Edgar, 89, 119, 121, 141
Speyer, Edward, 89, 114, 157, 164
Spohr, Louis, 18
Spray, Frederick, 18
Stamfordham, Lord, 169–70
Stanford, Sir Charles Villiers, 24, 33, 57,
    80, 85, 96, 99, 102, 135, 142, 148,
    183
Steinbach, Fritz, 72, 87, 96, 97, 134
Stephens, Jeffrey, 138
Steuart-Powell, Hew David, 36, 59, 62,
    63, 144
Stockley, William Cole, 25, 33, 38,
    79
Stoll, Sir Oswald, 132
Stosch, Leonora von (Lady Speyer), 119,
    164
Strauss, Richard, 44, 53, 72, 77, 79,
    81, 85, 88, 95, 97–8, 99, 105,
    114, 120, 121, 137, 140, 164, 165,
    166, 167
Stravinsky, Igor, 166

Stuart Wortley, Alice Sophie Caroline (*née* Millais) (Lady Stuart of Wortley) ('Windflower'), 4, 87, 89, 112, 116, 117, 119, 120, 121, 122, 123, 124, 125, 126–7, 128, 132, 133, 134, 135, 136, 137, 138, 140, 142, 143, 144, 146, 147, 148, 149, 150, 152, 153, 154, 155, 156, 157, 159, 160, 161, 163, 164, 165, 166, 168, 169, 171, 173, 174, 175, 176, 177, 178, 179, 181, 183, 185, 186, 188, 194, 195, 198, 200, 201
Stuart Wortley, Charles (Lord Stuart of Wortley), 87, 89, 116, 119, 120, 123, 143, 144, 147, 157, 166, 168, 174
Stuart Wortley, Clare, 116, 117, 137
Sullivan, Sir Arthur, 28, 33, 34, 57, 59, 62
Sumsion, Herbert (John), 179, 188
Swinnerton Heap, Charles, *see* Heap, Charles Swinnerton

Tallis, Thomas, 13
Tennyson, Alfred, Lord, 2–3, 5, 93
Terry, Charles Sanford, 123, 125
Tertis, Lionel, 148, 163
Thesiger, Ernest, 149
Thomson, Sir Arthur, 173, 197
Three Choirs Festival, 11, 13, 17, 24, 59, 166, 167, 187
Tietjens, Thérèse, 13
Tortelier, Paul, 160
Tours, Berthold, 47, 48, 50
Townshend, Richard Baxter, 38, 40, 62
Toye, Francis, 124
Trowell, Brian, 147–8
Tyler, Pollie, 10

Vandervelde, Emile, 143
Vandervelde, Lalla, 143, 154, 158, 185
Van Rooy, Anton, 89
Vaughan Williams, Ralph, 99, 143, 171, 177, 185, 188
Verdi, Giuseppe, 9, 18, 33, 36, 134, 185
Vert, Nathaniel (Vertigliano, Narciso), 66, 73

Victoria, Queen, 1, 51, 58, 69, 81, 114
Vine Hall, Rev. Edward, *see* Hall, Rev. Edward Vine
Volbach, Fritz, 97

Wagner, Richard, 19, 23–4, 25, 33, 35, 39–40, 41–3, 45, 55, 74, 77, 79, 80, 133
Walsh, Caroline, 9, 10, 12
Walter, Bruno, 172, 173, 193
Walton, Sir William, 60, 183, 192
Warlock, Peter, *see* Heseltine, Philip
Warrender, Sir George, 101
Warrender, Lady Maud, 89, 95, 101, 109, 120, 123
Weaver, Frank, 21, 25, 27, 147
Weaver, Helen Jessie, 21, 25, 26, 27, 28, 29, 30, 31, 121, 138, 147
Weaver, William, 21
Webb, Alan, 184
Webb, Frank, 37, 38, 184
Weingartner, Felix, 72, 81, 96, 97
Wensley, Shapcott, 51
Wesley, Samuel Sebastian, 18
Whiteley, Herbert, 181
Whitwell, Winifred, 50
Wilde, Oscar, 93
Wilhelmj, August, 19, 27
Wilkinson-Newsholme, Sarah Anne, 28
Williams, Joseph, 47
'Windflower', *see* Stuart Wortley, Alice Sophie Caroline
Wolf, Hugo, 195
Wood, Sir Henry J., 82, 85, 95, 114, 124
Worcester, 6, 8, 9, 12, 19, 21, 24, 26, 27, 29, 33, 37, 38, 39, 40, 41, 45, 46, 52, 64, 75, 148, 165, 176, 185, 186, 188, 197
Amateur Instrumental Society, 19, 22, 24
Glee Club, 6, 13–14, 18, 22
Musical Society, 18
Philharmonic Society, 18, 26
St George's church, 6, 8, 10, 13, 16, 17, 19, 32, 45, 200

Worcester (*cont.*)
  Worcester Festival, 11, 18, 22, 24,
    27–8, 33, 36, 37, 44, 47, 48, 69,
    73, 85, 86, 88, 100, 109, 131, 141,
    164, 169, 177, 179, 187, 190–2,
    194
  Worcestershire Musical Union, 25
  Worcestershire Philharmonic, 55, 82,
    88
Worthington, Julia, 100, 108, 112,
    135
Wortley, Lady Stuart of, *see* Stuart
  Wortley, Alice Sophie Caroline

Wortley, Lord Stuart of, *see* Stuart
  Wortley, Charles
Wüllner, Ludwig, 85, 89
Wylde, Leslie, 174–6
Wylde, Wendela, 174–6

Yale University, 100
Yeats, William Butler, 82
York, Duke and Duchess of (King George
  VI and Queen Elizabeth), 183
Ysaÿe, Eugène, 119, 124, 130

Zola, Emile, 22